Looking South

The Evolution of
Latin Americanist Scholarship
in the United States, 1850–1975

Helen Delpar

THE UNIVERSITY OF ALABAMA PRESS

Tuscaloosa

Copyright © 2008
The University of Alabama Press
Tuscaloosa, Alabama 35487-0380
All rights reserved
Manufactured in the United States of America

Typeface: Minion

∞

The paper on which this book is printed meets the minimum requirements of American
National Standard for Information Sciences-Permanence of Paper for Printed Library
Materials, ANSI Z39.48-1984.

Library of Congress Cataloging-in-Publication Data

Delpar, Helen.
The evolution of Latin Americanist scholarship in the United States,
1850-1975 / Helen Delpar.
p.   cm.
Includes bibliographical references and index.
ISBN-13: 978-0-8173-1594-8 (cloth : alk. paper)
ISBN-10: 0-8173-1594-2 (cloth : alk. paper)
ISBN-13: 978-0-8173-5464-0 (pbk. : alk. paper)
ISBN-10: 0-8173-5464-6 (pbk. : alk. paper) 1. Latin America—Study and teaching—United
States. 2. Latin America—Historiography. 3. Latin Americanists—United States. I. Title.
F1409.95.U6D45 2008
980.0307′073—dc22

2007021038

To the memory of Lewis Hanke and Howard F. Cline

Contents

Preface

Since the seventeenth century, Americans[1] have turned their gaze toward the lands to the south, seeing in them fields for religious proselytization, economic enterprise, and military conquest. Some have been motivated mainly by intellectual curiosity and the desire to learn more about the region and its people. In the nineteenth century these individuals were likely to be independent travelers and investigators. At the start of the twentieth century, with the emergence of the modern university, academics with specializations in Latin America began to appear, initially in history, anthropology, and geography. By the end of the century the number of dedicated Latin Americanists in these and other disciplines had increased dramatically, courses on Latin America had become apparently permanent features of university curricula, and research on Latin American topics was deemed a respectable activity for scholars.

Other non-European areas, notably the Middle East and Asia, also came under scholarly scrutiny in the United States in the nineteenth and early twentieth centuries. From an early date U.S. colleges and universities offered courses on the ancient Middle East and on biblical languages for the prospective ministers among their students. Of 122 doctorates in non-European international studies awarded by six leading universities between 1861 and 1900, more than half (66) pertained to ancient Hebrew. Archaeologists were also attracted to the ancient Middle East, often with the hope that their findings would either uphold or undermine biblical authority. During this period American missionaries stationed overseas produced many tomes not only about biblical lands but also about China and other parts of the "non-Christian world." Former missionaries and their children later played a decisive role in the development of academic Chinese studies in the United States.[2]

No dominant pattern can be discerned in the recruitment of the earliest Latin Americanists. Several historians, trained as U.S. or European specialists, turned to Latin America after finding employment at universities in western states that had once been ruled by Spain and Mexico. A few others, such as the geographers Mark Jefferson and George M. McBride, had experience in Latin America before undertaking academic careers. Early archaeologists and other anthropologists often looked to Latin America as a natural extension of their work on native peoples of North America.

In short, where Latin America was concerned, conditions and interests within the United States usually dictated the nature and intensity of academic interest. This became especially true with the expansion of U.S. military and economic power in the mid-twentieth century. During World War II and the cold war the federal government provided unprecedented funding for the support of research and teaching related to Latin America. At the same time, foundations and learned societies offered substantial sums to subsidize research that would foster inter-American understanding and contribute to the solution of contemporary problems. During these years Eastern Europe, Southeast Asia, and Africa also became subjects of study to a greater extent than before.

Because of federal and foundation funding, the decades after World War II also brought the apogee of area studies, though antecedents can be traced to the 1930s. The area studies approach to a geographical region entailed the combination of language learning with the study of the region's history, geography, politics, society, and culture. Ideally, scholars in university-based area programs would collaborate on research projects, graduate students would acquire multi-disciplinary expertise, and all would have opportunities for extended fieldwork in the area. Even during the heyday of area studies programs, however, there was tension between them and the universities' traditional discipline-based departments. I should also emphasize that Latin American studies were not synonymous with Latin Americanist scholarship and teaching in discrete disciplines, especially history and anthropology, which antedated the rise of area studies.

The first part of this book narrates the emergence of Latin America as the subject of academic inquiry in the United States in the first decades of the twentieth century. After an introductory chapter discussing nineteenth-century precedents, subsequent chapters trace developments to about 1935 in history, anthropology, geography, and other social science disciplines (political science, economics, sociology). Because a symbiotic relationship between scholarship and U.S. government policy is often alleged, a separate chapter probes linkages during this period. Here as elsewhere, I also consider the views of Latin Americanists toward the region, U.S. policy, and their own profession. Although they are not a primary focus, I make reference in this section and later to the presence of courses in the languages and literatures of Latin America in university curricula.

It is tempting to assert that the construction of Latin America occurred during the early twentieth century. However, the broad contours of the region were always understood to embrace the former New World colonies of Spain and Portugal. Haiti might be included, but not the English- and French-speaking colonies of the Caribbean. Of course, practitioners always made distinctions, sometimes invidious, among the countries of the region. As chapter 5 points out, in the early decades of the century the primary distinction was between the nations of the Caribbean Basin and those of the Southern Cone.

The term "Latin America" itself originated in the mid-nineteenth century, but it was not universally used in the early twentieth century.[3] Instead, "Spanish America" or "Hispanic America" was frequently preferred. This can be seen, for example, in the names of the journal *Hispanic American Historical Review (HAHR)*, founded in 1918, and of the contemporaneous Hispanic American History Group. In part, the use of "Spanish America" or "Hispanic America" was due to ignorance and neglect of Brazil—a perennial complaint throughout the century. In addition, some, including the first financial backer of the *HAHR*, insisted that Hispanic America embraced both the Spanish-speaking areas and Brazil.

The second part of the book traces developments from the mid-1930s through the mid-1970s, a period that witnessed the maturing and institutionalization of Latin Americanist scholarship in the United States. These decades were marked by two periods of growth, stimulated by World War II and by the accession to power in Cuba of Fidel Castro. In the intervening years (approximately 1945–1958) a "drought" ensued as Latin America became marginalized in terms of funding, graduate student enrollment, and general academic interest. By 1975 the study of Latin America in the United States was firmly established in nearly all American colleges and universities, buoyed by the growth of the previous fifteen years. Meanwhile, the U.S. expansion was paralleled by a similar expansion of scholarship in Latin America itself. Soon, however, developments in the international arena and within the academic community would combine to diminish or redefine the intense interest in the region characteristic of the previous fifteen years. Even so, Latin America remained a cynosure of scholarly interest in the following decades.

To date, little has been written on the development of Latin Americanist scholarship or of area studies in general except for biographies and memoirs of key individuals. Robert A. McCaughey traced the evolution of international studies, including those relating to Latin America, in a 1984 volume. His primary purpose, however, was to demonstrate the "enclosure" of international studies by university-based programs after World War II, an outcome about which he was avowedly ambivalent.[4] The book is especially enlightening in its discussion of the role of the Ford Foundation in stimulating international studies in academe. Latin American studies would be an important beneficiary of the foundation's largesse in the 1960s.

A few studies deal exclusively with Latin America. Mark T. Berger's *Under Northern Eyes: Latin American Studies and U.S. Hegemony in the Americas, 1898–1990* (1995) is packed with valuable information and insights, but as its subtitle indicates, it is primarily an attempt to show a fundamental connection between Latin American studies and U.S. hegemony in the Americas. Although it purports to cover the period 1898–1990, it deals mainly with the late twentieth century and with policy debates over Central America. An essay by Daniel W. Gade not only discusses early American geographers who studied Latin America but also speculates on "the scholarly pull" of the region, including the relative ease of learning Spanish and the role of mentors in countering negative stereotypes about Latin America.[5]

Several other works proved especially useful. Two were short pieces by Lewis Hanke that recount the early development of Latin American studies in the United States. The first, published in a collection of essays honoring geographer Preston E. James, discusses events of the 1930s; the second, which appeared in *The Americas* (1947), takes the story to 1945. In 1967 Howard F. Cline, Hanke's successor as director of the Hispanic Foundation of the Library of Congress, edited a compilation of previously published writings that he called *Latin American History: Essays on Its Study and Teaching, 1889–1965.*[6] Despite its title, many of the selections in this collection provide information about the development of Latin Americanist scholarship in fields other than history as well as on area studies related to Latin America.

Hanke and Cline were both productive historians whose books and articles made significant contributions to their respective fields—"the Spanish struggle for justice" and Bartolomé de Las Casas in Hanke's case and Mexican studies and Middle American ethnohistory in Cline's.[7] In addition, as these pages will show, the two men were also devoted to, and effective in, the promotion of Latin American studies in the United States, and it is therefore fitting that this book should be dedicated to their memory.

The present study pretends to be no more than an introduction that builds on the work of the aforementioned scholars and others cited in the notes. It aims to contribute to an understanding of the factors that can lead to the awakening, efflorescence, and occasional decline of academic scholarship devoted to a specific region. Although attention is devoted exclusively to Latin America, my findings may have relevance to scholarship related to other parts of the world. A secondary goal is to shed light on the discourse of Latin American specialists regarding Latin America during the years in question. Many previous studies have addressed the perceptions of travelers, journalists, diplomats, and others, but none has singled out those of Latin Americanists, arguably the most knowledgeable.

In addition to printed works such as those mentioned above, this study is based on the examination of several manuscript collections. Thanks are therefore due to the librarians and archivists who proved unfailingly helpful and cooperative at the following institutions: Bancroft Library, University of California-Berkeley; Rare Book and Manuscript Library, Butler Library, Columbia University; Research Center, Ford Foundation (especially Idelle Nissila); Manuscript Division, Library of Congress; Rockefeller Archive Center; Latin American Library, Tulane University; and Manuscripts and Archives, Yale University Library.

I would also like to express my appreciation for the suggestions of the anonymous readers of the manuscript and for the help of the staff of the University of Alabama Press. The editing of Kathy Swain greatly improved the manuscript.

1

Beginnings

The dislike of Anglo-Saxon Protestants for Spain and Roman Catholicism shaped early perceptions of the colonies that lay to the south of British North America. As the eighteenth century dawned, they were seen mainly as fields for missionary endeavor. The diary of the Massachusetts divine Samuel Sewall reveals a continuing interest in the possibility of Mexico's revolting against Spanish rule, which would presumably open the door to English colonization there and the introduction of Protestantism. In 1702 the appearance of a comet in the southern skies concentrated Sewall's thoughts on Mexico, and he wrote in his diary: "I have long pray'd for Mexico, and of late in those Words, that God would open the Mexican Fountain." His clerical colleague, Cotton Mather, went further and in 1699 composed a Spanish-language tract on the Protestant religion that he hoped to circulate in the Spanish colonies in the belief that "the Time for our Lord Jesus Christ to have glorious Churches in America" might be at hand. Mather's tract was the first work in Spanish to be printed in North America.[1]

Mather taught himself Spanish in a few weeks in order to write this tract. In the eighteenth century those who learned Spanish were likely to be self-taught or to receive instruction from private tutors. Thomas Jefferson was also self-instructed in Spanish, which he considered second only to French as an indispensable language for Americans. "Our connection with Spain is already important and will become daily more so," he wrote in 1787. "Besides this the antient [*sic*] part of American history is written chiefly in Spanish." Jefferson put his principles to work by insisting that his daughter Mary read ten pages of *Don Quijote* each day. It was through his influence that Spanish instruction was included among the offerings of the College of William and Mary in 1780. Benjamin Franklin, who had a reading knowledge of the language, was responsible for the teaching of Spanish at the Public Academy of the City of Philadelphia as early as 1766. Meanwhile, the first Spanish grammar to be published in the future United States appeared in New York in 1741.[2]

The intellectual curiosity stimulated by the Enlightenment encouraged individuals as well as libraries, universities, and other scholarly institutions to acquire books dealing with the history of the Spanish colonies. These books might be English language works, such as Thomas Gage's account of his years in Spanish America, or English translations of works by Francisco Javier Clavigero, among others. Titles in Spanish or Latin were also sought. While in France in 1787, for example, Jefferson purchased Garcilaso de la Vega's *Florida del Inca* and Antonio de Herrera's *Historia general.* Jefferson's library, which was sold to the fledgling Library of Congress, contained almost two hundred volumes about Latin America and the Iberian Peninsula.[3]

According to Harry Bernstein, Philadelphia was the "capital of Hispanic studies" during this period. In 1764 the Library Company there owned works by Garcilaso de la Vega and Juan de Solís, and the collection of the bibliophile John Logan, merged with that of the Library Company in 1792, included Francisco López de Gomara's history of the conquest of Mexico and the rare botanical treatise of Francisco Hernández. The libraries of Harvard University and the New York Historical Society also acquired books about the Spanish colonies. Meanwhile, institutions such as the American Philosophical Society of Philadelphia named Spaniards and Spanish Americans to be corresponding members, the first of the latter (1801) being Alejandro Ramírez, a botanist who had lived in Cuba, Puerto Rico, and Central America.[4] Two years later the society acquired a complete set of the *Mercurio Peruano,* the periodical published in Lima from 1791 to 1795.

Jefferson's *Notes on Virginia* (1785) reveals an acquaintance with Antonio de Ulloa and Clavigero. An expression of creole nationalism, Clavigero's history of Mexico (1780–81) was consciously intended to be a rebuttal to the work of scholars who he believed had maligned the New World and in particular its native inhabitants. The leading culprit in this respect was the Scottish clergyman, educator, and historian William Robertson. His *History of America* (1777) was undoubtedly the most influential work of scholarship on the Spanish colonies to circulate in North America in the late eighteenth and early nineteenth centuries. Robertson had already won distinction for his histories of Scotland (1759) and of the reign of Charles V (1769) when he embarked on a study of the Spanish colonies, originally envisioned as part of the latter project. He secured books and manuscripts from Spain, duly listed in a bibliography at the beginning of his text, and even prepared a questionnaire to be put to informants in Spain who had firsthand experience of the colonies, though he paid little heed to their replies. Instead, he relied heavily on the writings of Antonio de Herrera and other familiar accounts to produce a work that condemned the inhumanity and greed of the conquerors but portrayed the native Americans as occupying a low rung on the evolutionary ladder that led from savagery through barbarism to civilization. Influenced by the environmental and economic determinism of Montesquieu, David Hume, and Adam Smith, Robertson found even the most advanced societies—those of the Aztec and Inca empires—to be wanting in the development of commerce and the concept of property, which he considered fundamental to civilization.[5]

Robertson's *History of America* had wide circulation in the United States. The first American edition was not published until 1812, but copies of the many editions printed in London and Dublin circulated in the United States, and selections from the book were serialized in a magazine from 1789 to 1791. Robertson's work also served as a source for such authors as Joel Barlow and William Gilmore Sims, who dealt with themes related to the discovery and conquest of America in poetry and fiction.[6]

The long movement for Latin American independence, which began in 1810 and continued until 1825, quickened American interest in the region. A major force in disseminating information about Latin America and its prospects was the *North American Review*, founded in 1815 by William Tudor, who served as the first U.S. consul in Peru in the mid-1820s. Jared Sparks, a long-serving editor of the magazine (1817–18, 1823–30), was especially desirous of publishing information about the new nations. In 1825 he asked Lucas Alamán, the Mexican historian and conservative ideologue, for assistance in obtaining documents to be published in the *Review*. "There is universal sympathy in this country with the rising republics of the south," he explained, "but the knowledge of the actual state of things is limited and imperfect."[7] During Sparks's tenure as editor, the *Review* published numerous long articles related to contemporary developments in Latin America, often in the form of commentary about recently published books or official documents.

In articles in the *North American Review* and in comments elsewhere, two differing sets of perceptions about the present and future state of Latin America can be discerned. Like Sparks, some writers expressed sympathy with the aspirations of Latin America. Associated with this sympathy was the conviction that the new nations had been inspired by the North American example and would soon develop close political and commercial relations with the United States. Thus an 1827 article on conditions in Venezuela declared that the United States was the "leading star" guiding the "bravest and wisest and purest patriots" of the region.[8]

Other writers, however, expressed pessimism about the future of Latin America and suggested that the cultural differences between it and the United

States were too great to permit intimate and harmonious relations. Writing to Alexander von Humboldt in 1813, for example, Thomas Jefferson was confident that the Latin American colonies would achieve independence, but he was uncertain about the kind of government that would be established. "History, I believe," he observed, "furnishes no example of a priest-ridden people maintaining a free civil government." In 1821 a writer in the *North American Review* asserted that the people of the United States could have but scant political sympathy with Latin Americans as they sprang from different stock, spoke different languages, and professed profoundly different religions. He appeared to envision a neocolonial relationship for Latin America vis-à-vis the United States: "South America will be to North America . . . what Asia and Africa are to Europe." He attributed the dismal prospects of the region to its tropical climate, its Spanish cultural heritage, and its racial miscegenation. The writer did not see how good national character and political harmony could be produced by "such heterogeneous and odious confusions of Spanish bigotry and indolence, with savage barbarity and African stupidity."[9]

These gloomy pronouncements reflect the "disappointment or even contempt" with which, according to historian John J. Johnson, American policy makers had come to view the new Latin American nations by 1830. In his study *A Hemisphere Apart* (1990), Johnson argues that the cautious optimism with which the independence movement was greeted in the United States gave way to indifference and the belief that "Latin America would remain in an arrested state of development."[10] He attributes these attitudes to several causes, including the economic and political failures of the new nations. In addition, the United States was preoccupied with its own internal development and was willing to accept British hegemony in the region because the interests of the two nations were in basic harmony. Discounting hostility to Catholicism as a significant element in policy makers' negative perceptions, Johnson places emphasis on contemporary American prejudices toward Indians, blacks, and people of mixed race, all of whom were prominent in the Latin American populations.

As the previous reference to Spanish bigotry and indolence suggests, negative attitudes toward Spain persisted in the United States. The emphasis was now on Spanish decline. Accordingly, a writer in the *North American Review* in 1817 derided Spanish intellectual pretensions: "As a nation, the Spaniards are at present a full century behind every other nation of Europe in the arts of life, the refinements of society, and enlightened views of civil polity; and almost a millenium [*sic*], in the modes of education and intellectual culture. It may be questioned whether they have taken a step in the right road of learning since the days of the Cid." Moreover, the developments of the independence era offered writers a new opportunity to expatiate on Spanish misrule and folly. One article in the *North*

American Review called Spanish rule in Latin America a tyranny unmatched in world history, and another stated that the revival of mining in South America would be guided by motives different from those that had guided Spain. Then gold had fed the vanity and appetite of only a few and had brought Spain to its present degraded state at the bottom of the scale of nations.[11]

Yet amid the continuing denigration of Spain and official indifference toward Latin America, there were signs of interest in Spain that would lead indirectly to the dawn of American historical scholarship on Latin America. In the years after 1810 many additional colleges began to offer instruction in Spanish, among them Dickinson (1814), the University of Virginia (1825), Yale (1826), and Amherst (1827). In 1815 Abiel Smith, a Harvard alumnus, bequeathed the sum of $20,000 to his alma mater to support a professor of French or of French and Spanish. The Smith Professorship of the French and Spanish Languages was duly established and conferred on George Ticknor, who held it from 1819 until 1835. Ticknor himself gave no instruction in Spanish or French. That task was entrusted to instructors such as Francis Sales, a French émigré who had taught Ticknor and served on the Harvard faculty until 1854. Sales published a Spanish grammar based on a French original in 1822, as well as a collection of readings called the *Colmena española* (1825). During the same period Peter Babad, a French priest, offered courses in Portuguese at Saint Mary's College in Baltimore and produced a Portuguese grammar (1820). Pietro Bachi, a Sicilian, taught Portuguese to Harvard students from 1826 to 1846 and also published a grammar (1831).[12]

As Smith Professor, Ticknor's primary obligation was to give scholarly lectures on Spanish and French literature. To prepare himself for this assignment, he visited Spain in 1818 and, like many of his compatriots, found much that was repellent in Spanish culture and society, especially among the ruling classes and the clergy. He admired the common people, among whom he detected "more force without barbarism, and civilization without corruption" than he had seen elsewhere in Europe.[13] This ambivalence could also be detected in Ticknor's three-volume *History of Spanish Literature* (1849), to which he devoted himself after retiring from Harvard. Adhering to the belief, common in his day, that a country's literature reflects its civil society, Ticknor concluded that, like the nation, Spanish letters had degenerated since the mid-sixteenth century. He attributed the decline to the despotism of the Spanish monarchy and to religious intolerance as reflected in the workings of the Inquisition: "Through the whole period of the sixteenth and seventeenth centuries . . . the Inquisition, as the giant exponent of the power of religion in Spain, had not only maintained an uninterrupted authority, but, by constantly increasing its relations to the state, and lending itself more and more freely to the punishment of whatever was obnoxious to the government, had effectually broken down all that remained, from earlier days of intellectual independence and manly freedom."[14]

Historical Precursors: Irving and Prescott

Washington Irving had a longer and more intimate association with Spain than Ticknor and contributed to a more positive, if still ambivalent, portrait of that country. The first American writer to gain an international reputation, Irving became acquainted with Spanish literature in his youth. In 1825, at loose ends after his initial literary successes, he toyed with the idea of translating works by Cervantes. The Spanish language, he informed his brother, was "full of power, and magnificence and melody" and its poetry marked by "animation, pathos, humour, beauty, sublimity." In Spanish literature as a whole, he found an "oriental splendour."[15]

Irving lived in Spain from 1826 to 1829, travelling extensively throughout the country and writing several important works, including *Chronicle of the Conquest of Granada* (1829) and *Legends of the Alhambra* (1832). In 1842 he was astounded to learn that he had been appointed minister to Spain and accepted the position largely because he needed the salary and thought he might do some writing while there. Though tinged with the romanticism that characterized his writing about Spain, Irving's views of the country's people and culture evinced the ambivalence exhibited by Ticknor. In 1827 he considered Spain to be impoverished and "over grown with bigotry and ignorance," but he was lavish in his praise of the common people, whom he declared to be "Shrewd, sententious, proud, courteous, disinterested and Full of fire and courage, though all of no avail from want of good education and good government." Fifteen years later, soon after returning to Madrid, he wrote that he had been received as a friend of Spain, and indeed he was: "I cannot but feel a deep interest in the fortunes of this harrassed [sic], impoverished, depressed, yet proud spirited and noble country."[16]

Irving first travelled to Spain at the prompting of Alexander H. Everett, the American minister in Madrid and an old acquaintance. Everett had proposed that Irving undertake a translation of documents published by Martín Fernández de Navarrete in the first two volumes of his five-volume *Colección de viages y descubrimientos que hicieron por mar los españoles desde fines del siglo xv*. Irving quickly accepted the invitation, but on examining Navarrete's massive volumes after his arrival in Madrid on February 1, 1826, he concluded that the projected translation would be too dry to find a wide audience. In addition, Irving's London publisher was unwilling to commit himself to the work until he had seen a manuscript.[17] It was at this point that Irving decided to embark on a project—a life of Christopher Columbus—that would become the first major historical work on a Latin American subject by a citizen of the United States.

The idea of a Columbus biography was first broached to Irving by Obadiah Rich, the American consul in Madrid, with whom he found lodgings. A long-time resident of Spain, Rich had amassed a large collection of printed works and manuscripts relating to the New World, including a copy of part of Bartolomé de Las Casas's as yet unpublished *Historia y crónica de Indias*. Irving was therefore ideally placed to undertake a study of the discoverer, for he could consult not only documents in the Navarrete collection, which included the journal of Columbus's first voyage as transcribed by Las Casas, but also Rich's vast holdings, which the bibliophile put at his disposal. "The Books which Robertson was years in collecting," Irving told a friend, "are all within my reach." He would try, he added, to make his biography "the most complete and authentic account of Columbus & his voyages extant and, by diligent investigation of the materials around me, to settle various points in dispute."[18]

Irving's multivolume biography, published both in England and the United States in 1828, was indeed accompanied by the paraphernalia of scholarship, and a modern commentator has estimated that there was one citation for every four or five sentences.[19] All together, Irving cited 150 sources; the most frequently used, besides documents in Navarrete's collection, were Ferdinand Columbus's biography of his father and the histories of Las Casas and Antonio de Herrera. As a result, Irving's work garnered generally positive reviews from contemporary scholars such as Navarrete and William H. Prescott. The book quickly became an international best seller and proved to be "among the most profitable writing ventures" of Irving's career. During his lifetime it was translated into Spanish, Dutch, French, German, Greek, Italian, Polish, Swedish, and Russian, and three different editions were published in Latin America.[20]

Irving depicted Columbus as a romantic hero: farseeing, resolute, and benign in the face of incomprehension and hostility from men who were his inferiors. William H. Schurr considers Irving's Columbus well suited to appeal to contemporaries in the United States: "Like [North] America, he had shown himself superior to kings; he had faced and subdued a wilderness; finally, he had displayed a properly [North] American inventiveness and the nobility of the free individual." Schurr adds that Irving's biography expanded North Americans' conceptualization of their history: "He broadened the focus of [North] American identity from Protestant England exclusively to include the old Spanish world of the Caribbean with its still vitally important markets and manufactories." To Rolena Adorno, Irving's treatment of Columbus emphasized not only his accidental but "glorious" discovery of America but also his enterprise, "thus underscoring, in typical nineteenth-century language, the progressive economic goals that he attributed to Columbus."[21]

Historians ranging from Henry Harisse in the late nineteenth century to Samuel Eliot Morison in the twentieth continued to express favorable opinions of Irving's biography, though there were naysayers, notably Stanley T. Williams, who faulted him for what he considered excessive and inadequately acknowledged reliance on Navarrete's collection. More recently, Benjamin Keen criticized Irving for failing to consider Columbus's flaws, especially his mistreatment of the Indians, an omission he attributed to the biographer's conservatism and mediocre mind.[22] Indeed, Irving portrayed most of the native inhabitants of the Caribbean as gentle and ingenuous savages who received kindly and beneficent treatment from Columbus. Irving was critical of Columbus's proposal to Ferdinand and Isabella in 1494 that Carib captives, specimens of a reputedly ferocious and cannibalistic people, be enslaved. Columbus made this "pernicious" suggestion, Irving wrote, on the grounds that though enslaved, the Caribs would be Christianized, but "he was in reality listening to the incitements of his interest," for thus far his explorations had seemingly yielded little of value besides potential slaves. Irving was also critical of the abuses perpetrated by others besides Columbus, such as the royal governor, Nicolás de Ovando. In contrast to many other historians, however, he asserted that such atrocities were "commonly the crimes of individuals rather than of the nation," thereby exonerating the Spanish people of collective guilt in the fate that befell the Indians.[23]

While in Spain, Irving made plans to write an account of the conquest of Mexico, a subject that he said had engaged his imagination since childhood. He left Spain without having done the required research and then kept postponing the project until 1838, only to learn that William Hickling Prescott was engaged in writing a similar history.[24] Irving gracefully surrendered, though he later described his action as a sacrifice, and Prescott, already famous as the author of *The History of the Reign of Ferdinand and Isabella, the Catholic* (1837), proceeded to complete *The History of the Conquest of Mexico* (1843), generally regarded as his masterpiece.

As Irving had in effect created Columbus for the young United States, so Prescott viewed the story of the conquest of Mexico as part of American history as well. In 1838 he wrote to Martín Fernández de Navarrete that no portion of Spanish history had greater interest for Americans than that which was connected with their own country and was "singularly romantic" to boot, such as the conquest of Mexico and Peru. As had been the case with his work on Ferdinand and Isabella, Prescott, bound by his poor eyesight and family ties to his home in Massachusetts, obtained his research materials from book dealers and copyists in Europe. Angel Calderón, the Spanish minister in Mexico with whom Prescott had been acquainted while he was in the United States, urged him to visit Mexico City: a visit to the capital would enhance the authority of Prescott's work and help him to "understand the effects of time on the ancient Spanish race and on the Indians of which you must give the world an understanding."[25]

Although Prescott demurred, he obtained a portrait of Mexico from the letters of Angel's wife, Fanny, who provided him with caustic appraisals of Mexican society and answered his questions about the scenery and wildlife that Hernán Cortés might have encountered while en route to Tenochtitlán. He asked, for example, about the tropical vegetation in the hot lowlands: "Is not the road bordered with flowers and the trees bent under a load of parasitical plants of every hue and odour? I should like to get a peep into this paradise." Through Angel Calderón, Prescott was put into contact with Lucas Alamán, who provided information about a hospital founded by Cortés and about the conqueror's tomb. Prescott also gained insight into military matters as a result of conversations with General William Miller, a veteran of the Spanish American wars of independence.[26]

Prescott envisioned his narrative as an "epic in prose," in which European civilization was pitted against Aztec barbarism and the heroic figure of Cortés against that of Moctezuma, the Aztec emperor. But the pusillanimous and superstitious Moctezuma was no match for Cortés, who was represented as possessing remarkable qualities of leadership and character. Prescott condemned the bloody excesses committed by the Spaniards during the conquest period, but he attributed them to the sanguinary and intolerant spirit of the sixteenth century. On balance he considered the fall of the Aztec empire, which oppressed its subjects and engaged in human sacrifice on a massive scale, as a positive development.[27]

Prescott next turned to a history of the conquest of Peru, which was published in 1847. As before, he began with a description of the Inca empire, which he praised for its efforts to ensure the material well-being of even the humblest of its subjects. He was critical, however, of the regimentation imposed by the empire: "The power of free agency—the inestimable and inborn right of every human being—was annihilated in Peru."[28]

As Prescott was well aware, the conquest of the Inca empire by the Spaniards offered less scope for literary flourishes than the conquest of Mexico. Whereas the fall of Tenochtitlán was depicted as the climactic moment of the latter, the narrator of the conquest of Peru had to include the long period of internecine feuds and rebellion that followed the arrival of the Spaniards in the Inca capital of Cuzco—"quarrels of banditti over their spoils." Another problem lay in the person of Francisco Pizarro, whom Prescott viewed as far inferior to Cortés in character and military prowess. To him Prescott assigned the responsibility for the mistreatment and eventual execution of the Inca emperor Atahualpa, "undoubtedly one of the darkest chapters in Spanish colonial history." In short, Prescott presented Pizarro as an adventurer, "eminently perfidious," who seems to have been driven mainly by "avarice and ambition." By contrast, Pedro de la Gasca, the Spanish official dispatched to impose order and royal authority in Peru, emerged as the hero of Prescott's tale. To Prescott, Gasca was "a Spanish Washington—wise, temperate, humane, yet resolute & fearless."[29]

Prescott's accounts of the conquests of Mexico and Peru won him further acclaim in both the United States and Europe. His books were considered to have superseded Robertson's treatment of the same subjects not only because of their more extended narrative but also because of the much larger documentary base on which they rested. The sections on the Aztec and Inca civilizations were the best appraisals to date, though today they are considered the weakest portions of the two texts. Prescott has been faulted for slighting important aspects of the conquest, but no one has retold the story with greater narrative skill.

After completing his history of the conquest of Peru, Prescott turned to the reign of Philip II and had completed three volumes at the time of his death in 1859. Thus, his primary interest was in Spanish history, not that of the New World. Yet, according to Richard L. Kagan, for all his sympathy toward Spain, Prescott viewed it as the antithesis of the United States. In what Kagan calls "Prescott's paradigm," the religious fanaticism, despotism, and indolence of Spain, especially under the Hapsburgs, were for the first time contrasted with the rationalism and enterprise of the young republic: "Earlier New England writers, Cotton Mather and Samuel Sewall among them, had also espoused a negative view of Spain, but Prescott was the first to adopt a truly comparative perspective, setting the trajectories of the two nations side by side." It should be noted, nonetheless, that in his own estimation Prescott was a great friend of Spain. In 1844 he wrote: "I believe I may say without vanity or exaggeration . . . that with the exception of Irving I have done as much as any foreigner of the present day to exhibit the nation in a right and honourable point of view and have constantly endeavoured to hold up its great men and the achievements of its people to the admiration of the student of history."[30]

For all his devotion to Spanish subjects, Prescott retained some interest in Mexico and was pleased to learn that his account of the conquest was being translated there. He corresponded with the historian and bibliophile Joaquín García Icazbalceta as well as with Lucas Alamán, whom he nominated for membership in the Massachusetts Historical Society and the American Philosophical Society. He refused an invitation from General Winfield Scott to write a history of the Mexican War because he did not wish to deal with heroes who had not been under ground for at least two centuries.[31]

Early Studies in Anthropology and Archaeology

During his first sojourn in Spain, Washington Irving compared its population favorably with that of the native Americans at home: "There are more natural gentlemen among the common people of Spain than among any people I have known, excepting our Indians."[32] Here Irving was articulating a romantic conception of both Spaniards and Indians that saw both peoples as manifesting the traits of the "noble savage" of eighteenth-century myth. To many nineteenth-century Americans the Indians who inhabited the northern part of the New World were a source of intense interest, even as they were being dislodged from their lands. Scholars who probed the origins and capabilities of the indigenous peoples of North America were inevitably drawn to the indigenous peoples of the south and their histories, for it was believed that studying the latter would shed light on the former. Thus, scholarly investigation of the archaeology of Latin America can be seen as an extension of researches closer to home. The students of the indigenous peoples of Latin America, moreover, were the first investigators to travel to the region, informing their popular and scholarly accounts with the seeming authenticity of firsthand experience.

Inquisitive Americans of a scholarly bent sought answers to numerous questions about the Indians of the New World. Were they the descendants of migrants from Asia or some other part of the Old World? Or were they native to the Western Hemisphere, a possibility that cast into question the biblical story of a single creation? How were the different indigenous groups related? Did the Indians of the present day represent the pinnacle of indigenous civilization, or had they degenerated over the centuries?

Some, such as the Swiss-born statesman Albert Gallatin, studied native languages in the belief that philology could yield important information about a people's history and culture. The complexity that Gallatin and others discovered in indigenous languages suggested to them that a decline in the culture of the native peoples of North America had occurred. Unlike others who shared these views, Gallatin was optimistic about the Indians' capacity for improvement. A founder of the American Ethnological Society in 1842, Gallatin published in the first volume of its transactions "Notes on the Semi-Civilized Nations of Mexico, Yucatan and Central America" (1845). There he rejected the idea that Mesoamerican achievements in astronomy and mathematics were not auchthonous but of Old World origin. By attributing the relative advancement of Mesoamerican natives to their early development of agriculture, he was proposing an environmental explanation for cultural change that was increasingly out of favor in scholarly circles.[33]

Samuel George Morton, a physician from Philadelphia, collected and studied Indian skulls from both North and South America. Believing that cranial capacity was linked to mental development, he found Indians inferior to whites in both these spheres. Nor did he see significant differences between indigenous groups. The crania of South American Indians were as small as those of their North American cousins, and therefore, regardless of their achievements, they could not have attained a level of intellectual development comparable to that of whites. In fact, Morton inspired the "American school" of ethnology, whose followers adhered to a belief in polygenesis: that the various races of mankind were the result of multiple creations and represented distinct species.[34]

The study of the pre-Columbian civilizations of Mesoamerica received great impetus from the work of John Lloyd Stephens, whose narratives of travel in the region also acquainted contemporaries in the United States with a little-known portion of the former Spanish empire. Stephens, a native of New Jersey, was trained as a lawyer and practiced in New York City for several years before embarking on the first of his foreign journeys. He visited not only western Europe but also Poland, Russia, Greece, and Turkey and examined ancient monuments in Egypt and Petra. His accounts (1837, 1838) of this expedition were both profitable and well received.[35]

Stephens's interest in the antiquities of Central America is said to have been stirred by a New York bookseller, John Russell Bartlett, who showed him a copy of a recently published volume on Yucatan by Jean Frédéric Waldeck, a Frenchman who was one of the first modern travellers to visit and describe Maya ruins. Stephens enlisted as his travelling companion Frederick Catherwood, an English architect and artist whom he had met in London in 1836 and may have called his attention to an eighteenth-century description of the Maya ruins at Palenque. Stephens's plans received a further boost when he secured appointment as U.S. minister to the disintegrating Central American Federation.

Stephens and Catherwood sailed from New York for Central America in October 1839 and travelled through parts of Guatemala, Honduras, and Mexico before returning to the United States in July 1840. In October 1841, accompanied by Catherwood and Samuel Cabot, a young physician and naturalist, Stephens left for Yucatan and remained there until mid-1842. Stephens published long accounts of his two journeys: *Incidents of Travel in Central America, Chiapas, and Yucatan* (1841) and *Incidents of Travel in Yucatan* (1843). Enriched by Catherwood's superb illustrations, both works were favorably reviewed and gained huge popular success.

In many respects Stephens's narratives were typical of the accounts of travel to exotic places that gained a wide readership during the nineteenth century. Stephens observed and evaluated the landscape and the people, commenting, for example, on the seemingly harmonious relations between Indian servants and their white masters in Yucatan. While travelling through Central America, he frequently found fault with the local people; in particular, he accused them of indolence, though it is unclear whether he attributed this failing to an innate trait of the Indians, "the deathlike sleep of Spanish domination," the enervating effects of the tropical climate, or a combination of all of these. Like his compatriots, he was critical of the Roman Catholic Church, which he declared to be "at this day a pall upon the spirit of free institutions, degrading and debasing instead of elevating the Christian character."[36] Even so, he often praised individual priests whom he encountered on his travels, impressed by their dedication to their flock, their erudition and intelligence, and their eagerness to assist him.

But it was Stephens's descriptions of pre-Columbian ruins that won him fame in his own day and earned him a lasting reputation as the leading U.S. pioneer of Mesoamerican archaeology. During his two expeditions he visited numerous sites, notably Copán and Quiriguá in Central America, and Palenque, Uxmal, and Chichén Itzá in Mexico. Stephens's frequent references to the work of others who had surveyed the ruins before him, his own careful observations, and Catherwood's meticulous sketches combined to lend an air of authority to his conclusions.

Stephens addressed the principal issues that engaged contemporaries regarding the origins of Mesoamerican monuments and their relationship to contemporary native Americans. He forthrightly asserted that the monuments were worthy of comparison with those of antiquity and that the builders had been a civilized race, but he denied that they were the descendants of Egyptians, Greeks, or any other Old World people. Although he doubted that the ruined cities were of great age, he suggested that the builders had in most cases disappeared before the arrival of the Spaniards. Thus, he failed to make explicit any connection between the builders and the Maya speakers who still inhabited Chiapas, Yucatan, and parts of Central America, though he considered these a degraded remnant.

Undoubtedly adding to the appeal of Stephens's narrative was the highly romanticized imagery that he used to convey his impressions. Thus he mused about Copán at the start of his first expedition: "The city was desolate. No remnant of this race [the builders] hangs round the ruins, with traditions handed down from father to son, and from generation to generation. It lay before us like a shattered bark in the midst of the ocean, her master gone, her name effaced, her crew perished, and none to tell whence she came, to whom she belonged, how long on her voyage, or what caused her destruction—her lost people to be traced only by some fancied resemblance in the construction of the vessel, or, perhaps never to be known at all."[37]

Stephens was also a pioneer of what has been called "archaeological Monroeism." He acknowledged the intellectual curiosity and scholarship of some of the Central Americans and Mexicans he met, such as the Yucatecan Don Pío Pérez, but repeatedly asserted the indifference of local peoples, regardless of their race and position, to the antiquities in their midst. Their interest was likely to be excited only by the prospect of the pecuniary gain that might be derived from the ruins. Stephens could therefore feel justified in laying claim to the buried cities, to the exclusion not only of the natives but also of Europeans. On visiting Copán, he expressed concern that similar, more accessible sites might be discovered and that the friends of science and art in Europe would gain possession of them: "They belonged by right to us, and . . . I resolved that ours they should be." Accordingly, he negotiated the purchase of the ruins of Copán for $50 and claimed that the owner considered him a fool for paying so much.[38] Stephens also removed objects from the sites he visited, including wooden lintels from Uxmal and Kabah in Yucatan and sculptured stone doorjambs from the latter site. At a site near Ticul, also in Yucatan, he found a human skeleton that he gave to Samuel Morton.

Stephens intended to display the lintels and other objects at a Museum of American Antiquities that he planned to establish, but they were all destroyed by fire in 1842. The doorjambs arrived later and were given to a friend of Stephens, John Church, who sold them to the American Museum of Natural History in 1918. Despite the success of his two narratives, Stephens now turned from archaeology to entrepreneurship, becoming a leading investor in the transisthmian Panama Railroad, completed in 1855. While in Panama, he fell victim to malaria and died in New York in 1852. In 1844 Catherwood published a collection of *Views of Ancient Monuments in Central America, Chiapas, and Yucatan,* a limited edition folio containing twenty-five plates, but afterward he was employed mainly as an architect and engineer until his death at sea in 1854.

Stephens's writings on Mesoamerican antiquities and on Central America and Yucatan set a pattern that would be followed by Ephraim G. Squier (1821–88). Squier travelled extensively throughout Central America, especially Nicaragua, Honduras, and El Salvador, and carefully described the remains of pre-Columbian civilizations he encountered there, though he did not come upon buried cities as impressive as those visited by Stephens. Squier also resembled his predecessor in that he travelled, at least part of the time, in a diplomatic capacity and displayed entrepreneurial tendencies, but his favored project, a railroad across Honduras, would never be built. Squier's Latin American career would be more extensive than Stephens's, for after his Central American expeditions, he had an opportunity to travel to Peru and study pre-Columbian remains there.

Born into modest circumstances in Bethlehem, New York, Squier initially attained success as a Whig journalist and in 1845 moved to Chillicothe, Ohio, to become editor of the *Scioto Gazette*. There he met a physician, Edwin H. Davis, who was a student of the Indian mounds and earthworks of south-central Ohio. Together they explored and surveyed the mounds of the Middle West and South and published their findings and those of other investigators in *Ancient Monuments of the Mississippi Valley* (1848), still considered "an American archaeological classic." The well-illustrated volume not only described mounds and other indigenous artifacts but also addressed long-running controversies about the age of the mounds and the identity of the builders. Squier and Davis indicated that the Mound Builders had been a numerous sedentary people who practiced agriculture and that they had had a "more or less intimate" connection with the natives of Mexico and Central and South America.[39] Squier now desired firsthand experiences with indigenous people to the south and, with the help of Irving, Prescott, and others, obtained an appointment as chargé d'affaires in Central America with a base in Nicaragua.

Squier's year in Nicaragua (1849–50) led to the writing of the first of his nine books on Central America, *Nicaragua: Its People, Scenery and Monuments and the Proposed International Canal* (1852). In addition to relating his diplomatic activities, he described the landscape and people, including the Indians, some of whom he portrayed as "mild, brave but not warlike, industrious, intelligent, and law-abiding." He speculated that their ancestors, like those of the Aztecs, had been Toltecs, regarded in that era as representing the height of native American civilization, but in Nicaragua and in other parts of Central America this strain had been mingled with that of the barbarous Chichimecs. Nicaragua lacked the large pre-Columbian sites that Stephens had seen, but Squier took pains to describe the statues, paintings, and other antiquities he found. On seeing a group of large monuments on an island in Lake Managua, he determined to succeed where the British consul had failed and managed to send one of the monuments to the United States, where it was deposited in the Smithsonian Institution.

Squier's comments regarding Nicaragua's Spanish and Roman Catholic heritage echoed Stephens's in their relative mildness. He praised Spain's "conciliation" toward the Indians, by which both state and church accommodated themselves to their beliefs. Somewhat contradictorily, he attributed the failures of Nicaragua and other Spanish American republics not to flaws in the Spanish character but to the fact that colonization was directed by a greedy and corrupt royal court and aristocracy. Of the contemporary clergy he stated that "many of them, though not highly educated, are not only men of liberal sentiments, but amongst the most active promoters of measures of general improvement."[40]

The book also reflects two other themes that would be prominent in Squier's subsequent Central American writings.[41] He was critical of British pretensions in the region and stressed the friendly feelings of Nicaraguans toward the United States. He saw Nicaragua as an inviting field for American investment and immigration. Having visited the Bay of Fonseca in 1850, he became convinced that it would be a suitable Pacific terminus for a transisthmian railroad starting near Omoa on the Bay of Honduras. He found backers for the project in the United States and in 1853 led an exploring party to examine the route and initiate discussions with the shaky Honduran government, led by José Trinidad Cabañas, who saw in the railroad project a possible means of survival. Squier envisioned the railroad not only as a profit-making enterprise but also as one that might result in the annexation of Honduras to the United States. Failure to raise enough capital for the railroad in the United States led Squier to seek new sources of financing in Europe, and in 1857 a British group bought out the rights of Squier and his associates.

Despite his Anglophobia, Squier remained committed to the railroad project, even when it was apparently rendered superfluous by the construction of the Panama Railroad and the completion of the first transcontinental railroad in the United States in 1869. The railroad is in the background of three other books on Central America published by Squier: *Notes on Central America* (1855), *States of Central America* (1858), and *Honduras: Descriptive, Historical, and Statistical* (1870). The best known of these is *States of Central America*, which offers much information on the five republics. Honduras, Nicaragua, and El Salvador are praised for their liberal tendencies while Guatemala's government is condemned as "reactionary in the extreme, and it is difficult to say if political selfishness or religious bigotry be the leading element in its composition."[42] In *Notes on Central America* he attributed the political turbulence of the region to the indiscriminate mixing of races, which resulted in the deterioration of the superior stock. During this period Squier published his only novel, *Waikna, or Adventures on the Mosquito Shore* (1855). Ostensibly an account of the adventures of a young artist in Mosquitia, the book is actually intended to discredit British policy in the region. Also noteworthy is Squier's negative portrayal of the Miskito people, of whom he had virtually no firsthand experience. He described them as improvident, treacherous, and larcenous, absurd puppets of the British.[43]

During these years Squier also produced more narrowly focused works pertaining to Central American archaeology and ethnology. In 1853, for example, the New York Historical Society published his "Ruins of Tenampuá, Honduras, Central America," a paper that remained the fullest description of this site for nearly one hundred years. Like his contemporaries, he was interested in native languages and during his two trips to Central America compiled word lists on sheets provided by the American Ethnological Society. His only publication in this field, however, was an 1861 bibliography: *Monograph of Authors Who Have Written on the Languages of Central America, and Collected Vocabularies or Composed Works in the Native Dialects of That Country*. Meanwhile, Squier had amassed a collection of documents on Central America and Mexico that he hoped to translate and publish. Only one of these appeared (1860), a letter from Diego García de Palacio, a judge (*oidor*) of the Audiencia of Guatemala, in which he described the Indians as they were in 1576 and the ruins at Copán.[44]

These and other writings by Squier on Central America provided valuable information on antiquities and current conditions in a region virtually unknown in the United States. Herein lies Squier's greatest contribution to Latin American scholarship, but in the 1860s he turned his attention to Peruvian antiquities, about which he had published an article in 1853. In 1863 he secured appointment as a member of a mixed commission created to settle claims involving citizens of Peru and the United States. The commission completed its work in fewer than six months, but Squier remained in Peru for another eighteen months, studying the antiquities of that country. He recorded his impressions and findings in five articles in *Harper's New Monthly Magazine* in 1868 and in *Peru: Incidents of Travel and Exploration in the Land of the Incas* (1877). These writings constituted the earliest firsthand account by an American traveller with a professional interest in pre-Columbian Andean civilization and are still considered basic for Peruvian archaeology.[45] Prescott's account of Inca society was authoritative but was based solely on documents rather than his own archaeological inspection.

Squier travelled extensively in Peru, examining the remains of Chimú and sites in Cuzco and its environs; he also went to Bolivia to see the ruins of Tiahuanaco. A modern commentator has found his observations to be "quite thorough" and, though essentially descriptive, thoughtful and insightful.[46] Squier was also a pioneer in the use of photography to illustrate Andean archaeological sites; in addition to the photographs he took himself, he used others provided by August Le Plongeon, better known for his later work in Maya archaeology, who had been studying Peruvian antiquities since 1862.[47]

Squier could not assign dates to the monuments he studied, but he believed that they were very old. He was also convinced of the native origins of Andean civilization. If the Inca monuments of Cuzco resembled those of ancient Egypt, it was because "primitive architecture, as primitive ideas, must have a likeness." He was extremely impressed by the Inca walls of Cuzco: "The world has nothing to show in the way of stone cutting and fitting to surpass the skill and accuracy displayed in the Inca structures of Cuzco." He predicted that the walls would be standing long after the U.S. Capitol and London Bridge had crumbled.[48]

Despite his admiration for the ancient monuments of Peru, Squier found little to praise about contemporary Indians, especially the Aymara, whom he called "a swarthier, more sullen, and more cruel race" than the Quechua. He frequently censured the Roman Catholic clergy for drunkenness, sexual misconduct, and greed. The Peruvians he met had, with few exceptions, little interest in their own antiquities, except for the treasure they might contain. Squier was also harsh in his comments about the impact of the Spanish conquest on Peru: "There was, under the Incas, a better government, better protection for life, and better facilities for the pursuit of happiness than have existed since the Conquest or do exist today."[49]

Squier's Andean expedition marked the end of his Latin American travels, for the years after his return from Peru were marred by domestic upheaval and a period of mental derangement. In 1857 he had married Miriam Florence Folline, whose uncle had been connected with the Honduran railroad project. In the early 1860s both Squier and his wife were employed as editors by the publisher Frank Leslie. They later formed a *ménage à trois*, living and travelling together until Leslie and Folline divorced their respective spouses and were married in July 1874.[50] Soon afterward, Squier was placed in a mental institution for several months, and in 1876 his collection of books and documents was sold at auction.

One of the reviewers of Squier's book on Peru was Adolph F. Bandelier (1840–1914), who called it "the most valuable contribution to the archaeology of that country." Bandelier is remembered today mainly for his work in the southwestern United States, but he also carried out significant investigations into the prehistory of Mesoamerica and Peru. In addition, according to his biographers, Bandelier was "one of the first scholars to use a holistic approach to archaeology, applying botanical, historical, geographical, linguistic, and zoological data to archaeological interpretations." They attributed his failures largely to the inadequate data and the poor dating methods that existed in his day. Bandelier was also a pioneer in discerning connections between the prehistoric cultures of the Southwest and those of Mesoamerica.[51]

Like Stephens and Squier, Bandelier was self-trained but differed from them in other respects. He was not a native of the United States; he was born in Bern, Switzerland, and moved to Highland, Illinois, with his family when he was eight. Although he became a U.S. citizen in 1877, he cannot be considered a promoter of American territorial and economic ambitions. He was frequently critical of American policies and institutions and resented the business obliga-

tions that initially interfered with his scholarly activities. One of the major crises of his life occurred in 1885 with the failure of a local bank in which he had
only a minor interest but for the collapse of which he was held responsible.

By 1885 Bandelier had already become a student of indigenous peoples and
in the future would devote himself entirely to scholarship. He apparently became interested in Mexican antiquities in the late 1860s and soon found a mentor in Lewis Henry Morgan, whom he first met in 1873.[52] The architect of the
dominant ethnological paradigm of his era, Morgan asserted a uniformity of
development among all indigenous peoples at the time of their first contact with
Europeans. He placed them in the evolutionary category of savagery or, in the
case of Mesoamerica and Peru, in the middle sector of barbarism. None had
reached the level of civilization or established a state, that is, a political organization based on territory and property. Thus, in his long review essay "Montezuma's Dinner" (1876), which was based on material supplied by Bandelier,
Morgan questioned the accuracy of the sixteenth-century Spanish chroniclers
and maintained instead that Moctezuma was no emperor but a war chief ruling
over a tribal confederacy of limited range. Tenochtitlán was merely the largest
pueblo in America at the time of the Spaniards' arrival.

Bandelier at first defended the authority of the Spanish chroniclers, but he
quickly came to embrace Morgan's views. This was evident in his review of
Squier's book, for he remarked that ancient Peru had no civilizations, only linguistic groups, and suggested that Tiahuanaco was no more than "an Indian
pueblo after the ordinary form." In letters to the Mexican scholar Joaquín García Icazbalceta, Bandelier expressed his opinion that Moctezuma presided over
a military democracy like that of the Iroquois, not a monarchy, and claimed to
find similarities in the line of succession as well. "In general terms," he wrote
to García Icazbalceta, "the analogies between the aborigines of your country
and those of the North seem to me to be much more marked than modern authors admit."[53]

Morgan proved helpful to his disciple. He helped arrange the publication of
Bandelier's first major papers—on Aztec warfare and land tenure—in the reports
of the Peabody Museum of American Archaeology and Ethnology. He was also
instrumental in obtaining for Bandelier his first opportunity to do fieldwork.
In 1880 Bandelier was engaged by the recently founded Archaeological Institute
of America to undertake a program of archaeological and ethnographic investigation in New Mexico. For the next twelve years Bandelier worked mainly in
the Southwest, though he also conducted archaeological surveys and archival
research in central and northern Mexico. His career entered a new phase in 1892
when he and his friend and fellow archaeologist Charles Lummis were engaged
by the railroad magnate Henry Villard and *Century* magazine to travel to Peru

and Bolivia to collect antiquities for the former and to write articles for the latter about their experiences. After Villard's support ended, the American Museum of Natural History agreed to sponsor Bandelier's work in South America, an arrangement that lasted until 1906, three years after his return to the United States. While in Peru, Bandelier surveyed and conducted excavations at several sites, notably Chan Chan. He also explored the region around the north coast of Lake Titicaca as well as islands in the lake. In his last years he was employed by the Carnegie Institution of Washington (CIW) to copy archival documents in Mexico City and Seville, where he died.

Bandelier's extensive bibliography, written in English, German, and French, contains scholarly works and collections of documents along with writings designed for general readers, such as articles and book reviews in the *Nation*. Most of his writings are the products of his work in the U.S. Southwest. Among them is a history of the colonization and the missions of Sonora, Chihuahua, New Mexico, and Arizona before 1700. Bandelier drafted the fourteen-hundred-page manuscript in 1886, but only portions of it have been published. Also relating to the Southwest is a novel, *The Delight Makers* (1890), now considered valuable because of its ethnographic material.[54] The principal work originating from his South American sojourn is *The Islands of Titicaca and Koati*, published in 1910 by the Hispanic Society of America, with which Bandelier was affiliated for several years after his return to the United States. This massive volume exemplifies the "holistic" approach that had become characteristic of Bandelier. He discusses not only the pre-Columbian remains he observed on the two islands on the lake but also the physical environment and the present-day condition of the Aymara-speaking inhabitants of the region as well as native traditions and myths. As sources he uses his own observations and surveys, supplemented by citations from the writings of the principal Spanish authors.

According to his biographers, Bandelier moved away from Morgan's "extreme evolutionism" about 1881, by which time he had begun his fieldwork. This was also the year of Morgan's death. Even so, one can find evidence of Bandelier's adherence to Morgan's views long after that. For example, in an 1885 address to the New York Historical Society, Bandelier faulted Prescott and other contemporary historians for failing to go beyond the accounts of the sixteenth-century chroniclers and for failing to see similarities among all native Americans: "No attention is paid as yet to the fact that the religious creeds of the Indians *over the whole American continent were moulded on the same pattern*, that their social organization was fundamentally the same . . . , that the system of government of the Iroquois differed from that of the Mexicans but very little, and that the same principles pervade the aboriginal architecture from one arctic circle to the other, varying only in *degree* and *not in kind.*" In *The Gilded Man (El Do-*

rado) and Other Pictures of the Spanish Occupancy of America (1893), Bandelier includes a chapter titled "The Massacre of Cholula," in which he asserts that Moctezuma was not a crowned monarch but merely the commander in chief of three confederated tribes of the Valley of Mexico. He scoffs at Prescott's depiction of Cholula with its pyramid and dense population and questions the accuracy of the Spanish chronicles: "Everything was misunderstood at first, or not understood at all."[55]

Nor did Bandelier find any reason to alter his views as a result of his stay in Peru and Bolivia. In an article in *Harper's Monthly* (1905) he offered "The Truth about Inca Civilization," arguing that the Inca were a tribe somewhat more successful than most but essentially no different from all the others that occupied the Americas in the sixteenth century. He minimized their number and the extent of their conquests and insisted that they treated conquered people as tributary allies or confederates without altering their mode of government or religion. In short, there was no effort to create a homogeneous nationality or an integrated empire. Though focusing on a narrower topic and writing for a specialized audience, Bandelier expressed similar opinions in *The Islands of Titicaca and Koati*. The Inca ruler is called a "war chief," and the vaunted Inca roads are said to be no more than trails. Moreover, the sixteenth-century chroniclers who bestowed the terms "gorgeous" and "splendid" on the monuments and ceremonies they witnessed on Titicaca were exaggerating: "All these reports suffer from the failings of their time, that is, from lack of means of comparisons with other peoples and countries, and an inclination to accept without reserve all that was told."[56] He did not reject the chroniclers' testimony out of hand but believed that it should be used critically.

The year 1881 was significant in Bandelier's life for another reason besides his fieldwork in Mexico and the death of Morgan. On July 31 he was baptized a Roman Catholic at a church in Cholula; García Icazbalceta acted as his godfather. Bandelier kept his conversion secret from his family in the United States for a time, realizing that it would make his father unhappy. He remained a Catholic until his death, and his newfound faith in the church is reflected in his interpretations of its role in Spanish America and in his view of Indians. He often expressed negative views of contemporary Indians, being especially critical of the Aymara whom he encountered around Lake Titicaca: "Cupidity, low cunning, and savage cruelty are unfortunate traits of these Indians' character." Ephraim Squier, it will be recalled, also had an unflattering opinion of the Aymara, but he believed that the people of Peru had been better off under Inca rule than at any time since then. Bandelier, by contrast, was convinced that the missionary work of the Catholic Church and by extension the Spanish regime were responsible for whatever degree of civilization the Indians possessed. Thus, he wrote in a letter to García Icazbalceta in 1882, however backward the Indians of New Mexico might seem, they had advanced a great deal since their first contact with Spain: "Everything they have and can do today they owe to the Church." Regarding the disagreeable traits of the Aymara, these were "not, as sentimentalism would have it, a result of ill-treatment by the Spaniards, but *peculiar to the stock*, and were yet more pronounced in the beginning of the Colonial period than at the present time." Where the Spanish and Catholic presence was withdrawn, as had occurred in Casas Grandes, Chihuahua, in the eighteenth century, the Indians reverted to their original rude condition.[57] In short, Bandelier's positions were diametrically opposed to those of Stephens and Squier, who had exalted the achievements of pre-Columbian populations and denigrated the Spanish colonial record.

Hubert Howe Bancroft: Businessman and Bookman

Prescott and the Spanish chroniclers found a defender in Hubert Howe Bancroft (1832–1918), the controversial businessman and collector who was responsible for the production of a multivolume history of the Pacific Coast region of North America (including Mexico and Central America) and for the creation of the Bancroft Library of the University of California. Lewis Morgan's essay titled "Montezuma's Dinner" originated as a dismissive review of the second volume of Bancroft's *Native Races*. Bancroft responded to Morgan in an essay of his own, "The Early American Chroniclers" (1883), in which he declared "presumptuous" the willingness of Morgan and his followers to ignore the eyewitness testimony of sixteenth-century Spaniards. He was also critical of what he considered Morgan's simplistic assignment of peoples into the three categories of savagery, barbarism, and civilization, as the distinctions among them were never sharp. In any event, he believed that the people of central Mexico were indeed civilized in 1519. "Compare [Nahua culture] with the European civilization or semi-civilization of that day on the one hand, and with the savagism of the Iroquois and the Ojibways on the other," he said, "and then judge of the two which it most resembled."[58]

Bancroft, a native of Ohio, became engrossed in scholarship unintentionally. After settling in San Francisco, in 1856 he founded a company that sold books and stationery and later expanded into printing and publishing. He initially acquired materials for use in the preparation of a Pacific Coast handbook published by the firm; as his interests expanded to encompass the western half of North America from Alaska to Panama, the collection grew apace. He travelled to Europe and to Mexico to make acquisitions and purchased part of Ephraim Squier's Central American collection in 1876. He eventually acquired at least sixty thousand volumes. In 1905 he sold his library to the University of California for $250,000, of which he contributed $100,000.[59]

Meanwhile, he had become interested in using his library to write a history of the region covered, but realizing that such a task was beyond the capacity of a single individual, he decided to apply business methods to the endeavor. He engaged a team of individuals to index relevant materials, take notes, and write large portions of the narratives that were published under his name. The fact that Bancroft himself wrote only small segments of the history produced criticism, especially from collaborators who believed that their contributions were not adequately acknowledged. The methods he employed in selling the volumes by subscription also generated criticism.[60]

Published between the mid-1870s and 1890, Bancroft's *Works* comprise thirty-nine volumes, of which five are the books in the *Native Races* series. Of the others, three deal with Central America, six deal with Mexico, and most of the others discuss territories once ruled by Spain that had passed to the United States. The first two volumes in *The Native Races* are titled *Wild Tribes* and *Civilized Nations*, the former embracing the northern peoples, the latter those of Mesoamerica. The remaining three cover myths and language, antiquities, and primitive history. The nine volumes on Central America and Mexico place greatest emphasis on the conquest period, then offer a narrative history relating events through the late nineteenth century. All are copiously documented with citations from materials in Bancroft's collections, but neither he nor his collaborators conducted archaeological surveys or archival research. Bancroft's Central American experience was limited to several transisthmian crossings by way of Panama or Nicaragua while travelling to and from California. He visited Mexico in 1883 and 1886 and purchased books there and obtained orders for his history. Although he commented on the poverty, ugliness, and mendacity of the Mexicans, he wrote a laudatory biography (1884) of Mexico's dictator Porfirio Díaz, as well as a popular history of Mexico (1887).

Bancroft's volumes on Mexico and Central America can still be mined today for factual data not readily available elsewhere in English. Writing in the early 1970s, ethnohistorian Howard F. Cline found *The Civilized Nations* still useful as an introduction to Aztec and Maya society. The general surveys in *Primitive History* also retained value.[61] In these works and in other writings his general outlook is similar to that of most of his predecessors. Although Bancroft expressed admiration for the "civilized city-builders" of Central America and the "refined and intelligent" Maya, he was critical of what he considered Spanish bigotry and misrule, though he could praise individual clergymen and administrators. Recalling his first trip to Mexico in his autobiography and the "squalid misery" he encountered, he declared: "Infinitely happier and better off, and far less debased and wretched were the people of this plateau before ever a European saw it." At the same time he considered Spanish policies toward the Indians to be well intentioned and compared them favorably with those of the United States.[62]

Even as Bandelier and Bancroft were still writing, the age of the self-educated scholar was drawing to a close. The rise of the university-trained academic specialist was evident by the late nineteenth century, along with the philanthropic institutions and learned societies that would help to finance and direct investigations in the future. The work of Bandelier himself, it will be recalled, was supported initially by the Archaeological Institute of America and by the CIW. In addition, the deepening interest of U.S. political and business leaders in Latin America created conditions conducive to more intense investigation of the region.

During their heyday, however, the gifted amateurs discussed here—Irving, Prescott, Stephens, Squier, Bandelier, and Bancroft—as well as many others had laid a respectable foundation for subsequent studies of Latin America. By surveying and describing pre-Columbian ruins and studying Spanish chronicles of the colonial era, they publicized the ancient civilizations of Mesoamerica and the Andes in the United States and greatly added to the contemporary fund of information. Their writings also provided much information about the conquest era, though all but Bandelier evinced an anti-Catholic, anti-Spanish bias to some degree. To a large extent their study of Latin America was driven, initially at least, by their interest in issues linked to the United States, particularly the nature and history of indigenous peoples and the history of once-Spanish territories that had been acquired by the United States. They tended to see the conquest narratives of Latin America as part of U.S. history as well, or as a means of contrasting the Spanish and English experiences. In the future, the independent scholar of Latin America would be relegated to a minor role, but the linkage of Latin America studies with U.S. concerns would remain strong.

PART I

LAYING THE FOUNDATIONS

With the dawn of the twentieth century, the study of Latin America in the United States experienced substantial growth as a result of several developments. Perhaps the most important was the increasing interest in the lands south of the border exhibited after 1870 by industrialists, statesmen, and naval strategists. As the geopolitical doctrines of naval strategist Alfred Thayer Mahan gained currency and prompted the expansion of the U.S. Navy, areas of Latin America, and especially the Caribbean Basin, were seen as potential sites of naval bases and coaling stations. Economic and commercial ties with the region also became stronger. The economic crises of the late nineteenth century convinced many that the surplus production of American factories might be sold in Latin America, many of whose exports, such as coffee and bananas, did not compete with U.S. goods. The conference of American states convened in Washington in 1889 was intended mainly to promote U.S. exports, a goal underlined by a six-week recess during which conference delegates were given an extensive tour of factories in the Northeast and Middle West.[1] Great Britain remained the principal trading partner of Southern Cone nations, but commerce with Mexico, Cuba, Colombia, Brazil, and others became increasingly important for the United States. Direct investment also increased significantly as American capital was employed in Peruvian and Mexican mining, Cuban sugar production, Central American banana cultivation, and many other enterprises. These trends are often seen as marking a decisive shift in U.S. orientation toward Latin America that was part of what has been characterized as the New Diplomacy, a more aggressive and calculated approach toward foreign policy beginning in the 1880s.[2]

Scholars have long debated the relative importance of economic motives, strategic interests, and ethnocentric paternalism in leading the United States to direct intervention in Mexico, Central America, and the Caribbean starting in the late nineteenth century with the war against Spain. This brief conflict yielded the first colonial possession in the region—Puerto Rico—as well as the first protectorate: Cuba. The separation of Panama from Colombia in 1903 with U.S. assistance created a second protectorate and permitted the realization of a long-held ambition, the construction of a transisthmian canal, the defense of which now became a major concern in Washington. The long Mexican Revolution (1910–20), with its disturbances near the border and the intervention of U.S. forces in 1914 and 1916, served to direct attention to that country. Meanwhile, the United States established protectorates in the Dominican Republic, Haiti, and Nicaragua that lasted well into the twentieth century.

These new ties with Latin America not only created greater interest but also generated new sources of information about the region. The principal concrete result of the Washington conference of 1889 was the creation of the International Bureau of the American Republics (later known as the Pan-American Union), which produced a monthly bulletin as well as publications on Latin American commerce, agriculture, cities, and other subjects. Meanwhile, travel to Latin America for pleasure, business, and instruction also rose and contributed to an increase in the production of travel literature about the region, to the point that in 1912 a book reviewer was moved to comment: "With the ever-increasing flood of Latin-Americana, there seems little need for a further essay in a field which for the last ten years has been covered to satiety."[3]

Accompanying the heightened interest in Latin America was a demand for individuals with expertise in the economics, politics, and culture of the region. This demand occurred as colleges and universities were becoming the training ground for experts in a variety of fields besides the traditional professions of medicine, law, and the ministry. Undergraduates contemplating business careers that might take them to Latin America could be advised to enroll in courses related to the region. In 1919 an American banker who had spent eleven years in the field asserted that the prospective businessman in Latin America "can be made very much more effective if he is able to talk about the history and customs of the country with the people with whom he is dealing."[4] This trend continued after World War I as undergraduate enrollments increased, nearly doubling between 1919–20 and 1929–30, and the emphasis on practical learning in fields such as business administration intensified.

In the late nineteenth century, as American higher education began its expansion, postbaccalaureate training in the German mold became the model for aspiring academics and all serious students. Initially, this training required a period of residence in a German university, but American institutions soon began to offer advanced degrees themselves, starting with Yale, which in 1861 became the first U.S. university to award an earned PhD. More significant was the establishment of separate schools for graduate study, as undertaken by Johns Hopkins University in the 1870s, Columbia in 1880, and many other universities in subsequent years. Soon the doctorate became the sine qua non for the college professor, "the label of academic respectability, the mark of professional competence, the assurance of a certain standard sameness of training, experience, and exposure to the ideals, the rules, the habits of scientific Germanic scholarship."[5]

Meanwhile, knowledge and scholarship were fragmented into disciplines whose practice and performance within the university were the exclusive province of academic departments. The emergence of the new academic departments was accompanied by the establishment of societies intended to facilitate practitioners' communication with each other and the dissemination of their research through newsletters and journals. Whereas earlier societies, such as the American Philosophical Society and the American Association for the Advancement of Science, had been notable for the breadth of their interests and membership, the newer groups were much more narrowly focused and directed mainly to the professional scholar. The American Philological Association (1869) was the first of the new societies, followed by the Modern Language Association (1883), the American Historical Association (1884), and the American Economics Association (1885), among others. The proliferation of scholarly journals and the establishment of university presses in the 1890s attested to the importance of research in determining academic careers: not only were dissertations to be published, but future success in the chosen discipline required the steady production of books and articles.[6]

The importance assigned to scholarly productivity meant that academics without independent incomes required released time and money in order to undertake research, especially in fields that necessitated foreign travel. Professors might tap their own institutions for sabbatical leaves and grants, but private foundations and institutions could also provide funding. After World War I the American Council of Learned Societies (ACLS) and the Social Science Research Council (SSRC), which were established in 1919 and 1923, respectively, served as conduits for research funds. Representing the principal professional associations in the humanities and the social sciences, the two councils received funding from Rockefeller philanthropies and other external sources and through their grants attempted to promote research and improve scholarly communication.[7] Museums and other institutions also supported selected researchers outside the universities. Notable in this respect was the Carnegie Institution of Washington, established in 1901 with a donation of $10 million from Andrew Carnegie, the steel magnate and philanthropist. Although the CIW was committed mainly to research in the natural sciences, in its early decades it also made substantial investments in history, archaeology, anthropology, and other social sciences.[8]

Initially Latin America played a negligible role in the expansion of graduate education in the United States. Of the 122 PhDs awarded by six leading universities between 1861 and 1900 identified by Robert A. McCaughey as falling under the general category of international studies (excluding western Europe), only 6, or 5 percent of the total, pertained to Latin America.[9]

Three of the 122 PhDs were awarded for studies in modern languages, and one of these was on Latin American Spanish. As interest in the region grew after 1900, it was reflected in an increase in the number of persons who studied the Spanish language, on both the secondary and the college levels. In 1910, approximately five thousand high school students were studying Spanish, or 0.7 percent of those enrolled in a foreign-language course. By 1915, the figure had risen to 33,172, or 2.7 percent of the total. Spanish-language enrollments mushroomed during World War I, reaching approximately 263,000 by 1922, an increase attributed at least in part to a decline in the study of German. Similar gains were registered in higher education as the number of students studying Spanish in 210 colleges surveyed grew from 1,736 in 1916–17 to 9,579 in 1917–18.[10] To be sure, Spanish continued to lag behind French and German at the college level, but the field expanded sufficiently to produce the formation of the American Association of Teachers of Spanish in 1917 with more than four hundred members. Its journal, *Hispania*, appeared in 1918.

The study of Spanish, especially at the high school level, was promoted at this time as a practical tool for those interested in business careers relating to Spanish America. This sudden "Spanish craze" produced discomfort among some college and high school teachers and administrators, who considered the trend undesirable for several reasons.[11] Critics questioned the much-touted commercial usefulness of Spanish as well as the value of Spanish literature and culture as compared with that of France, Germany, or Italy. Others maintained that Spanish was easy to learn and therefore attracted fraternity boys and others in search of "snap" courses. Defenders of Spanish were quick to refute such canards, denying that it was easy and extolling the merits of Spanish literature. Although they also stressed the desirability of Americans' learning the language of their neighbors to the south, they placed less emphasis on the value of the literature and culture of Spanish America.

Whatever their sentiments about Spanish America, devotees of Spanish agreed that instructors should impart Castilian pronunciation to their students, specifically that of the "educated people of Castile." A survey of seventy-five teachers and other interested persons published in 1917 revealed that seven-eighths of the respondents favored the retention of Castilian. Some instructors also believed that commercial students should be separated from those mainly interested in literature.[12]

Although Spain was still perceived as the font of Hispanic civilization, the years after 1900 saw the beginning of scholarly interest in the literature of Spanish America as well as the first college courses on the subject. An important pioneer in the promotion of Spanish American letters was J. D. M. Ford, who was named to the Smith professorship at Harvard in 1907. In addition to producing numerous publications in the field, he encouraged the work of Alfred Coester, who received a doctorate in Spanish from Harvard in 1906 and taught for fifteen years at a Brooklyn high school before moving in 1920 to Stanford University, where he became professor of Spanish American literature in 1928. In 1912 he published a bibliography of Spanish American literature in the *Romanic Review*, and his *Literary History of Spanish America* (1916) is considered the first important book on the subject in the United States. In his preface to the latter work, Coester asserted that Spanish American literature was not a mere appendage of Spanish or French letters but a subject worthy of study in its own right, even though it was imitative in form and extremely provincial.[13]

Despite such ambivalence, the number of colleges and universities offering courses in Spanish American literature grew substantially in the early twentieth century. A 1931 survey showed that 109 courses in Spanish American literature were being taught at 75 institutions (of 251 questioned): 14 of the courses were for graduate students only, 37 were for graduate students and advanced undergraduates, and 58 were for undergraduates only.[14]

In the early twentieth century the study of Portuguese and of the literature of Portugal and Brazil remained marginal at best, though the language and its literature had some advocates. Isaac Goldberg, who received a doctorate from Harvard in 1912 with a dissertation on the Spanish dramatist José Echegaray, published a translation of six Brazilian stories in 1921 and a survey of *Brazilian Literature* in 1922. Ford coauthored a Portuguese grammar in 1925. John Casper Branner, a geologist and former president of Stanford University with extensive experience in Brazil, was an admirer of Luso-Brazilian culture, but in a 1919 article in *Hispania*, he stressed the utility of Portuguese for those who wished to do business in Brazil.[15]

At this time Brazilian culture was often subsumed under the label of Spanish America because champions of Spanish civilization saw it as the source of everything that emanated from the Iberian Peninsula. In 1918 Aurelio M. Espinosa, a professor at Stanford and the first editor of *Hispania*, denounced the increasing use of the term "Latin America" to refer to the region south of the U.S. border. He considered the name an "intruder" and its use "improper, unjust," and "unscientific" because the region's languages and culture originated in Spain, not France, Italy, or Romania. The correct term was "Spanish America." Three years later Espinosa was elated when the Second Spanish-American Congress of History and Geography, meeting in Seville, resolved that the only appropriate name for the former New World colonies of Spain was either Spanish America or the Hispanic American republics.[16]

In the preface to his *Literary History of Spanish America*, Alfred Coester stated that the Hispanic Society of America and Harvard University possessed the only valuable collections of writings by Spanish American authors. During the first three decades of the twentieth century, these collections would be supplemented by others as U.S. libraries began to amass significant holdings of books, manuscripts, and other materials pertaining to Latin America.

The Hispanic Society of America was founded in New York in 1904, thanks to the largesse of Archer M. Huntington, son of railroad tycoon Collis P. Huntington, who dedicated his life to the promotion of Spanish culture and letters. Its purpose was to "advance the study of the Spanish and Portuguese languages, literature, and history, and advancement of the study of the countries wherein Spanish or Portuguese are or have been spoken." In 1927 Huntington donated $105,000 to the Library of Congress for the purchase of books dealing with Hispanic or Portuguese history, literature, and art. The following year Huntington made an additional donation of $50,000 to help support a consultant in Hispanic literature. In 1928–29 another significant gift came to the Library of Congress from the philanthropist Edward S. Harkness, who donated manuscripts and documents related to the conquest of Mexico and Peru.[17]

Harvard's holdings of Latin American materials were expanded during this period as a result of the efforts of Archibald Cary Coolidge, who was a professor there and director of the library. In 1908–9, during a visit to Chile, he purchased the four-thousand-volume library of Luis Montt, that country's national librarian; five years later he purchased another nine thousand volumes for Harvard. In 1915 Yale's Latin American holdings were augmented by the purchase of the Mexican collection of Henry R. Wagner, an alumnus and businessman with extensive experience in that country and in Chile who later retired to devote himself to the writing of history.[18]

During this period the foundation for the Latin American library at the University of Texas was laid with the acquisition in 1921 of the collection of Genaro García, a Mexican historian and educator. It consisted of 25,000 printed items and 300,000 manuscript pages covering a span from the pre-Columbian era to modern times. The university purchased the collection from García's widow for approximately $100,000. In 1916 the Catholic University of America accepted an offer from Manoel de Oliveira Lima, a Brazilian scholar and diplomat, for his

collection of approximately sixteen thousand books on Latin America. He inaugurated the Oliveira Lima Library in 1924 and served as its keeper until his
death four years later.[19]

Archibald Cary Coolidge promoted the study of Latin America at Harvard
in other ways besides the acquisition of library materials. In 1902 he played an
important role in securing the appointment of Roger B. Merriman, who introduced Spanish history to the university and, by 1906, was including Latin
America in his course on the Spanish empire. Coolidge was also influential in
persuading Robert Woods Bliss to donate $125,000 for the creation of a chair
in Latin American history and economics in 1913. Bliss, a Harvard alumnus and
career diplomat who served as ambassador to Argentina from 1927 to 1933, was
also a serious collector of pre-Columbian art and Byzantine materials, all of
which were given to Harvard, along with his estate, Dumbarton Oaks, in Washington, D.C.[20]

In short, by the second decade of the twentieth century, conditions were
propitious for the emergence of Latin America as a subject worthy of study in
the American university. To the traditional sources of American interest in the
region were now added geopolitical and economic concerns. The expansion
of Spanish-language instruction, the acquisition of library materials, and the
greater availability of funding for researchers all contributed to the trend. Even
so, advances would be notable primarily in history, anthropology, and geography while the other social sciences lagged behind.

2

Early Historians

The awarding of PhDs in history in the United States began in 1882 when Johns Hopkins and Yale conferred the first two doctorates in that field. Graduate study in history expanded rapidly in the following years: by 1901–2 eighteen institutions offered the PhD, and an average of nineteen history doctorates was being awarded each year, though this figure represented only 6.5 percent of all doctorates.[1] The recipient of the first Johns Hopkins doctorate was John Franklin Jameson, who became a pivotal figure in the development of historical studies in the United States, not so much because of his own scholarship but because of his work as the head of the Carnegie Institution's Department of Historical Research (1905–28) and his long connection with the American Historical Association and the *American Historical Review*, of which he was managing editor for most of the period 1895–1928. His last position was as head of the Manuscript Division of the Library of Congress.[2]

In the late nineteenth century, undergraduate and graduate training in history was confined almost entirely to the study of the United States and Europe. As a result, the first courses in Latin American history were perforce offered by instructors who had no formal training in the field. The first person known to have taught a course related to Latin American history was Daniel De Leon, who is remembered chiefly as a leading socialist thinker and political activist. A native of Curaçao, De Leon received a law degree from Columbia University in 1878. Five years later he won the first prize lectureship to be awarded by Columbia's new School of Political Science. Required to offer a series of lectures, De Leon chose South American diplomacy as his subject. He initially covered the "relations of Spain and Portugal to America during the colonial period" as well as the relations of the independent republics to imperial Brazil; in 1885 he added a unit on European intervention in Latin America in the mid-nineteenth century. The lectureship was renewed for a second three-year term in 1886, but in 1889 his connection with Columbia and the academic world was severed as he became more deeply involved in radical politics. His only publication during his lectureship was a campaign pamphlet in 1884 critical of James G. Blaine's Latin American policy.[3]

More lasting was the commitment of Bernard Moses, a professor at the University of California at Berkeley, who in 1895 initiated the study of Spanish American history in the United States with a one-semester course ranging from the colonial period to the postindependence development of the new republics. The son of a Connecticut farmer, Moses graduated from the University of Michigan in 1870; he spent the next five years in Europe, mainly in Germany, and was awarded a doctorate by the University of Heidelberg. Beginning his long career at Berkeley in 1876, Moses was for a time not only the sole history professor at the university but also, in 1880, the first to offer a course there under the rubric of political science. During this period his principal publications were in the field of Swedish history and politics. By the late 1880s he had decided to shift his emphasis to Latin American history, "moved perhaps by an instinctive sense that California, a former Spanish territory, did not present an advantageous point for viewing Swedish affairs." He taught himself Spanish, visited Mexico, and spent part of the academic year 1891–92 in Spain.[4]

Moses began to publish articles on Mexican history in the 1880s. In 1898 he urged teachers and scholars to study what he called the "neglected half of American history."[5] Acknowledging that it might be inopportune to make such a plea on the eve of war with Spain, he argued that studying the Spanish role in America would give a more accurate view of the development of the Western Hemisphere and would lessen the provincialism of Americans. The same year saw the appearance of Moses's first book on a Latin American topic, *The Establishment of Spanish Rule in America*, which has been described as the "first scholarly history of colonial Hispanic America by a professor of the subject, with a student following, to be published in the United States." Moses intended the book to be an introduction for students and general readers. In it he repeated his belief that the history of colonial Spanish America was an important part, albeit a neglected one, of the history of the United States. Based entirely on printed sources and consisting of discrete chapters, the book surveys the development of administrative, ecclesiastical, and economic institutions in various regions and, despite its title, extends its coverage to the eighteenth century. Like his predecessors but more explicitly than most, Moses compared Spanish and English colonization in his concluding chapter. The most significant contrast he found was in the degree of local control exercised by the English colonists in North America as opposed to the "rigid rule" of the Council of the Indies and its subordinates, from which the Spanish colonists learned only one lesson, the

"necessity of obedience." As a result, the people of the Spanish American republics were unprepared for self-government and "were perfect material for the
demagogue, or the pliant tool of revolutionists." In a shift from the conventional
view of Spanish treatment of the native population, he contrasted the pitiless
attitudes of the English toward the Indians with those of the Spanish, who in-
termingled with them and sought to gradually raise them to the level of civilization. The English measures seemed "merciless and unwarrantably cruel," but
he admitted that they might have been beneficial for "social progress," presumably of the two regions as a whole.[6]

Moses went on to write six other books on Spanish American topics. In 1899–
1900 he introduced a course on Spanish constitutional history, and even after
he became head of a separate Department of Political Science, he continued to
teach a history course on the colonization of Latin America. In 1908–9 he had an
opportunity to visit Chile when he was a U.S. delegate to the First Pan-American
Scientific Congress, which was held in Santiago. It was the fourth such conference in Latin America but the first to which Americans had been invited. The
topics discussed by the seven hundred to eight hundred delegates in attendance
included not only the natural sciences but also the social sciences, education,
and philosophy.[7]

On the East Coast, Latin American history was introduced to Columbia University by William R. Shepherd. Though a native of Charleston, South Carolina, and the son of a former Confederate officer, he was raised in Brooklyn,
New York.[8] At Columbia University he wrote a dissertation on colonial Pennsylvania under Herbert L. Osgood and received his doctorate in 1896. His brilliant
record at Columbia earned him a prize lectureship in 1896. It was after his appointment as an instructor in history in 1902 that his attention turned to Latin
America, and he began to teach a course on the region in 1904. In 1905 he went
to Spain as one of several historians engaged by J. Franklin Jameson on behalf
of the Carnegie Institution of Washington to travel to foreign archives for the
purpose of preparing guides to sources of American history there. In 1907 he
was in Buenos Aires, where he visited museums, libraries, and other cultural institutions for Columbia, the Hispanic Society of America, and the Bureau of
American Republics. Late the following year he took part in the Pan-American
Scientific Congress in Santiago.

After Shepherd's sudden death in Berlin in 1934, Alfred Hasbrouck, a former
student, called him the "pioneer who cleared the soil for the growth of the study
of Latin American history."[9] This is an apt description, for Shepherd became a
publicist of Latin America rather than a conventional historian. After the publication of his Carnegie Institution guide in 1907, he appears to have produced
nothing based on documentary research. A visit to the rich archive at Simancas

in 1926 yielded a humorous article in which he described the difficulties of doing research there. He also related the discomforts of life in the "poor decrepit
village" of Simancas, itself symbolic of Spain in decline, "bereft of all its splen-
dors, with all its glories vanished." It should be noted, however, that elsewhere
he, like Moses, stressed Spanish contributions to the development of the United
States, ranging from the introduction of new plants and animals to the concept
of community property in marriage. He went so far as to envision the United
States, along with Spanish America, as the base of a triangle whose sides, representing history and civilization, stretched forth like gigantic arms toward the
Spanish apex. If the mother of the United States was England, he was quoted as
saying in a Spanish newspaper, the former could not forget that the first European settlements on its soil were Spanish.[10]

On Latin America itself, his principal contribution was a short overview
(1914) of the region's history and present state of development for the Home
University Library of Henry Holt and Company. Adopting a thematic approach,
Shepherd reviewed the colonial history of Latin America as well as contemporary topics, such as commerce, international relations, and the fine arts. Given
the brief length of the book, he could not provide extensive coverage of any
single country but divided the republics into three groups in accordance with
the degree of advancement shown by each. In the first group he placed the
Southern Cone nations, Brazil, and Costa Rica; in the second, Mexico, Cuba,
Peru, and Colombia; and in the third, Ecuador, Paraguay, and several countries
of the Caribbean Basin. A reviewer in the *Independent* praised Shepherd's ability
to "generalize without being rash or hazy, and he can particularize without fill-
ing his pages with confusing figures and details."[11] Shepherd wrote a somewhat
similar work for the multivolume series Chronicles of America. Called *The Hispanic Nations of the New World* (1919), the book ended with a discussion of the
persistence of the Iberian heritage in Latin America.

Bourne and Bingham at Yale

The conviction of Moses and Shepherd that the history of the United States
should be expanded to embrace colonial Spanish America reached brilliant fruition in E. Gaylord Bourne's *Spain in America, 1450–1580* (1904), which was the
third volume in the American Nation historical series edited by Albert Bushnell Hart and published by Harper. At the time of its publication Bourne was
on the faculty at Yale University, where he had received a doctorate in history
in 1892 with a dissertation on the demarcation line of Pope Alexander VI. After
seven years of teaching at Adelbert College in Cleveland, Ohio, he returned to
Yale in 1895 and taught European and American history, introducing graduate

students to historical criticism. Several of the themes he developed in *Spain in America* were adumbrated in his introduction to the documents in *The Philippine Islands, 1493–1898* (1903–9), edited by Emma Helen Blair and James A. Robertson. Here he compared Spanish policies toward native populations favorably with those of Anglo-Saxons in North America, Hawaii, and other colonies and asserted that overall Spanish rule had been "benevolent."[12]

Because *Spain in America* is universally regarded as the outstanding scholarly synthesis produced during the pioneer era of Latin American historical studies in the United States, it is ironic that Bourne initially wanted to contribute the volume on the Federalist period (1789–1801) to Hart's series. It was Hart who suggested that Bourne tackle the Spanish background, but the latter readily acquiesced, partly because of his interest in the subject and partly to accommodate Hart.[13]

Bourne was hard pressed to deliver the manuscript on time, but the final product revealed his breadth of knowledge, his mastery of the sources, and his unusual degree of detachment in comparing Spanish and English colonization. More than half of the text is devoted to the early voyages of exploration and expeditions to North America, the remainder to the Spanish colonial system. Bourne begins the second part of the book by paying tribute to the achievements of sixteenth-century Spain in conquering and colonizing the New World and in undertaking the "magnificent if impossible task of uplifting a whole race numbering millions into the sphere of European thought, life, and religion." As he went on to describe Spanish administration, he noted the crown's paternalism toward the Indians, whereas in the English colonies "they were left in the main to take their chances in a sort of struggle for existence." Spain's protective attitude, he added, had been overlooked by those who were influenced only by the writings of Las Casas. Also countering the belief that the Spanish colonial system was "pre-eminently oppressive" was the fact that Spanish slave codes were "far more humane" than those of the French and English and encouraged the attainment of freedom by slaves. The final chapter emphasizes the transmission of education and the production of learning, especially by the clergy. "That the Spanish authorities in church and state did much to promote education is abundantly evident, and the modern sciences of anthropology, linguistics, geography, and history are profoundly indebted to the labors of the early Spanish-American scholars and missionaries."[14] Thus, while not glossing over what he considered defects in the Spanish colonial system, such as curbs on intellectual freedom imposed by the Inquisition, his overall assessment was positive.

William R. Shepherd praised the book in a personal letter to Bourne in which he said that it was "but a tantalizing foretaste of what ought to be done for the history of colonial Spanish America." In a published review Shepherd noted that although the treatment of Spanish colonial policy and institutions had little direct relevance to U.S. history, the book "easily surpasses in value anything hitherto offered in the field." He also observed the revisionist nature of Bourne's discussion: "The actual degree of intellectual culture and material prosperity which the author shows to have existed in the Spanish-American colonies ought to dissipate some of the clouds of ignorance and prejudice which have enveloped so long the tale of Spanish colonization in the New World." Shepherd's judgment was prescient. In fact, the modern historian Benjamin Keene has credited Bourne with initiating a "scholarly reaction in the United States against . . . the 'black legend' of Spanish cruelty and fanaticism."[15]

By 1905 Bourne was widely recognized as an expert in Spanish exploration and colonization. In that year he was asked to travel to Cambridge, Massachusetts, to examine a Harvard doctoral candidate in Spanish American history, Hiram Bingham, because there was no appropriate scholar on the Harvard faculty to perform that role.[16] Bingham passed his examination, completed his dissertation, and soon found himself at Yale, where he continued a course in Latin American history introduced by Bourne, who died in 1908. The History Department's doubts about the value of the field made Bingham's position a tenuous one, however.

Born in Hawaii, Bingham was the son and grandson of missionaries. He received his bachelor's degree from Yale and a master's degree from the University of California. He wrote his thesis, which discussed U.S. interest in Hawaii, under the direction of Bernard Moses, who encouraged his growing interest in Latin American history. His Harvard dissertation dealt with the stillborn seventeenth-century Scottish colony in Darien. Meanwhile, he had married the granddaughter of the founder of Tiffany and Company, and her family's wealth made it possible for him to live in affluence despite meager earnings.[17]

After receiving his doctorate in 1906, he accepted a three-year appointment as a preceptor or tutor at Princeton University but found the work uncongenial. He took a year's leave of absence for a tour of the Caribbean and northern South America, during which he travelled overland from Caracas to Bogotá in an effort to reconstruct the 1817 trek of Simón Bolívar, of whom he planned to write a biography. He also made purchases of Latin American materials for the Harvard and Princeton libraries. This expedition produced a book (1909) as well as a paper for the American Political Science Association (1907), in which he emphasized the importance of South American history and politics as fields for research and described source materials available in the region as well as in the United States and England.

Bingham was eager to return to Yale, and the president of the university, Arthur Twining Hadley, favored the teaching of Latin American history there.

He was unable to obtain departmental support for an appointment in the field, however, and could offer Bingham only a position as an assistant professor of geography or as a lecturer in history. If he accepted the latter position, he would not be a member of the History Department and would receive an occasional honorarium rather than a salary. Even so, Bingham accepted the lectureship and was soon planning an ambitious program of courses in Latin American history and geography that would create a specialization in the field. His proposed course in South American geography duplicated that offered by Isaiah Bowman, who had been named an instructor in 1905 (see chapter 4), and Bingham had to content himself with teaching courses in history.[18]

At the end of his first academic year (1907–8), Yale renewed Bingham's appointment as a lecturer and gave him a token salary of $400 per annum. For the year 1908–9 he received a leave of absence, the highlight of which was a second trip to South America. In December 1908 he was in Santiago, Chile, where he joined his Berkeley mentor, Bernard Moses, and William R. Shepherd as a delegate to the First Pan-American Scientific Congress. He had travelled from Buenos Aires to Santiago by rail, mule, and steamer with the goal of retracing the Spanish commercial route across the continent and, after the conclusion of the conference, continued his journey by travelling to Bolivia and Peru.[19]

In Peru, Bingham and his companion, Clarence Hay, were treated as distinguished guests, especially in Abancay in the department of Apurimac. The departmental prefect, J. J. Núñez, had been instructed to show Bingham a set of ruins that was thought to be the last Inca capital. The site in question—Choqquequirau—was not the Inca stronghold, but Bingham's survey of the ruins was a turning point in his career. In the future his exploits as an Andean explorer and as the "discoverer" of Machu Picchu in 1911 would eventually overshadow his work as an instructor and historian.[20]

Bingham organized and led three Yale-sponsored expeditions to Peru: in 1911, 1912, and 1914–15 (see chapter 3). Bingham included two fledgling historians on the expeditions: Osgood Hardy and Philip Ainsworth Means. Hardy, a Yale student fluent in Spanish, was Bingham's assistant in 1912 and in 1914–15. Meanwhile, he had enrolled in one of Bingham's courses and was giving occasional lectures in another. It was his goal to obtain a doctorate in Latin American history and to return to teach at Yale.[21]

Less happy was Bingham's experience with the future ethnohistorian Philip Ainsworth Means. A Harvard undergraduate in 1914, Means asked to join the advance party in Peru that summer, explaining: "I am very eager to be an archaeologist although I fully realize that there is a vast amount of drudgery to be gone through before the original research work begins." His path undoubtedly smoothed by a $2,100 contribution to the expedition by his father, Means arrived in Peru in July 1914 but soon notified Bingham of his intention to leave in mid-September because the onset of the rainy season and the expedition's other activities would interfere with his archaeological work. Bingham was furious, reminding Means that he had warned him that the work would be tedious and accusing him of deserting his post. He later refused to sell Means photographs of the expedition, wondering why he should want them. Means replied that it was natural for him to "desire a little something"—the photographs—"to show for the $2100 you charmed from me."[22] Despite this contretemps, in 1923 Bingham asked Means for assistance in preparing a manuscript on Machu Picchu. Means submitted a booklength draft that Bingham abridged and revised and published as *Machu Picchu: A Citadel of the Incas* (1930) without acknowledging any contribution by Means.[23]

Meanwhile, Bingham had remained on the Yale faculty through the academic year 1916–17. By that time the university had given him the title of professor of Latin American history in the graduate school, but he was still not a member of the Yale college faculty. Moreover, the History Department found fault with his use of nonacademic guest lecturers and his tendency to include what they considered an excessive amount of contemporary material in his classes. According to his son and biographer, Bingham was now inclined to sneer at academics.[24] His growing celebrity as an Andean explorer and his changing attitudes toward Latin America, to be discussed later, also probably contributed to his departure from Yale.

The University of California Carries On

While Yale remained ambivalent about Latin American history, the University of California built on the foundation created by Bernard Moses. In the first three decades of the twentieth century, it became the leading center of teaching and scholarship on Latin American history in the United States, thanks to the efforts of three men: Charles E. Chapman, Herbert I. Priestley, and, above all, Herbert E. Bolton, all three of whom are said to have "charged across the Western Hemisphere as if on a polo field."[25] Especially significant was their training of several cohorts of younger historians whose own contributions further cemented the bases of the field in the United States.

Bolton was born in modest circumstances in rural Wisconsin and struggled to gain an education that would enable him to avoid farm life, which, according to his brother, he regarded as "drudgery and too drab and unrewarding."[26] In 1893, after normal school and several years of teaching, he entered the University of Wisconsin with the intention of eventually studying law, but was drawn to history by Frederick Jackson Turner, Charles Haskins, and other professors.

Having earned bachelor's and master's degrees at Wisconsin, he won a fellow-ship that enabled him to complete a doctorate in American history at the University of Pennsylvania under John Bach McMaster in 1899.

In 1901 Bolton accepted a position at the University of Texas. Because he was initially engaged as a temporary replacement for a professor of European history, the courses Bolton offered there were in that field. The department chair, George Pierce Garrison, had staked a claim to American and Texas history, but Bolton quickly determined to carve a niche for himself in the study of the Spanish background of the Southwest. He began to study Spanish, travelled to Mexico in the summers, and in 1904 offered a course on Latin America, which was completed by only three students. In 1906 J. Franklin Jameson asked him to prepare a guide to materials in American history in Mexican archives for the Carnegie Institution; the resulting work, published in 1913, established his mastery of southwestern history. Although Bernard Moses, William Shepherd, and others had asserted the significance of the Spanish antecedents of much of what became the United States, no other historian became so closely identified with this field as Bolton. In 1907, however, Garrison made it clear that neither southwestern nor Latin American history had a future at Texas.[27] In 1909 Bolton moved to Stanford, but despite Garrison's animadversions, Latin America did become part of the Texas history curriculum. William R. Manning, who had written a prize-winning dissertation on the Nootka Sound controversy at the University of Chicago, began to teach Latin American history, along with English history, at Texas in 1910.

In 1911 Bolton left Stanford for the University of California, lured to Berkeley by the existence there of the Bancroft Library. To his former mentor Turner, he explained: "I hate very much to leave here [Stanford], but the Bancroft Collection was too great a temptation for me to resist. . . . I hope that we shall be able to build up there a strong department in Western and Spanish American History for both of these are in the center of the stage." His own personal interest, he added, lay at the intersection of the two fields.[28] Bolton would spend the remainder of his long career at Berkeley, serving extended periods as chairman of the History Department and as curator of the Bancroft Library.

As his letter to Turner indicated, his own research would be focused on what came to be called the "borderlands," a name that was popularized by the title of his most widely read book, *The Spanish Borderlands* (1921). One of the ironies that attended the publication of the book, which appeared in the Chronicles of America Series, is that it is unclear who first suggested the title. When he heard of the series in 1916, Bolton wrote to the editor, Allen Johnson of Yale University, to propose a "popular, scholarly sketch of the expansion of New Spain, with especial reference to the northern frontier" and on receiving encouraging replies, suggested "The Spanish Pioneers" as a title. When he dispatched the manuscript a year later, he stated that he preferred "The Spanish Borderlands" to any of the other titles that had been proposed.[29]

To Bolton's chagrin, Johnson found the manuscript boring and pedantic even after substantial revisions. He suggested that "a reviser" be engaged to rewrite the book, though Bolton was to check the work for historical accuracy. Bolton was unenthusiastic after his first look at the manuscript drafted by the reviser, Constance Lindsay Skinner. In particular he objected to Hispanophobic suggestions that the Spaniard and his institutions in the Southwest crumbled before the Anglo-Saxon advance. "Two thirds of America and some eighty million people are still under Hispanic institutions and are likely to remain so," he told Johnson. "There is no excuse for another book written in the old spirit of ignorance and prejudice."[30] In the end, Bolton's organization and historical interpretations were retained, but much of the wording was Skinner's. Bolton appeared as the sole author, however, and merely acknowledged Skinner's "able assistance."

Meanwhile, Bolton had been developing the second historical concept with which he is associated: the idea, related to his work on the borderlands, that the Americas have a common history and can and should be studied as a unit. He had formulated this concept at least as early as 1919 when the sudden death of the department chairman, Henry Morse Stephens, catapulted Bolton into that post, and he took advantage of the opportunity to revamp Berkeley's introductory courses. One was a survey of European history since 1500. The other (History 8) covered the history of the Americas "from the North Pole to the South Pole and from Columbus to now," as he described the course to a correspondent. He was optimistic about the prospects for his idea. "If it succeeds here, I predict that it will spread all over the country and mark a new departure in the teaching of American history."[31] He presented his views to an audience of his peers in 1932 when, as president of the American Historical Association, he spoke on "The Epic of Greater America." In his presentation he stressed the similar experiences of Europeans in the New World as they encountered native peoples, adjusted to the American environment, and later threw off the domination of their respective mother countries. Bolton never developed his ideas in a full-length book, but spurred by his reputation and the influence of his former students, many institutions, especially in the West, began to offer similar courses. Ginn and Company published his syllabus for the course in 1928.[32]

Bolton attracted more than seven hundred undergraduates to his course on the history of the Americas when it was first offered in the fall of 1919, and he continued to draw large numbers of students to this and his more advanced courses. A former student, John W. Caughey, called him "a teaching machine, a one-man assembly line, a taxpayer's dream of efficiency in the degree factory."[33] It was perhaps as a mentor to a large number of graduate students that Bolton had the greatest influence on Latin American history. Although his own scholarly production was confined to the borderlands, many of his students became leading historians of Latin America itself. Bolton's training of graduate students was facilitated by the existence of fellowships financed by the Native Sons of the Golden West. Established in 1910 through the efforts of Henry Morse Stephens, the fellowships were awarded annually and allowed one and later two students to spend a year in Seville searching for manuscripts relevant to California history.

One of the first recipients of a Native Sons fellowship, Charles E. Chapman, began teaching in Berkeley's History Department even before he received his doctorate and spent his entire academic career there. Born in New Hampshire of old New England stock, Chapman received his bachelor's degree from Tufts University in 1902 and earned a law degree from Harvard in 1905.[34] During this period, however, his principal interest was baseball. He played and coached for Tufts, and played for several minor league teams until an injury he suffered in 1906 while demonstrating baseball for a high school in Japan ended his playing days. He remained devoted to the sport and was Pacific Coast scout for the St. Louis Cardinals from 1921 to 1932 and later acted in the same capacity for the Cincinnati Reds.

Having settled in San Francisco, Chapman found employment with the Western Electric Company, but later decided to become a teacher of history, a subject he had enjoyed in college. He enrolled at the University of California to earn the requisite teaching certificate and was told that he would have to enroll in a seminar that would involve using Spanish-language materials from the Bancroft Library. Chapman managed to acquire a reading knowledge of Spanish and earn the teaching certificate and a master's degree in history in a single year (1908–9).

After a year of teaching at Riverside High School, he returned to Berkeley in 1910 to work for the doctorate, with the expectation that he would eventually be invited to join the faculty. Later he recalled the enthusiasm with which he had faced the future: "I would not have exchanged my prospect for the Doctor's degree and a professorship for a place as a millionaire at the head of the best business in the world."[35] After two years in Seville as a Native Sons fellow, Chapman received his doctorate in 1915. His dissertation, "The Founding of Spanish California," was published the following year. His stay in Seville also yielded *Catalogue of Materials in the Archivo General de Indias for the History of the Pacific Coast and the American Southwest* (1919).

Despite the subject of his dissertation, Chapman became increasingly committed to Latin American history, especially of the national period. In contrast to Bolton, who made his first and only trip to South America in 1938, Chapman went to Buenos Aires in 1916 as the university's representative to the American Congress of Bibliography and History and visited Brazil, Uruguay, Chile, and Peru. In 1920 he returned to Chile as an exchange professor and published several articles on his experiences there. Chapman also travelled to Mexico and Central America, and in 1924 spent two months in Cuba doing research on what became his best-known and most controversial book, *The History of the Cuban Republic* (1927), which he wrote on behalf of the Carnegie Endowment (see chapter 5).

Starting in 1917, Chapman regularly taught courses in Latin American history as well as the history of California and Spain. He attracted large numbers of undergraduates and surmised that his popularity with students created resentment among his colleagues, who looked down on his baseball connections and claimed that his courses were "snaps." Another possible reason was suggested by a former student, J. Fred Rippy, who recalled that Chapman laced his lectures with baseball jargon and with jokes that "skirted so near the edge of the *risqué* that the ladies present were rarely free from alarm." By contrast, Chapman's graduate seminars in Spanish American history could be terrifying to the careless or unprepared. To Chapman, who believed that his efforts at the university were inadequately rewarded, "students are the joy of a professor's life and one's professional colleagues are its curse."[36]

Chapman occasionally clashed with his colleague in Latin American history, Herbert I. Priestley, who was both friend and rival.[37] A native of Michigan, Priestley received bachelor's and master's degrees from the University of Southern California. From 1900 to 1912 he was a teacher and administrator in schools in California and the Philippines. From 1907 to 1910 he was a teacher of Spanish at Riverside High School, where he met Chapman. He came to Berkeley in 1912 as assistant curator of the Bancroft collection but obtained a doctorate in history in 1916 and joined the department the following year.

Priestley's dissertation was the basis of his most important published work, a massive institutional study of the career of José de Gálvez, the reforming inspector-general (*visitador*) of New Spain. He next published *The Mexican Nation: A History* (1923), intended for general readers. He devoted approximately half of the long text to the colonial period, contrasting the paternalism, absolutism, and monopolistic practices of Spanish rule with British methods of colonization. His *Coming of the White Man, 1492–1848* (1929) was a Boltonian social history dealing with the Spanish, French, Swedish, and Dutch settlements in North America.

While Chapman focused on teaching Latin American history of the postindependence period, Priestley taught courses on the colonial era and one on Mexico. Their emphasis, along with Bolton's contributions, brought occasional murmurings that the region received excessive attention from the History Department. In 1923, for example, Chapman and Priestley, with the help of Bolton, beat back an effort by the university's executive committee to cut their year-long surveys of colonial and modern Latin American history to one-semester courses.[38] So long as the three professors continued to be active, Latin American history and the history of the Americas remained fixtures at Berkeley.

The Second Generation of Pioneers

By the early 1930s a substantial cadre of Latin Americanists had appeared to carry on the work of the first generation. In most cases they had received formal training in the field, usually at the University of California under the direction of Bolton. Many of these younger scholars had an opportunity to do research in Seville as Native Sons of the Golden West, and, as might be expected, their dissertations and early writings focused on the borderlands or on other aspects of the colonial period. One such scholar was Texas-born Charles W. Hackett, whom Bolton said he loved like a son. Hackett followed Bolton from the University of Texas to Stanford to Berkeley, receiving his doctorate in 1917 with a dissertation titled "The Revolt of the Pueblo Indians in New Mexico in 1680." In 1918 he returned to Austin, where he succeeded Manning as professor of Latin American history. Remaining at Texas until his death in 1951, he directed approximately seventy master's theses and thirty-five doctoral dissertations and helped establish the university's leadership in Latin American studies.[39]

Other prominent historians of Latin America who were trained under Bolton included J. Fred Rippy (1920), John Tate Lanning (1928), Irving A. Leonard (1928), and Charles Nowell (1932). Leonard was distinctive in that he committed what he called "the unforgivable apostasy" of obtaining doctorates in history and literature while employed as an instructor and professor of Spanish at Berkeley (1923–1937). Lesley Byrd Simpson, a student of Priestley, committed a similar "offense."[40] He received his doctorate in 1929 with a study of the *encomienda* (a grant of indigenous tribute and/or labor to a deserving Spaniard) but spent his entire teaching career in Berkeley's Spanish Department. Charles E. Chapman's first student was Bingham's former aide, Osgood Hardy. Even before receiving his doctorate in 1925 with a dissertation on U.S.-Chilean relations, Hardy had joined the faculty of Occidental College in Los Angeles, where he remained until his retirement.

Even in this era, Berkeley did not have a monopoly on the training of Latin American historians. Scottish-born William Spence Robertson developed an in-

terest in diplomatic history while studying at the University of Wisconsin. Enrolled at Yale for his doctorate, he came under the influence of E. G. Bourne,
who steered him toward Latin America and directed his dissertation (1903),
titled "Francisco de Miranda and the Revolutionizing of South America," which
won the Herbert Baxter Adams prize of the American Historical Association. A
member of the faculty of the University of Illinois from 1909 to 1941, Robertson
wrote extensively on the Spanish American independence movements as well
as on the region's diplomatic relations with the United States.[41] Roscoe R. Hill,
who received his doctorate from Columbia in 1933 under William R. Shepherd,
differed from most of his colleagues in that he spent almost his entire career in
government service. From 1920 to 1928 he served with the High Commission
for Nicaragua, an experience that provided the subject of his doctoral dissertation, published in 1933 as *Fiscal Intervention in Nicaragua* (see chapter 5). From
1935 to 1946 he was employed by the National Archives.

Stanford University became another West Coast center for Latin American
history under the leadership of Percy Alvin Martin. Trained as a medievalist in
European universities and at Harvard, Martin had turned his attention to the
region by 1911–12, when he offered a two-semester course on Spain and Spanish
America.[42] He coauthored one of the first textbooks dealing with Latin America
and wrote an influential article on the causes of the fall of the Brazilian empire.
At Stanford the study of Brazil was furthered by the support of John Casper
Branner, who arranged for lectures by Manoel de Oliveira Lima and by Ambassador Joaquim Nabuco and donated his collection of Brazilian materials to
the library.

Perhaps the most influential of this second generation of pioneers was
Clarence H. Haring. A native of Philadelphia, Haring graduated from Harvard
in 1907, having developed an interest in Latin America while enrolled in a class
on the Spanish empire taught by Roger Merriman. Latin America "took," Haring later said, "like the measles." A stay at Oxford University as a Rhodes scholar
yielded his first book, *The Buccaneers in the West Indies in the Seventeenth Century* (1910).[43]

Haring returned to Harvard for his doctorate (1916) and joined the Yale faculty the same year but was disappointed by the university's lack of commitment to the Latin American field. As a result, he was happy in 1923 to accept an
invitation from Harvard to become the Robert Woods Bliss Professor of Latin
American History and Economics. He remained affiliated with Harvard until
his death in 1960.

Haring's contributions to Latin American history were substantial and varied. He published two major books on the colonial era—*Trade and Navigation
between Spain and the Indies in the Time of the Hapsburgs* (1918) and *The Span-*

ish Empire in America (1947)—as well as numerous works on contemporary affairs and a short history of the Brazilian empire (1958). His students at Harvard included several scholars, notably Lewis Hanke and Howard F. Cline, who themselves became major figures. Finally, in the 1930s he was active in the promotion of area studies in the Latin American field (see chapter 6).

Early American historians of Latin America were nearly all white men of northern European ancestry. An exception was Carlos E. Castañeda, a native of Tamaulipas, Mexico, who came to the United States in 1906.[44] He earned bachelor's, master's, and doctoral degrees at the University of Texas, the last with a dissertation (1932) based on an eighteenth-century history of Texas by Fray Juan Agustín Morfi, an unpublished manuscript he had discovered in Mexico. From 1927 to 1946 he was curator of the Latin American collection at Texas, during which time his acquisitions included the library of the nineteenth-century Mexican scholar Joaquín García Icazbalceta and that of the Paraguayan statesman Manuel B. Gondra. In 1946 Castañeda became a full-time member of the History Department, where he had taught on a half-time basis since 1939. According to his biographer, there was some prejudice against Castañeda, but it may have been caused as much by his Catholicism as by his Mexican origins. He was active as a Catholic layman, served as president of the American Catholic Historical Association, and was appointed a knight of the Holy Sepulchre in 1941. His most important historical contribution was a seven-volume history of the Catholic Church in Texas.

Another exception was Abraham P. Nasatir, whose Jewish ancestry was noted by Bolton even as he praised the abilities of this precocious student, only fourteen when he arrived at Berkeley in 1919. Nasatir received his doctorate in 1926 and went on to publish extensively on the Spanish role in the Mississippi Valley. Despite strong recommendations from Bolton, he had difficulty finding permanent employment because of his "race." Finally, in 1928 he joined the faculty of San Diego State University, where he remained until his retirement.[45]

It should be noted that regional or social origins might count against even young men of Anglo-Saxon background. When William Spence Robertson, a graduate of the University of Wisconsin, was first recommended to Bourne in 1901, the latter was assured that even though Robertson was a westerner, he was not "one of the obstreperous kind." Similarly, in 1916 Bolton noted that one of his students, Charles H. Cunningham, was well trained, ambitious, and energetic, but he had been raised on a midwestern farm and might be deemed too "uncurried" in appearance for a faculty position at Princeton.[46]

A few women evinced interest in Latin American history during this period, but the way was hard, for they could not expect to win positions at major public or private institutions. At Berkeley Bolton was accused of hostility to women students, and he did discourage them from undertaking doctoral work because of the limited number of positions open to them.[47] Neither of the first two women scholars of this generation was formally trained in Latin American history, nor could they boast of academic affiliations. Alice Bache Gould lived in Argentina as a child while her astronomer father was in charge of an observatory there, and later she vacationed in Puerto Rico, developing an interest in the history of the West Indies. She was trained as a classical scholar and mathematician, but a chance visit to Seville in 1911 led to a drastic change in direction. For the next forty years she devoted herself to the identification of the crew of Columbus's first voyage, relentlessly seeking documents in Spanish archives, even the jail in Moguer. She published her findings in a series of articles in the *Boletín de la Real Academia de Historia* (Madrid).[48]

Gould's younger contemporary, Irene A. Wright, turned to scholarship after several years as a journalist in Cuba, during which she published a book on social and economic conditions on the island (1910). Desiring to learn more about Cuba's origins, she moved to Seville, devoting herself for the next twenty years to the Archive of the Indies. To help support herself she offered her services as a researcher who could also arrange for the copying and translation of documents; later she helped set up a photographic workshop at the archive.[49] Meanwhile, she published prolifically: *The Early History of Cuba, 1492–1586* (1916), collections of documents related to English and Dutch voyages to Spanish America, and numerous articles.

Mary W. Williams and Lillian Estelle Fisher followed more conventional paths to scholarship. They were both productive historians, yet their gender confined them to positions in women's colleges. Williams received her PhD from Stanford University in 1914 with a prize-winning dissertation published as *Anglo-American Isthmian Diplomacy* (1916). She produced several articles on diplomatic subjects as well as a biography (1937) of Pedro II, emperor of Brazil. From 1915 until her retirement in 1940 she taught at Goucher College. During her career Williams was an active feminist and advocate for women's interests in the American Historical Association. In 1919 she complained about their second-class status within the organization: "All that any twentieth century woman of sense asks is a fair field and no favors;—to her chivalry merely means a 'square deal,'—but the woman who is so unfortunate as to have specialized in history largely asks in vain."[50]

Lillian Estelle Fisher also taught mainly at women's colleges. Her primary mentor at Berkeley was Priestley, under whom she received her doctorate in 1924 with a dissertation on viceregal administration in Spanish America that became her first book. Priestley was concerned about her employment prospects and welcomed the possibility that a professorship open only to women might be available at the University of Michigan. For his part, however, he was not prepared to countenance the presence of women in male-dominated departments. To Arthur Aiton, a former Bolton student at Michigan, he wrote: "I think we also recognize that the intrusion of a female personage in a history department will have its complications, and I believe that the supremacy of man should be pronounced and enunciated on all possible occasions." Priestley predicted that Fisher would be a "big producer of authoritative material," and indeed she published several more monographs.[51] After teaching for a year at Whittier College, she was on the faculty of the Oklahoma College for Women from 1926 to 1942, then served briefly at Hunter College and in the extension division of the University of California.

Institutional Foundations

By 1918–19 courses in Latin American history had become regular offerings at many American colleges and universities. The field, however, was acknowledged to be a new one that had arisen from "practical rather than from purely cultural considerations," and there was little consensus on the length and content of such courses. A survey in 1926 showed that approximately 175 colleges and universities offered regular or occasional courses devoted to Latin American history or to the history of U.S. relations with the region. According to the survey, however, several leading institutions, such as Princeton, Yale, and Wisconsin, did not teach Latin American history.[52]

In his early years of teaching at Yale, Hiram Bingham asked his students to read general works, such as his own *Across South America* (1911), which one student had the temerity to declare monotonous, as well as James Bryce's *South America* (1912) and Pierre Denis's *Brazil* (1911).[53] Textbooks soon began to appear, and by 1932 six histories of Latin America for college use had been published. The earliest were *A History of Latin America* (1919), written by William Warren Sweet, a professor at DePauw University, and *History of the Latin American Nations* (1922) by William Spence Robertson. A statistical analysis of the most recent editions of the six texts in 1934 showed that they were substantial tomes, the shortest (Sweet) consisting of 382 pages of written material. Robertson's weighed in at 805 pages, and *The People and Politics of Latin America* (1930) by Mary W. Williams totalled a daunting 836 pages. All of the texts, except *The Republics of Latin America* (1923) by Herman G. James and Percy A. Martin, devoted at least one-third of their content to the colonial and independence eras. All devoted varying amounts of space to individual countries, with Brazil, Mexico, Argentina, and Chile receiving the most attention. Central America and Panama also received substantial allotments in several of the texts.[54]

Given the development of scholarship and teaching about Latin America, it was to be expected that practitioners should desire a publishing outlet dedicated to articles about the region and a mechanism for providing information about new books and other publications. The Spanish historian Rafael Altamira recommended the creation of such a journal when he visited California in 1915, and the idea received further encouragement at the American Congress of Bibliography and History held in Buenos Aires in 1916. The delegates hoped that each country might establish a periodical to provide scholars with bibliographical data concerning all branches of learning.

William Spence Robertson and Charles E. Chapman, both of whom attended the conference, decided to pursue the matter formally, though their goal was a journal devoted exclusively to Latin American history.[55] Because Robertson remained in Argentina for nearly a year, it fell to Chapman to lay the groundwork for the endeavor, which was discussed at a dinner in Cincinnati during the December 1916 meeting of the American Historical Association. The approximately thirty persons present agreed to launch the *Ibero-American Historical Review* no later than January 1918, and two committees were established to bring the project to fruition.

The first issue of the new journal did not appear until February 1918. Partly because of the demands generated by American participation in World War I, the journal was on shaky financial footing from the start. Those involved had hoped that an endowment of $10,000 could be obtained, but less than half of that was subscribed, most of it by Juan C. Cebrián, a Spanish-born resident of San Francisco. Although the journal's name had been a subject of discussion for some time, Cebrián's contribution may have tipped the scales in favor of *Hispanic American Historical Review*. In Cebrián's view, the term "Hispanic" embraced all that pertained to Spain and Portugal, and to refer to the region south of the Rio Grande as Latin America was as inaccurate as referring to Canada and the United States as "Teutonic America."[56]

The first editor of the review was James A. Robertson, coeditor of *The Philippine Islands*. The inaugural number contained supportive statements from President Woodrow Wilson and J. Franklin Jameson as well as articles by Hackett, William Spence Robertson, and Charles H. Cunningham. There were, however, only fifty subscribers, and in subsequent years increased printing costs and the failure to enlarge the list of subscribers further weakened the journal's tenuous financial base. Bolton attempted to raise funds for the journal, explaining to Jameson in September 1921 that publication costs totalled about

$3,000 per year, of which subscriptions accounted for only $900. They could no longer lean on Cebrián, who had already contributed $5,000.[57] The efforts of Bolton and others were unavailing, and the journal was forced to cease publication in 1922. In 1926 Duke University agreed to assume financial responsibility for the review, which reappeared in that year, again under the editorship of James A. Robertson.

Articles in the journal during its first years paralleled the monographic production of specialists. Colonial institutions received much attention, as did relations between the United States and Latin America. From the beginning, contributions by Latin American scholars such as Gilberto Freyre and Ricardo Levene were also included.

During the early years of the twentieth century, historians of Latin America met regularly during the annual conventions of the American Historical Association to present papers and to hold a luncheon or dinner. As early as 1919 they called themselves "the conference on Hispanic American History," but later adopted the name Hispanic American History Group. By the mid-1920s some believed that their activities warranted greater structure, but in 1928 a committee appointed to study the matter recommended against establishing a formal association. Instead, they voted to adopt the title of Conference on Hispanic American History and to elect officers, whose primary responsibility would be to arrange for the annual meeting of the group.[58]

As the 1930s began, the field of Latin American history had attained a measure of respectability and status within the profession. The field had blossomed in the wake of the growing American commercial and political ties to the region, especially in Mexico and the Caribbean Basin. A cadre of trained historians had established themselves, mainly in the West, and were offering courses in the field to undergraduates and preparing graduate students to succeed them. Textbooks and monographs had been produced, and a historical journal had been created to disseminate the results of research and other communications. Other signs pointed to the novelty of the field: the shaky initial financing of the journal, the nebulous relationship of the Conference on Hispanic American History to the American Historical Association, and the fact that courses in Latin American history were still absent from the curricula of many institutions.

3

The Rise of Anthropology

In the emerging social sciences of the late nineteenth and early twentieth centuries, Latin America was an important subject of teaching and research mainly in the field of anthropology. As chapter 1 showed, Latin America and especially Mesoamerica had been a major source of interest for nineteenth-century archaeologists and ethnologists. This interest remained keen as the twentieth century began, all the more so as native Americans in the United States seemed to be on the verge of disappearance. In many parts of Latin America, by contrast, there remained not only the physical remains of the vanished civilizations so eloquently described by John Lloyd Stephens but also indigenous peoples who lived in traditional communities seemingly touched only lightly by the forces of modernity. Moreover, these communities were vibrant and healthy and in no danger of dying.[1]

Archaeological and ethnological research focused on the Americas during this period was shaped by the fact that the two fields were increasingly subsumed under the new discipline of anthropology. In 1900 the American Ethnological Society counted 73 members, but it was soon overshadowed by the American Anthropological Association, which had 172 members at the time of its foundation in 1902. Members of the older society were automatically enrolled in the new association, and the latter's journal, *American Anthropologist*, became its organ.[2]

In the United States anthropology was usually divided into four subfields with often blurred boundaries: archaeology, linguistics, physical anthropology, and ethnology, which evolved into cultural anthropology. It should be noted that only archaeology of the Americas fell within the purview of anthropology departments in colleges and universities. Old World archaeology was included in classics departments or was the province of special institutes. The gap between the two fields was also seen in the trajectory of the Archaeological Institute of America, founded in 1879. Although the institute supported work by Adolph Bandelier and funded a study of Quiriguá, a Maya site in Guatemala, it gradually moved away from American projects to devote itself to Old World archaeology.[3]

The twentieth century saw leadership in the New World field pass increasingly from museums and similar institutions to academic departments within universities and from autodidacts such as Stephens and Bandelier to university-trained professionals. Anthropology was formally established in U.S. higher education with the creation in 1885 of Harvard's chair of American archaeology and ethnology, to which Frederick W. Putnam, curator of Harvard's Peabody Museum, was appointed. It was not until 1890, however, that a degree-granting department was created. Two years later Clark University awarded the first American doctorate in anthropology to a student of the German-born Franz Boas. By 1930, eighty-one doctorates had been conferred, most of them by a handful of institutions, including Harvard, Columbia, and California, that emerged as leaders of academic anthropology. Ten years later more than 60 percent of 273 institutions surveyed offered undergraduate courses in the field, though the number of anthropology departments remained small.[4]

With the relative decline of museum leadership came a decreased emphasis on the collection of artifacts. During the same period, governments in Latin America became more protective of their pre-Columbian remains and enacted legislation to regulate archaeological projects and to prevent the removal of antiquities. Mexico created the position of inspector of archaeological monuments in 1875, and legislation enacted in 1897 declared all such monuments to be the property of the nation. The government of Peru issued decrees in 1893 and 1911 declaring that all antiquities were the property of the state and requiring government permits before excavation could be undertaken. These laws were laxly enforced, however, and both natives and foreigners routinely ignored them.

Also noteworthy was the erosion of nineteenth-century cultural evolutionism as propounded by Lewis Morgan. Scholars became less inclined to believe that human beings everywhere progressed through the stages of savagery, barbarism, and civilization. The new paradigm, associated primarily with Franz Boas, emphasized the need to study cultures in terms of their environment and historical circumstances and eschewed the ethnocentrism implicit in the evolutionary model. Boas was also active in efforts to professionalize anthropology and to shift leadership from the museum to the university, and his American career illustrates the trajectory of anthropology during the four decades after 1890.[5] After a four-year stay at Clark University, Boas was employed by the World's Columbian Exposition in Chicago and by the American Museum of

Natural History. In 1896 he joined the Anthropology Department of Columbia
University as an instructor, and he became a professor in 1899.

Archaeology: Mesoamerica

Changes in the structure and organization of archaeological and ethnological
investigation did not occur overnight, and well into the twentieth century self-
taught individuals such as Bandelier remained active, working alone and receiving limited support from various institutions. Two such transitional figures
were Frederick Starr and Edward H. Thompson. Starr had a doctorate in geology, but neither he nor Thompson had formal training in anthropology. Both
made Mexico their major area of study—for only a decade in Starr's case, for a
lifetime in Thompson's. Both were to become notorious for their removal of pre-
Columbian objects from Mexico despite laws forbidding such actions.

In 1892 Starr became the first anthropologist at the University of Chicago,
where he proved to be a popular lecturer. Until his retirement in 1923, however,
he was the only anthropologist there, and the field remained wedded to sociology in a single department. Starr also remained committed to the concept of
cultural and social evolutionism, rejecting Boasian relativism. During the decade 1894–1904 Starr made a dozen trips to Mexico and became an avid collector of both artifacts and people. He collaborated with W. D. Powell, a Southern
Baptist missionary, in excavating in Toluca and in acquiring pre-Columbian objects, including a collection sold to Powell by a Mexican archaeologist, Antonio
Peñafiel. In 1897, when Powell was experiencing financial difficulties, Starr purchased the Peñafiel collection, which he in turn sold to the Field Museum of
Natural History in 1905, along with other objects he had obtained in Mexico.
Meanwhile, he toured Indian villages in central and southern Mexico, making photographic records of the communities and their inhabitants and taking
measurements of a sample of the latter. He also made plaster busts of the villagers, to their intense dismay.[6]

A native of Worcester, Massachusetts, Thompson came under the influence
of the French cleric Charles Etienne Brasseur de Bourboug, who believed that
the ancient people of Mesoamerica were the descendants of the lost continent
of Atlantis.[7] In 1879 Thompson published an article, "Atlantis Not a Myth," in
Popular Science Monthly, which came to the attention of Stephen Salisbury, Jr.,
vice president of the American Antiquarian Society. Several years later Salisbury invited Thompson to undertake studies of the ancient Maya in Yucatan on
behalf of the society and the Peabody Museum of Archaeology and Ethnology.
To help support his research, Thompson would be named American consul in
Mérida.

Accepting with alacrity, Thompson arrived in Yucatan in 1885. He remained there for approximately four decades, dedicated to archaeological work that can be divided into two principal phases. Initially he was engaged in surveying and describing several sites, notably Labná, but lacked the manpower and resources to engage in extensive excavation. His principal achievement was the study of the subterranean cisterns (*chultunes*) of Labná.

The second phase began in 1895 when he acquired the hacienda of Chichén Itzá, thanks to the largesse of a wealthy Chicago businessman, Alison Armour, Jr. The boundaries of the ruined hacienda were unclear, but its ownership allowed Thompson to devote himself to the study of the nearby ruins. His best-known feat was the dredging of the sacred cenote, or waterhole, at the site with the financial assistance of his Massachusetts patrons. The cenote yielded human bones and objects of gold, copper, and jade, thereby confirming Thompson's belief that it had been a place of sacrifice. Thompson sent many of the objects found in the cenote to the Peabody Museum, ignoring Mexican regulations regarding the export of antiquities. Nor, according to the government, did he even seek permission to dredge the cenote until 1911, seven years after the work got under way. Although Thompson had made no secret of the dredging, the government did not act until 1926, presumably spurred by several recent publications in the United States that referred to the export of objects from the cenote. In September of that year the government formally charged Thompson with illegally removing artistic treasures from Mexico and attached his hacienda to guarantee civil responsibility. The litigation embittered Thompson's last years and was not settled until after his death in 1935.

Mesoamerica, and primarily the Maya zone, remained the principal field of activity for U.S. archaeologists. European and Mexican investigators dominated work in central Mexico, with relatively little participation by Americans at this time. Marshall H. Saville, who studied at Harvard from 1889 to 1894, conducted excavations in Mitla and other sites in Oaxaca for the American Museum of Natural History and acquired a valuable collection for the museum. In 1903 he was named to a chair in American archaeology at Columbia University funded by Joseph F. Loubat (Duc de Loubat), who was also an important museum patron.[8]

Boas was responsible for the most important projection of U.S. academic influence in central Mexico through his efforts to establish the International School of American Archaeology and Ethnology. Boas obtained the support of the governments of Prussia and Mexico as well as of several U.S. universities—Columbia, Harvard, and Pennsylvania—and the Hispanic Society of America for the school, which was formally inaugurated in 1911. Headed by a rotating director from one of the sponsoring institutions, the school was intended to finance the research of promising graduate students and to publish their findings promptly. The Mexican Manuel Gamio, University of Pennsylvania graduate student John Alden Mason, and others carried out important research under the auspices of the school, which focused on two major problems: (1) stratigraphic investigation of the Valley of Mexico to establish the chronology of civilization there, and (2) study of the structure and distribution of Mexico's indigenous languages. Although the school was never formally disbanded, it had ceased operations by 1916, a casualty of World War I and the Mexican Revolution, which brought not only political upheaval but also new priorities in anthropological research in that country.[9]

In the 1920s several scholars conducted archaeological investigations in central Mexico on behalf of American institutions. From 1922 to 1925, for example, Byron Cummings of the University of Arizona excavated a mound at Cuicuilco in the Federal District that proved to be a temple and the oldest building known up to that time. Most important was the work of George C. Vaillant of the American Museum of Natural History. From 1927 to 1934 he carried out stratigraphic investigations at several sites in the Valley of Mexico that "changed the course of Mexican archaeology and placed it on a new and professional footing." In particular, his work demonstrated the existence of cultures that antedated those of the so-called Archaic era, which had been considered the earliest but which Vaillant now described as a middle period.[10]

Americans might have made relatively few contributions to understanding the prehistory of central Mexico, but they played what some might call a hegemonic role in the Maya zone of Mesoamerica, which embraced Yucatan and other Mexican states and parts of Central America, notably Guatemala and Honduras. The foregoing is not meant to suggest that Americans monopolized foreign archaeological investigations in the area. The Englishman Alfred Maudslay and other Europeans made significant contributions as well, but long-running and well-financed institutional programs developed only in the United States.

Initially sparked by the writings of Stephens, American interest in Maya civilization had remained keen, as seen in the sponsorship of Edward H. Thompson's work. Maya achievements gained a wider audience when Thompson was asked to prepare moulds of parts of Maya structures at Labná and Uxmal. Casts were made from the moulds for exhibition at the World's Columbian Exposition of 1893 in Chicago and attracted much favorable comment.[11] The Maya structures also served to persuade any remaining doubters that the New World had produced a civilization perhaps not comparable to those of classical antiquity but certainly deserving of serious study.

The head of the fair's anthropology section was Frederick W. Putnam, who was a key figure in promoting Maya studies in the United States. Remaining at Harvard until his retirement in 1909, he also helped to cement the university's leadership in Maya studies during the early twentieth century, when individuals trained or employed there—the so-called Maya crowd—dominated the field.

In the late nineteenth century the Peabody Museum was able to finance Maya archaeological expeditions partly because of funding supplied by Charles Bowditch, who had become interested in Maya culture, especially in the decipherment of Maya glyphs, while travelling in Central America. In addition to subsidizing the work of Thompson in Yucatan, the museum undertook a larger project in Honduras, where in 1891 it obtained a ten-year concession for a study of the ruins at Copán and other sites with the right to take away half the objects found. Marshall Saville and John G. Owens led the first expedition in 1891–92, and Owens the second in 1892, but he died of yellow fever in February 1893. Work continued under G. Byron Gordon and Alfred Maudslay, but more difficulties arose when a new government in Honduras cancelled the concession. Although an agreement was eventually reached, work resumed for only two additional seasons (1899–1900, 1900–1). The museum's work at Copán consisted mainly of exploration rather than excavation, but also yielded five hundred photographs of the site and operations there, some of which were displayed at the 1893 fair.[12]

Bowditch had long been looking for an individual who could test one of his theories: that there might yet be unacculturated Maya who could read the glyphs of their ancestors. Several candidates for this role had been tried and found wanting when Putnam suggested Alfred M. Tozzer, a recent Harvard graduate.[13] After successfully completing two summers of fieldwork in California and the Southwest, Tozzer was sent in 1901 to Yucatan, where he learned Maya and toured the ruins of Chichén Itzá with Thompson. He eventually decided to concentrate on the remote and relatively unacculturated Lacandon Maya in the Usumacinta River region. His fieldwork was the basis of his doctoral dissertation, published as A Comparative Study of the Mayas and the Lacandones (1907). Tozzer found no understanding of Maya glyphs among the Lacandones.

Tozzer joined the Harvard faculty in 1905 and offered for the first time his celebrated Maya seminar—Anthropology 9—which would be attended by several generations of Mayanists. He returned to the Maya region for fieldwork in Guatemala in 1909–10, and in 1913–14 was director of the International School in Mexico City. Meanwhile, in 1913 he had been named curator of Middle American Archaeology and Ethnology at the Peabody Museum.

Tozzer's list of publications included a Maya grammar (1921) as well as a monumental edition (1941) of Diego de Landa's Relación de las cosas de Yucatán. Another major work was the posthumous Chichén Itzá and Its Cenote of Sacri-

fice: A Comparative Study of the Contemporaneous Maya and Toltec (1957). His influence as a teacher, however, was as great as his impact as a scholar. Of the thirty-four contributors to *The Maya and Their Neighbors* (1940), a festschrift in his honor, twenty-five had been trained under his direction, and the other nine had taken courses with him.

Two of Tozzer's students—Sylvanus G. Morley and Alfred V. Kidder—were to play leading roles in the largest Maya project sponsored by an American institution in the first half of the twentieth century. In 1912–13 Morley presented to the Carnegie Institution of Washington a long-term plan for excavation at Chichén Itzá, which he believed would shed light on such problems as the evolution of Maya writing and architecture.[14] Morley had been a member of Tozzer's first Maya seminar in 1905, and though he never earned a doctorate, he acquired considerable experience as an archaeologist in the U.S. Southwest and Mesoamerica, including a visit to Chichén Itzá in 1907. His specialty was the study of Maya glyphs, which he was convinced related mainly to chronology and astronomy.

After much internal discussion, the Carnegie Institution approved Morley's proposal in 1914 and appointed him to its staff. Morley led expeditions to Guatemala and Honduras for the CIW, but the Mexican Revolution and World War I delayed implementation of the Chichén Itzá project. It was not until 1923 that Morley went to Mexico to obtain a concession from the government. After several months of negotiation, a contract was signed that granted the institution the right to explore, excavate, and preserve the ruins at Chichén Itzá for ten years under the supervision of the Mexican government, which was also to take part in the project.[15] All objects that might be found during exploration of the site were to be the property of the government. The CIW was apparently scrupulous in observing this provision, refusing to renew the employment of an English physician who smuggled a jade piece out of Mexico by taping it to his back.

The work at Chichén Itzá, which got under way in 1924 under Morley's direction, is now seen as a testament to his belief in the glories of ancient Maya civilization. Although George Vaillant and other specialists studied Maya glyphs and pottery, the emphasis was placed on the excavation and repair of monumental structures, such as the Temple of the Warriors and the Caracol. Mexican archaeologists did similar work in the Castillo–Ball Court group. As a result, Maya achievements were magnified, an outcome that dovetailed with the government's current efforts to exalt Mexico's Indian heritage and with the desire of local authorities to develop tourism in the area. In July 1923 a twenty-five-kilometer road linking the town of Dzitas to Chichén Itzá was inaugurated.

Tourists might now ride by train from Mérida to Dzitas and then travel by car to the ruins.

A second major focal point of CIW archaeology was the remote site of Uaxactún in the northeastern Petén of Guatemala, which Morley had discovered in 1918. He found there a stela bearing a date that showed Uaxactun to be the earliest Classic era site yet found in the Maya region. In 1925 the CIW signed a contract with the Guatemalan government authorizing it to conduct excavations at the site, and work began the next year under the supervision of two Harvard graduates: Oliver G. Ricketson and Augustus Ledyard Smith. Because of the inaccessibility of the site, Uaxactún did not draw many visitors, and little attention was paid to preservation. Instead, efforts were concentrated on "dirt archaeology" rather than on ethnohistorical work or on studying dated monuments and stelae. According to a modern student, "By demonstrating the validity of archaeologically constructed culture history through stratigraphic excavation, the excavators of Uaxactun set the major research agenda for decades of Maya field archaeology."[16]

The CIW's Maya program took a new direction in 1929 when the institution's trustees decided to broaden the scope of the inquiry through an interdisciplinary approach. They created a new Division of Historical Research and named Alfred Kidder as its chairman.[17] After receiving his doctorate from Harvard in 1914, he conducted landmark stratigraphic investigations at the ruins of Pecos pueblo in north-central New Mexico from 1915 to 1929. In 1926 he was named a research associate of the CIW and the following year was put in charge of its archaeological activities. The Division of Historical Research embraced all the CIW's historical endeavors, including archaeology, history, and the history of science.

Kidder envisioned a "panscientific attack" on the problems of the Maya area that would involve physical anthropology, medicine, ethnology, linguistics, history, nutrition, and agriculture. The contributions of scholars from these and other disciplines would be necessary in order to understand Maya prehistory, a task that archaeology alone could not accomplish. Accordingly, the CIW expanded its program to include, among others, a major ethnographic study directed by Robert Redfield (see below) and various historical projects. In 1933 the institution decided not to undertake any new excavation projects at Chichén Itzá but rather to concentrate on studying the questions raised by the work already done. In the same year the Mexican government extended the CIW's concession for another five years.

Efforts to explore the Maya past through ethnohistory were led by France V. Scholes and Ralph L. Roys, both of whom joined the CIW in the early 1930s.

Roys, who was self taught as a Mayanist, was first employed part-time by Tulane's Department of Middle American Research while he managed his family's
lumber business in the Northwest. He joined the CIW in 1932, also on a part-
time basis. Scholes, trained as a medievalist, searched Spanish and Mexican archives for documents about the Maya, which he published with Eleanor Adams
and others. Scholes collaborated with Roys on several major works, notably
*The Maya Chontal Indians of Acalan-Tixchel: A Contribution to the History and
Ethnography of the Yucatan Peninsula* (1948), which is considered a model work
of ethnohistory.[18] Of Roys's other publications for the CIW, the best known is
probably *The Book of Chilam Balam of Chumayel* (1933), his translation with
commentary of a set of pre-Columbian prophecies, history, and Maya lore compiled after the conquest. Another CIW historian, Robert S. Chamberlain, wrote
monographs detailing the conquest and colonization of Yucatan and Honduras
and published in 1948 and 1953, respectively.

Although they did not match the magnitude of the CIW program, other
U.S. institutions undertook research into Maya prehistory during this period.
The Department of Middle American Research at Tulane, established in 1924
with funds provided by banana magnate Samuel Zemurray, sponsored an expedition in 1925 by Frans Blom and Oliver LaFarge that took them to Maya-
speaking areas in Mexico and Guatemala. In addition, their finds at LaVenta, in
central Mexico, helped to arouse interest in the builders of the site, soon to be
named Olmecs.[19]

Blom, who had received a master's degree from Harvard (1924), became head
of the department in 1926. Although he had difficulty raising funds, Blom expanded the holdings of the department's library and museum, and in 1927 he
recruited the German-born Herman Beyer, a specialist on Maya glyphs who
had been working in Mexico since 1904.[20] Blom also led subsequent expeditions
(1928, 1930) to Maya zones in Mexico and Guatemala.

The University of Pennsylvania and its museum began a long association
with Maya archaeology in the 1930s. In 1930 J. Alden Mason, curator of American archaeology and ethnology at the museum, visited the Maya site of Piedras Negras in northwestern Guatemala and made arrangements for excavating
there. The site had been visited by Teobert Maler in 1901, as well as by Morley,
who gave it extensive coverage in his *Inscriptions of Petén* (1938).

According to Morley's biographer, it was he who convinced Mason to undertake an archaeological project there. Work began in 1931 and continued until
1939, mainly under the guidance of Linton Satterthwaite, who became field director in 1933. The nature of Maya construction at Piedras Negras required especially careful and laborious digging, which had to be completed during a short
dry season of two and one-half months. The site was also distant from sources

of labor and from the nearest port (Alvaro Obregón) on the Gulf of Mexico. Raising funds for the annual expeditions proved difficult during the Depression years and came mainly from private benefactors and the American Philosophical Society. The project resulted in the careful mapping of the site and the excavation of buildings and carved monuments. Eight of the latter went to Guatemala City and others to Philadelphia on loan.[21]

The Tozzer festschrift, *The Maya and Their Neighbors* (1940), offered impressive evidence of the maturity attained by Mesoamerican archaeology during the early decades of the century. More than thirty contributors, nearly all of them Americans, surveyed existing knowledge and identified problems to be solved. Morley, for example, pointed out that approximately one-third of the characters in Maya writing had been deciphered and surmised that the remaining, non-numerical glyphs dealt with religious and ceremonial matters. The collection contained one cautionary note by Clyde Kluckhohn, who faulted Mesoamerican specialists for their inattention to theory. To him, many of the scholars in the field were "but slightly reformed antiquaries" who engaged in "obsessive wallowing in detail of and for itself." He urged specialists to develop and articulate conceptual frameworks that might guide their research and enable their findings to contribute to the understanding of human behavior.[22]

Archaeology: South America

The attraction of early twentieth-century American archaeologists to the Maya zone is not surprising given the relative propinquity of the area and the long tradition of interest dating back to the mid-nineteenth century. By contrast, Andean South America, though known to be the center of advanced civilizations, could be expected to generate relatively little archaeological activity by Americans. Not only was the region farther away from the United States, but the cultures that had flourished there in prehistoric times had left fewer monumental structures comparable to those in Mesoamerica. Moreover, the study of Maya glyphs, which was so important to American scholars, could have no counterpart in South America, where pre-Columbian writing in any form was non-existent.

The first foreigner to make a major contribution was not an American but a German, Max Uhle, considered the founder of Andean archaeology, who held a doctorate in linguistics (1880) from the University of Leipzig.[23] His first fieldwork in South America was an ethnographic, linguistic, and archaeological reconnaissance begun in 1893 under the sponsorship of the Prussian government and the Berlin Museum. In 1895 he began to work under the patronage of the University of Pennsylvania, surveying the ruins at Tiahuanaco in Bolivia. Unable to gain permission for his activities, he moved to Peru in 1896 and spent a year in a major excavation project at Pachacamac north of Lima. From 1897 to 1899 he was in Philadelphia, writing a report on his work at Pachacamac, which was published in 1903. The death of Uhle's patron at Pennsylvania led him to find a new sponsor in the University of California. From 1899 to 1901 he explored numerous sites along the Peruvian coast and identified pottery styles produced by the Chimu, Moche, and Nazca cultures. He also measured and photographed the Inca palace at Tambo Colorado. After a two-year interval in California, during which he studied the collections he had shipped from Peru, he returned to the field, where he again concentrated on coastal excavation. From 1906 until he retired and returned to Germany in 1933, he was employed in various positions related to archaeology by the governments of Peru, Chile, and Ecuador.

Because of his peripatetic career, Uhle did not leave disciples to carry on his work, though students in the United States would later study the pottery and other objects he had sent to California. Meanwhile, Hiram Bingham was making more spectacular discoveries in Peru. While on the faculty at Yale, he led three expeditions to Peru (1911, 1912, 1914–15). It was during the first of these that he made his most celebrated find—that of the "lost city" of Machu Picchu.

After Bingham's initial foray into archaeology at Choqquequirau, described in chapter 2, he shelved plans to write biographies of Bolívar and San Martín and to revise his dissertation for publication. Instead, he made plans for an expedition to Peru that would have three primary objectives: an ascent of Mount Coropuna, which Bandelier had believed to be the highest peak in the Andes; a geographical reconnaissance of the Andes from the Urubamba Valley to the Pacific Ocean along the seventy-third meridian of longitude; and a search for Inca ruins. With expenses budgeted at nearly $12,000, Bingham had to scramble for financing, raising funds from United Fruit Company founder Minor C. Keith and philanthropist Edward S. Harkness as well as his own resources.[24]

Besides Bingham, seven men made up the personnel of the expedition. Isaiah Bowman, an assistant professor of geography at Yale and an experienced South American traveller, was largely responsible for the survey along the seventy-third meridian and functioned with virtual independence from Bingham (see chapter 4). Bingham succeeded in climbing Coropuna, but barometric measurements and triangulations by his companions made it clear that the mountain was not the "apex of America."

Bingham's 1911 expedition is best known for his "discovery" of Machu Picchu, but he had been alerted to ruins in the vicinity by scholars in Cuzco and others, and he found three Indian families living at the site. Moreover, despite what he wrote in subsequent accounts, he was not overly impressed by what he had found and spent only five hours there. Two weeks later, guided by a local official, he reached the ruins of Vitcos, which he concluded had been the capital founded by Manco Inca in the 1530s. His third major find was at Espiritu Pampa, where the ruins appeared to match Spanish accounts of Vilcabamba, where Manco's sons, Tito Cusi Yupanqui and Tupac Amaru, ruled.[25]

On his return to the United States, Bingham began preparing for the classes he was scheduled to teach during the spring semester of 1912. He also wrote a variety of pieces on his expedition, including a scholarly monograph on Vitcos for the *Proceedings of the American Antiquarian Society* and three articles for *Harper's Weekly*. A lecture at the National Geographic Society in February 1912 had far-reaching consequences, for it led to an offer from the director of the society, Gilbert Grosvenor, to sponsor the new expedition Bingham was already planning.[26]

The National Geographic Society contributed $10,000 to the expedition and was listed as cosponsor along with Yale University. In return, the society was to receive one or two articles on the expedition by Bingham, along with photographs, for publication in the *National Geographic Magazine*. Edward Harkness again made a contribution, apparently conditioned on Bingham's ability to excavate in Peru and bring objects found to the United States.[27] As it turned out, the archaeological aspects of the 1912 expedition would provoke controversy in Peru.

Although Machu Picchu had been surveyed and mapped during the 1911 expedition, and bones apparently dating from the glacial era had been unearthed near Cuzco, no archaeological excavations had been undertaken. The 1912 expedition, however, although announced as being primarily geographical, was clearly intended to have a strong archaeological focus as well. Its plan of work called for excavation in the Cuzco area and in the ancient province of Vilcabamba, and Bingham assured Harkness that George Eaton, the expedition's osteologist, had experience with pottery and other archaeological remains as well as ancient bones.[28]

Although Peru's 1911 decree had been issued while Bingham was at work in the country, he had had little difficulty in dealing with Peruvian officials, probably because of the low priority assigned by the expedition to archaeology. In 1912, however, he sought from Peru a concession of ten or twenty years duration that would allow Yale University to carry out archaeological excavations and export some material.[29] While Bingham was still in New Haven, the American minister in Lima, H. Clay Howard, presented the Yale proposal to President Augusto B. Leguía, who was willing not only to approve a twenty-year concession but to give the university exclusive rights to archaeological exploration in Peru. According to Howard, "[Leguía] said that he would rather have such rights placed in the United States than in Europe; and granted to such a university as Yale, rather than be the subject of indiscriminate concessions of conflicting rights, and perhaps to irresponsible concessionaires."[30] Leguía foresaw no difficulty in obtaining the approval of the Peruvian Congress, which was dominated by his supporters, though he was to leave office on September 24, 1912.

Bingham expressed some concern over whether the grant of a monopoly to Yale was appropriate, fearing that it would arouse opposition, but soon after arriving in Lima in June 1912, he left for Cuzco before the final draft of the contract had been prepared, let alone approved by the Peruvian Congress.[31] Signed by Howard in Bingham's absence on August 19, 1912, the concession as drafted was to run for ten years only but included the monopoly and allowed Yale to export any artifacts it might uncover.[32] As Bingham had feared, the concession aroused a storm of criticism. An article in Lima's *El Comercio* called the concession a threat to Peru's national culture and noted the opposition of the Instituto Histórico del Perú, which the Peruvian Congress had asked for an opinion. The institute opposed limitations on the freedom to do research and predicted that Peruvians would someday have to go to Germany or the United States to study their own culture. More serious was the opposition of Peru's new president, Guillermo Billinghurst, who had succeeded Leguía after a stormy election cycle. According to Howard, Billinghurst told Bingham, who had returned to Lima to deal with the problem, that "the entire idea upon which the proposed concession was predicated was little less than a disgrace to the country, because [it was] a confession of inability to properly exploit her own treasures." In the United States, Alfred M. Tozzer and Thomas Barbour of Harvard's Peabody Museum also complained about the grant of exclusive rights to Yale.[33]

Bingham wrote a letter to *El Comercio*, attempting to mollify the critics, but privately he attributed his difficulties to antipathy to the United States and to the political timidity of the Billinghurst administration, which did not comprehend what Yale wished to do for Peru.[34] In the end the contract was withdrawn, and after some dickering a new agreement was drawn up to cover the expedition then under way. Dated October 31, 1912, it allowed the expedition to continue its work in the department of Cuzco until December 1 under the inspection of a government official. The decree also allowed Yale, as a special favor, to export objects that had been unearthed during the expedition, but the government reserved the right to claim unique objects or duplicates.

Despite the difficulties encountered, the expedition could claim some accomplishments. With the help of local farmers, Eaton found more than one hundred graves near Machu Picchu, mainly in caves. The site of Machu Picchu was cleared and photographed. When Bingham left Peru on December 1, 1912, he took with him seven hundred photographs and one hundred cases of bones and potsherds.

Undaunted by past problems with the Peruvian authorities, Bingham made plans to return to South America with an even larger expedition. The National Geographic Society, with a grant of $20,000, was again a cosponsor, and a large staff was recruited, headed by Osgood Hardy, veteran of the 1912 expedition, who travelled to Peru in 1914 to lead an advance party that included two topographical surveyors.[35] Bingham himself did not arrive in Peru until April 1915, accompanied by a zoologist and two botanists. From the expedition's headquarters at Ollantaytambo, Bingham made journeys south and west of Machu Picchu, trying to identify Inca trails.

Considering his difficulties in 1912, Bingham showed remarkable insouciance about his relations with the Peruvian authorities. In January 1915 he informed officials in Lima and Cuzco of his intention to excavate at various points but apparently did not obtain the permits required by law. As a result, on May 25, 1915, the prefect of Cuzco ordered all excavation to stop. Sentiment against the expedition was stirred by Luis Valcárcel, then a young professor who headed the Instituto Histórico del Cuzco and who charged that Bingham and his colleagues were smuggling Peruvian treasures out of the country. After Bingham promised that any objects destined for removal from Peru would first be sent to the National Museum for evaluation, the prefect stated that any new excavation would have to be conducted under Peruvian supervision.[36] Bingham apparently decided to end the expedition and left Peru soon afterward. He later told Harkness that the work had had to be halted because the inspectors appointed by the government refused to have any contact with the expedition.[37]

Two members of the expedition who had been recruited in Peru took charge of shipping excavated objects to the National Museum in Lima. In early 1916 permission was granted for their export—seventy-four cases in all—on condition that they be returned in eighteen months. It is not clear whether Yale ever returned the material. In any event, Bingham's archaeological researches in Peru were at an end, at least partly because of his annoyance over the treatment he had received: "I hope I may never have to go back to Peru," he wrote on February 4, 1916. "The whole experience has taught me a great deal about the character of the South Americans."[38]

Bingham now moved on to military service during World War I and a career in politics. Meanwhile, his writings on Machu Picchu and other Inca sites had enhanced the visibility of Peruvian antiquities among both academic and general audiences. Ironically, however, although his original identifications of Vitcos and Vilcabamba have endured, this has not been the case for the somewhat confusing account of Machu Picchu that he elaborated in his writings: that it was both the cradle of Inca civilization and the last Inca capital. The scholarly consensus has been that the site was a fortress or royal residence constructed during the reign of the fifteenth-century Inca ruler known as Pachacuti.

In the decades immediately following Bingham's retirement from the field, few American archaeologists ventured into the Andean area. The most prominent was Alfred L. Kroeber, who made contributions in linguistics and the theoretical aspects of anthropology as well as in archaeology. One of the first persons to receive a doctorate (1901) at Columbia under Franz Boas, Kroeber moved to the University of California, where the Anthropology Department had just been founded as a result of the financial aid of Phoebe Apperson Hearst, who later supported the work of Max Uhle on behalf of the university. Kroeber met Uhle during the latter's stay in Berkeley in 1901–3, and the collections gathered by the German archaeologist formed the basis of Kroeber's first publications in the Peruvian field. Alone, or with graduate students William Duncan Strong and Anna H. Gayton, Kroeber analyzed the Uhle specimens from Moche, Chincha, Ica, Nazca, and other sites with the aim of classifying them stylistically and establishing their chronology. According to John Howland Rowe, this work, published in a series of monographs in the mid-1920s, "formed the basis for all subsequent contributions to the area for 20 years," and parts of it had not been superseded at the time of Kroeber's death.[39]

Kroeber went to Peru himself for two seasons of fieldwork (1925, 1926) under the sponsorship of the Field Museum of Natural History in Chicago. During his first trip he met the Peruvian anthropologist Julio C. Tello, who became a friend and collaborator. Kroeber concentrated his archaeological investigations in Peru's central and southern coast areas, especially the Cañete and Nazca valleys. He returned to the Nazca Valley in 1926 and, with Tello and his colleague William E. Schenck, he examined ancient burial sites in different locations. He also discovered the famous desert lines and markings of Nazca, sighting several of them on the dry plain of La Calera.[40]

Kroeber published several important monographs and articles on his work in Peru. He planned a five-year program of research in Peru under the aegis of the Field Museum, but financial constraints prevented its realization, and he did not return to South America until 1942. Meanwhile, he had introduced a course on the ancient civilizations of Peru at Berkeley in 1925–26 and graduate work in Peruvian archaeology in 1927–28.

Wendell C. Bennett was the second American to win recognition for his work in Andean archaeology during this period.[41] After receiving his doctorate in 1930 from the University of Chicago with a dissertation on Polynesian religious structures, he spent a year doing fieldwork in the Tarahumara region of northern Mexico, an experience that marked the beginning of his interest in Latin America. In 1931 he was employed by the American Museum of Natural History, and although his previous archaeological experience was limited, he travelled to Bolivia in 1932 to study Tiahuanaco in an effort to determine the nature and extent of its influence.

Having obtained the requisite permission from Arturo Posnansky, a former Prussian army officer who was the head of Bolivian antiquities, Bennett dug ten test pits at Tiahuanaco, the results of which enabled him to establish three ceramic periods for the site: Early, Classic, and Decadent. During this process he came upon the carved face of a large stone sculpture that became known as the "Monolito Bennett." Returning to Bolivia in 1934, he excavated at Chiripa in the highlands southeast of Tiahuanaco and at Arani in the lowlands, but his permit to export materials to New York was revoked by Posnansky. These seasons of fieldwork and subsequent excavations in Peru (1936, 1938) studying the antiquity of the Chavín horizon had made him, by 1940, in the words of Gordon R. Willey, the "leading North American Andean archaeologist actively engaged in field research."[42]

Ironically, the principal synthesis in the field, *Ancient Civilizations of the Andes* (1931), was not produced by a dirt archaeologist but by Philip Ainsworth Means, whose interests had turned increasingly to history. After his disagreement with Bingham, he had obtained a master's degree from Harvard (1917) and made two subsequent trips to Peru under the auspices of the U.S. National Museum, the Smithsonian Institution, and the American Geographical Society. In 1920–21 he headed the archaeological section of Peru's National Museum.[43] *Ancient Civilizations of the Andes*, which summarized existing knowledge from the earliest cultures through the era of the Inca empire, remained the standard textbook in the field for years.

By the mid-1930s American archaeologists had contributed substantially to understanding the prehistory of Mesoamerica and Andean South America, especially the identification and sequencing of cultural traditions. Elsewhere, relatively little had been done. A few researchers studied cultures in Central America outside of the Maya region and in South America outside of Peru and Bolivia. Samuel K. Lothrop, for example, received his doctorate from Harvard in 1921 with a dissertation on the pottery of Costa Rica and Nicaragua; in the 1930s he directed archaeological excavations at Sitio Conte in central Panama that brought to light gold ornaments, ceramics, and other objects associated with the Coclé culture. Lothrop was also one of the few Americans to conduct archaeological work in the Buenos Aires area. In the mid-1930s Junius B. Bird of the American Museum of Natural History found remains in the Strait of Magellan that indicated to him the presence of human beings at the southern tip of South America about 4000 BC, a date earlier than any previously suggested.[44]

The Birth of the Community Study

From the days of Stephens, Squier, and Bandelier, students of the prehistory of Latin America had commented, often derisively, on living peoples in the regions they visited. Starting in the 1920s, the study of contemporary Latin Americans was furthered by changes in the focus and methodology of American anthropologists. Boas and his followers had initially concentrated on what has been called "salvage ethnography": tracing and recording the material and cultural aspects of North American Indian life, which seemed on the verge of extinction, especially as the U.S. government was encouraging assimilation. Boas warned in 1906: "Day by day the Indians and their cultures are disappearing more and more before the encroachments of modern civilization, and fifty years hence nothing will remain to be learned in regard to this interesting and important subject." The emphasis was on the accumulation of data rather than on the formulation of theories or generalizations.[45] Moreover, little work was done on groups other than Indians living in the United States or Canada.

After World War I, however, several important changes came to the field. The study of contemporary culture and the processes of change became dominant concerns, and groups in regions other than the United States or Canada attracted larger numbers of researchers. Fieldwork—sustained participant observation of a small group perceived as tribal, primitive, or traditional—became the sine qua non for the aspiring anthropologist.[46] Meanwhile, the Social Science Research Council had emerged to direct the funds of philanthropic foundations to anthropological projects that might clarify if not solve contemporary problems.

All these trends can be seen in the background of Robert Redfield's *Tepoztlán, A Mexican Village* (1930), a landmark in the ethnography of Latin America.[47] Redfield, who received a law degree in 1921, was the son-in-law of Robert E. Park, a prominent sociologist at the University of Chicago. In 1923 Redfield and his wife, Margaret, visited Mexico, then in the midst of a cultural and artistic renaissance in which the country's indigenous traditions were assigned a leading role. While in Mexico, Redfield became acquainted with Manuel Gamio, who had received a doctorate under Boas at Columbia in 1921 and was now engaged in a major archaeological and ethnographic project at Teotihuacán near Mexico City. Gamio hoped that his work on the contemporary village at the site would contribute to its social and economic development and to its integration into the Mexican nation.

On his return to Chicago, Redfield enrolled in the university's Sociology and Anthropology Department. Frederick Starr had recently retired, and his successor, Fay-Cooper Cole, was attempting to revive the field of anthropology there.[48] Although Redfield's primary field was anthropology, he took several courses in sociology and in 1924–25 received a $500 grant to carry out a survey of Mexican immigrants in Chicago. This experience, as well as his 1923 Mexican visit, influenced his decision to devote his dissertation to a community in Mexico. To secure funding, he turned to the SSRC. In his application Redfield asserted that a study of a village such as those that sent immigrants to Chicago would facilitate understanding of the problems caused by the growing Mexican presence in the United States. He wanted to do more than produce an ethnographic monograph, however; what he envisioned was a "study of comparative mentality" that would relate patterns of thought in the selected village to Mexican communities in the United States.[49] In 1926 the SSRC awarded Redfield a $2,500 fellowship.

According to Redfield, it was Gamio who suggested Tepoztlán, sixty miles south of Mexico City, as a site for his study. Redfield and his family were enchanted by the beauty of the town, but less than three months after their arrival, they decided to leave because of a flare-up of political violence. Redfield later returned to Tepoztlán while his wife and children stayed in Tacubaya, near Mexico City. After returning to the United States in July 1927, Redfield took up a position as instructor of anthropology at the University of Chicago and completed his dissertation the following year.

In 1930 Redfield published his dissertation with only minor revisions as *Tepoztlán, A Mexican Village: A Study of Folk Life.* Alfred Kroeber and other reviewers immediately recognized the book as a landmark study. In it Redfield discussed marriage and the family, religion, and other aspects of Tepoztlán society, as was customary in ethnographic works; more novel was the emphasis on the contemporary life of a nontribal group and on the process of cultural change as the town's "folk culture," itself created by the fusion of Indian and Spanish traits, was being transformed by the spread of city ways.[50] Also notable was Redfield's attention to the psychological factors in cultural change. The book's appeal may have been enhanced by its depiction of a seemingly tranquil and stable community where cooperative labor was common, where religious festivals entailed as much play as worship, and where "the pulse of life [was] measured . . . by the great clocks of the sky." In an era when social critics railed at the fragmentation, uniformity, and hectic pace of life in modern industrial society even as the Great Depression was beginning, Tepoztlán as portrayed by Redfield seemed almost idyllic, because he failed to mention the disturbances that had caused his family's departure from the town. The economist Stuart Chase would expand on this view for popular audiences in his best-selling *Mexico: A Study of Two Americas* (1931), in which he compared Tepoztlán to "Middletown" (Muncie, Indiana), to the latter's disadvantage. Ironically, in reviewing Chase's book, Redfield took issue with the former's portrayal, noting that the villagers were often "underfed" and "underslept" and that some were "sodden with drink."[51]

By the time *Tepoztlán* appeared, Redfield had become involved in a larger, decade-long project for the Carnegie Institution of Washington. Part of Kidder's

"panscientific attack" on the Maya, it aimed to study the process of modernization as it affected four communities stretched along a folk-urban continuum
from primitive tribal settlements in Quintana Roo to the city of Mérida. The
first volume to be published (1934) was devoted to Chan Kom, a "peasant village" of 250 inhabitants fourteen kilometers south of Chichén Itzá. Redfield's
collaborator in the study was Alfonso Villa Rojas, a native of Mérida who was
the Chan Kom schoolteacher and later did graduate work at the University of
Chicago. Another collaborator was Asael T. Hansen, who had received a doctorate in sociology at the University of Wisconsin and, with his wife, Greta, was
given the task of studying Mérida.[52]

The Carnegie Institution extended its ethnographic study of the contemporary Maya to Guatemala as well as the Yucatan Peninsula. The principal investigator was Sol Tax, a graduate student at the University of Chicago who had
studied native Americans of the Southwest and Middle West. After completing
his doctoral work in 1934, he and his wife, Gertrude, left for Guatemala, where
they would spend part of each year until 1941.[53]

At the time, Guatemala was little studied by foreign ethnographers. The
Taxes set up their base at Chichicastenango. When life here was disrupted by a
Hollywood crew filming scenes for a Tarzan movie, Tax toured western Guatemala and visited Panajachel and other towns near Lake Atitlán, which also became foci for his research. Tax was assisted by Antonio Goubaud Carrera, who
later received a master's degree from Chicago, and by Juan de Dios Rosales, a
Panajachel Indian who was one of his principal informants.

Redfield's work in Tepoztlán and in the Yucatan Peninsula marked the beginning of a series of studies of small Latin American communities, though it
would be some time before ethnographers ventured outside Mexico and Central
America. Among the best-known of the early Mexican studies was *Mitla: Town
of the Souls* (1936) by Elsie Clews Parsons, who was interested in the accultura-
tion of indigenous peoples and their adoption of Spanish traits. A wealthy New
Yorker, Parsons received a doctorate in sociology from Columbia in 1899 and
turned to anthropology only after visits (1910–13) to the U.S. Southwest.[54] Her
interest in the culture of the Pueblo and other southwestern Indian groups later
led her to Mexico, where she travelled extensively from 1929 to 1933, often in the
company of Ralph Beals, brother of the journalist Carleton Beals and a young
anthropologist himself. She acknowledged that Mitla, a town of 2,000–2,500 inhabitants in Oaxaca, was too large for intimate acquaintance, but the people re-
minded her of her Pueblo friends, and she knew that she would be "very happy"
there.[55] The book is a personal, discursive account, notable for a long chapter on
"Town Gossip," in which she described her impressions while visiting various
homes and gossiping.

The prominence attained by Elsie Clews Parsons, who was president of the American Anthropological Association at the time of her death in 1941, might suggest that the barriers to women in the field were not as great as in history. Indeed, anthropology had a reputation for being more welcoming to women than the other social sciences. More recently, anthropologists of a younger generation have called this belief into question, asserting that women were often marginalized within the profession and their contributions ignored.[56] The case of Parsons was anomalous, for she was a wealthy woman who financed the work of many scholars and never required or sought a permanent paying position in a university or museum.

Two other women anthropologists of the era gained some renown for their work on topics related to Latin America, but their career paths were less conventional than those of their male counterparts. Ruth Bunzel was employed as Boas's secretary in 1924 when he suggested that she undertake an anthropological project of her own in the Southwest. The result was *The Pueblo Potter: A Study of Creative Imagination in Primitive Art* (1929), her doctoral dissertation, now considered a "landmark in the anthropology and sociology of art."[57] Having won a Guggenheim fellowship in 1930 for a Mexican project, she decided to go to the less-studied Guatemala instead. Settling in Chichicastenango, she helped formulate plans for the Carnegie's ethnographic work there and was led to believe by Kidder that she would have an important role in it. She was therefore incensed when the permanent position went to Sol Tax, who knew little of the region. She later taught occasionally at Columbia but never won a permanent position.

Lila Morris O'Neale was initially trained in "household art" with a specialty in textile and clothing history and design and taught these subjects at several colleges and universities in the West. In 1926 she enrolled at the University of California as a graduate student in household art, but turned to anthropology after meeting Kroeber, who encouraged her to work with the university's collection of pre-Columbian Peruvian textiles, which became the subject of her master's thesis. Her doctoral dissertation (1932) was on Indian basket-weavers of the Northwest, but a Guggenheim fellowship enabled her to continue her work on Peruvian textiles, about which she published extensively. She was also employed by the CIW to study the contemporary textiles of Guatemala. She did not find a permanent home in an anthropology department, but rather from 1932 until her death in 1948 was a professor of household art or decorative art at Berkeley.[58]

Although anthropology was also reputed to be welcoming to minorities, men of northern European and Protestant ancestry predominated among its practitioners, especially in archaeology. Franz Boas was a Jew, as were several of his students. Conflict over the direction and control of anthropology in the early twentieth century has been interpreted partly as a clash between museum men of traditional native stock and university-oriented men of immigrant origins, such as Boas.[59] Sol Tax was the son of Russian Jewish immigrants.

The nature of anthropology as a discipline made its evolution as a field of inquiry in the Latin American region different from that of history. Its practitioners regarded themselves as social scientists who formulated and tested hypotheses about aspects of human society that were expected to be valid regardless of the regional context. This orientation was obscured but by no means obliterated by the archaeologist's attention to the prehistory of the New World or the ethnographer's concentration on small groups in rural or traditional settings. Moreover, scholars in the early twentieth century often evinced broad regional or topical interests. Archaeologists whose specialty was Mesoamerica often had prior experience in the Southwest. Others, such as Kroeber, achieved professional distinction in both archaeology and ethnology.

In this environment it is not surprising that no professional organization or journal strictly devoted to Latin America was established along the lines of the Conference on Latin American History or the *Hispanic American Historical Review*. In 1934, however, the Society for American Archaeology was founded, and its journal, *American Antiquity*, was launched the following year. The society grew out of the Committee on State Archaeological Surveys, which had been created in 1921 as an advisory body in the field of North American archaeology, but the constitution of the new group stated that it embraced the entire Western Hemisphere.[60] George Vaillant was named to the society's council, and Alfred Kidder became its second president. The first volume of the new journal was devoted entirely to archaeology of the United States, but the second carried some articles on the Maya and one on a South American topic. Likewise, approximately one-third of the papers on the programs of the society's first two meetings (1935, 1936) dealt with Latin American topics.

By the mid-1930s, then, the linkages between investigation into the peoples of both North and South America remained as strong as they had been in the nineteenth century. The study of prehistoric civilizations in Mesoamerica and Andean South America was deemed central to the development of New World archaeology, and those who worked in Latin America were highly respected members of the profession. In a similar way, the impact of community studies by Redfield and others ensured that Latin America would be a focal point for anthropologists interested in the culture of contemporary peoples.

4

Geography and
the Other Social Sciences

Of the other disciplines considered social sciences during the early twentieth
century, only geography developed a cadre of academic specialists on Latin
America who regularly conducted research and taught courses on the region.
By contrast, in political science, sociology, and economics, a few individuals
studied Latin America, but they did not constitute a group that was identified
with, and sought to advance, scholarship about the region. In part this discrep-
ancy was due to the relatively late emergence of the latter three as more or less
discrete disciplines with distinctive methodologies and concerns. The American
Economic Association was founded in 1885, but the American Political Science
Association (APSA) was not founded until 1903, and the American Sociological
Society was launched two years later. Disciplinary boundaries dividing these
fields from one another and from history long remained blurred, however, and
individuals trained in one might well teach and publish in another. Bernard
Moses, for example, though trained as a historian, introduced political science
to the University of California in 1880 and was a founding member of the APSA.
A survey of 401 colleges and universities by the APSA ten years after its founding showed that only 38 had separate departments of political science.[1] In most
institutions, political science was part of departments of history, philosophy,
economics, sociology, or some combination of these. Many institutions offered
no courses in the field at all.

Students of economics and sociology and to a lesser extent political science
directed their energies overwhelmingly to domestic topics, with little attention given to international problems and issues that did not concern the United
States. The aforementioned APSA survey showed that a few institutions offered
courses in English or comparative government, with the latter limited to Europe. In fact, the committee that conducted the survey recommended that the
content of comparative government courses be expanded to include other im-

portant areas, among them South America. The organs of the various associations carried few articles devoted to Latin America, which was represented slightly, if at all, on the programs of their annual meetings.

Geography differed from these social sciences in several respects. Its study, if only by amateurs, had a long history in the United States. In addition, as the field was redefined and professionalized in the early twentieth century, the importance of regions in the conceptual framework espoused by scholars created a situation wherein parts of Latin America were deemed appropriate sites for research. The early linkage of geography with departments of business and economics at a time of increased trade and investment in Latin America contributed to this orientation. Finally, the study of geography with a Latin American focus undoubtedly acquired prestige because of the eminence of many of the early scholars in the field—Isaiah Bowman and Carl O. Sauer, to name but two—who reached the very top rungs of their profession.

Latin Americanist Geography in Ascendance

Americans had long been concerned with geography in its most primitive sense, which they defined as the description and mapping of the earth, and supported exploratory expeditions to fill in the many blank spaces that still remained on maps. These concerns prompted the organization of the American Geographical Society in New York in 1851. South America and its exploration were among the topics that interested its early members, and those who attended the first public meeting of the society in 1852 heard a paper by the American diplomat and promoter Edward A. Hopkins titled "The Geography, History, Productions, and Trade of Paraguay."[2]

As an academic discipline geography was still in its infancy at the turn of the twentieth century. The first geography department was established at the University of Chicago in 1903, but at Yale and many other institutions, geography remained part of the Department of Geology or was linked to programs in economics and business, as at the University of Pennsylvania. These linkages reflected strains and uncertainty in the conceptualization of the field, in particular the relationship between the physical environment and human development. In the early years of the century, practitioners frequently embraced environmental determinism, which treated culture and socioeconomic processes as the products of conditions in the natural world.

Geographers never fully resolved these ambiguities, but by 1924, state universities, as well as private colleges and universities, offered nearly five hundred courses in the field. In 1904 the Association of American Geographers was founded to promote research by professional geographers; membership was limited to those who had produced original work in some branch of geography. Forty-eight persons were admitted to the new association, which until the years following World War II, required prospective members to show evidence of "mature scholarship."[3]

An early figure of great importance in the development of scholarship in Latin American geography was Mark Jefferson, who was significant not only because of his own research and writing but also because of his influence on Isaiah Bowman, another leader in the field.[4] In 1883 Jefferson was a student at Boston University when he was offered a position as assistant to Dr. Benjamin Gould, director of the Argentine National Observatory in Córdoba and the father of Alice Bache Gould. Jefferson accepted the position and spent approximately six years in Argentina, three of them at the observatory and two as an employee of a sugar plantation in Tucumán.

Employed as a teacher and school administrator after his return to the United States, Jefferson took a summer course in physical geography at Harvard and decided to pursue studies in geography there, receiving a master's degree in 1898. In 1901 he accepted a position as a geography instructor at the State Normal School in Ypsilanti, Michigan, where he remained until his retirement in 1939. In the latter year he published an important work, "Law of the Primate City," based in part on his observations of Latin American capitals.

At Ypsilanti, Jefferson's best-known student was Isaiah Bowman, who was born in Canada in 1878 but raised in Michigan.[5] Following Jefferson's advice, he pursued his studies at Harvard, where he earned a bachelor's degree in 1905. In the same year he became an instructor at Yale and taught what was probably the first course on South American geography ever offered in the United States. He received his doctorate from the same institution in 1909. His dissertation, "The Geography of the Central Andes," was the first to be written in the United States on a South American subject.

Bowman's dissertation was based on his first fieldwork in South America, which took place in 1907 and was partly funded by Archer M. Huntington, who was the principal benefactor of the American Geographical Society.[6] On this expedition he examined land forms in a little-studied region lying between 12° and 26° south latitude and embracing part of the Atacama Desert, the Maritime Andes, and the Eastern Andes of Bolivia. The trip not only provided data for his dissertation and for several articles but also led to an invitation from the Rand McNally Company to write a geography text on South America. Published in 1915, it was one of the first on that continent to be written in English and was widely used in high schools and colleges.

Bowman's second field trip to South America took place in 1911 when he was part of Hiram Bingham's expedition to Peru. Operating independently from Bingham, Bowman made a topographical survey of the Andes along the seventy-third meridian from the junction of the Urubamba and Timpia rivers south to Camana on the coast. The survey proved hazardous as Bowman's canoe was overturned and nearly lost on the Urubamba, and he broke a bone in his right foot. In 1916 Bowman published *The Andes of Southern Peru*, an account of this and his previous expedition. The volume received high marks from most reviewers, including former president Theodore Roosevelt, who asserted: "The work is of high value from the scientific viewpoint—and possesses the additional merit, not always found in scientific books, of being exceedingly interesting even to the layman."[7]

Bingham invited Bowman to join him on his next expedition, but the geographer demurred, partly because of the differences in their interests and partly because of personal tension between the two men. Instead, with the help of a $4,000 grant from the American Geographical Society, Bowman undertook a third trip to South America in 1913. After travelling east across the Atacama Desert from Iquique, Chile, he and his companions ascended the Andes, suffering from altitude sickness and the effects of winter. This trip provided much of the material for *Desert Trails of Atacama* (1924). Drawing on his earlier South American journeys as well, Bowman in this volume describes the physical and human geography of a wide swath of northern Chile and parts of Bolivia and Argentina. According to Bowman, the area covered—the Atacama Desert and the high ranges and plateaus of the Central Andes, which end in the Puna de Atacama—attracted him more than any other part of South America.

Meanwhile, Bowman had become a mentor to two younger geographers. One was English-born Gladys W. Wrigley, whose 1917 dissertation titled "Roads and Towns of the Central Andes" was the first in geography to be written by a woman in the United States. The other geographer was George M. McBride, who had earned a doctor of divinity degree from Auburn Theological Seminary in 1901 and gone on to teach in Protestant mission schools in Chile and Bolivia. An encounter with Bowman in 1915 in La Paz led him to enroll at Yale as a graduate student in geography; he received his doctorate in 1921 with a dissertation titled "Land Tenure in Latin America."[8] McBride then joined the faculty of the University of California, Southern Branch, as it was being transformed into an independent institution: the University of California at Los Angeles.

Many of McBride's publications, including two major monographs, related to landholding in Latin America. *The Land Systems of Mexico* (1923) and *Chile: Land and Society* (1936) both traced the historical roots of existing patterns in the various natural environments of each country as well as their effects on contemporary society. In the former work, which was based on his dissertation, he anticipated the demise of the large hacienda, which was "disappearing before the combined attack of the landless mestizo politician, the equally landless soldier, the social reformer, and the agriculturalist Indian." Such a development was desirable, he maintained, and would result in a system of land tenure more in keeping with "modern democratic and individualistic notions."[9] For Chile he concluded that its agrarian problems stemmed from the haciendas of the central part of the country, which had also outlived their usefulness.

Apparently at the suggestion of Archer Huntington, the American Geographical Society named Bowman its director in 1915, a position he held until 1935, when he resigned to become president of Johns Hopkins University.[10] As director, Bowman reenergized that venerable institution, establishing a new, research-oriented publication series and replacing the society's *Bulletin* with the new *Geographical Review*, of which Gladys Wrigley served as editor from 1920 to 1949. Bowman also expanded the holdings of the society's library; from 1917 to 1919 McBride served as assistant librarian.

Bowman did little research on Latin America after 1915, but his interest in the region remained keen. This was evident when he became the dominant figure of the Inquiry, an organization created to provide maps, statistics, and other data that might be useful at the peace conferences after World War I. Although Latin America was marginal to the postwar settlement, a substantial proportion of Inquiry resources were devoted to that region (see chapter 5).

In 1918 the American Geographical Society allocated $6,000 for an expedition to be led by Mark Jefferson to temperate South America to study recent European colonization there.[11] Accompanied by Alfred Coester, the future Stanford professor, Jefferson spent approximately four months in mid-1918 in Chile, southern Brazil, and Argentina, where he renewed relations with families he had known in the 1880s. Despite the times, he saw German settlers in South America as a generally positive element, just as they had been in the United States. In *Recent Colonization in Chile* (1921), one of three monographs stemming from the expedition, Jefferson also derided the widespread belief that southern Chile had been "Germanized." In *Peopling the Argentine Pampas* (1916), Jefferson discussed conditions in European colonies in Santa Fe and Entre Ríos provinces and immigration in general. He viewed immigration as an unalloyed boon to Argentina, but believed that it was being inhibited by the reluctance of landowners to allow immigrants to acquire land.

After the war, Bowman committed the American Geographical Society to a program of research related to Latin America. In part it entailed the publication of the monographs by Bowman, Jefferson, and McBride already mentioned as well as by others. Its most important component, however, was the compilation and drafting of the Millionth Map of Hispanic America. The map, produced on a scale of 1:1,000,000 (15.78 miles to one inch), was a major undertaking, the cost of which was borne mainly by Archer Huntington and James B. Ford, another longtime supporter of the society. Raye R. Platt, a student of Jefferson's at Ypsilanti, became head of the project in 1923. The first sections of the maps appeared in the 1920s, but it was not completed until 1945.[12] Depicting the Western Hemisphere south of the U.S.-Mexico border, the map comprised 107 separate sheets, which, when joined together, covered an area of approximately 320 square feet. Even as it was being produced, the map was put to use by scientists and engineers, by Latin American governments in drawing boundaries, and by the U.S. government during World War II.

As Bowman was contributing to the acquisition and diffusion of knowledge of Latin American geography from his base in the Northeast, Carl O. Sauer was beginning to play the same role on the West Coast. Unlike Bowman, Sauer did not develop an interest in Latin America until he was well established as a geographer. He also differed from Bowman in that he spent his entire career as an academic.

Sauer was born in 1889 in Warrenton, Missouri, where his father and uncle were professors at Central Wesleyan College, which the younger Sauer attended.[13] After receiving his doctorate from the University of Chicago with a dissertation on the Ozark Highland district of Missouri, he joined the faculty of the University of Michigan. By the early 1920s he was being courted by the University of California. Geography constituted a separate two-man department at Berkeley, whose senior member, Ruliff S. Holway, had met Sauer at a meeting and became convinced that he was the person "to present the human element—the influence of Geographic conditions on man and his activities" and in general modernize and expand the department.[14]

Sauer accepted California's offer in 1923. Because Holway retired the same year, Sauer had an opportunity to revamp the department's faculty and courses. With John Leighly, whom he had brought with him, he reorganized the introductory course on physical geography and launched a new course on cultural geography. In 1925 he brought to the department as a senior teaching fellow the German-born Oskar Schmieder, who had been working in Argentina on settlement and agriculture. Schmieder remained at Berkeley until 1930.

Sauer's interest in Latin America, and especially Mexico, began after his move to California. In 1926 he made the first of a series of field trips, usually accompanied by students, to northwestern Mexico. These excursions exposed him to interesting and relatively untouched terrain and led him to study not only contemporary landscapes but also historical periods earlier than any he had previously considered. "I started in on Mexico," he wrote in 1948, "thinking I would go back no further than Spanish colonial institutions; and then I found myself back at the origin of man and his cultures."[15] One of his companions on these journeys recalled his skills in conversing with local people. "He was genuinely interested in them and they took to him," a former graduate student wrote. "His colloquial Spanish and his unpretentious, avuncular manner made for easy rapport."[16] His interest in the human past also led him to study archaeological remains and to engage in archival research in the Bancroft Library and elsewhere.

Sauer's broad and humanistic conception of geography—"an understanding of how things came to be"—was bolstered by the ties he developed with the university's anthropologists, especially Alfred L. Kroeber. With Kroeber and Herbert Bolton, he formed a nucleus of Latin Americanists who sought support within the university and from external sources for interdisciplinary studies.[17] An early result of their efforts was the establishment (1932) of the Ibero-Americana series, of which the three scholars were editors. Among its first publications was Sauer's *The Road to Cibola* (1932), the by-product of five field seasons in Arizona and northwestern Mexico. Here he traced the history of the old Indian highways that were subsequently used by Spaniards to explore and colonize the region.

Spurred by the departure of Schmieder, Sauer began to offer courses on Latin America in 1932. Former students attested to his prowess in the classroom. "He had an extraordinary gift for colorful language," one recalled, "and we all felt that we were witnessing the process of literary creation in action." At the same time he had his foibles. The same student recalled a dispute over the origin of the coconut, an argument that "lasted more than a dozen years—during which we hardly spoke to each other!"[18]

Sauer did not actively encourage students to concentrate on Latin American problems, but it appears that in the early years at least travel funds were available only to those working on Mexico. During the period 1927–36, 37 percent of the geography doctorates granted at Berkeley dealt with Latin American topics; during his total thirty-four years of service there, his students earned thirty-seven doctorates, of which nineteen dealt with Latin America.[19] Through these students Sauer's cultural-historical approach spread far beyond the University of California to constitute a Berkeley School.

In 1923, the year of Sauer's move to Berkeley, the University of Michigan engaged Preston E. James, another young geographer who became a leading Latin American specialist. A Harvard undergraduate, James did his graduate work at Clark University, where he was told that he had to develop a regional focus and chose Latin America, perhaps because Bowman and others had shown its possibilities, yet the competition "did not seem too hot" compared with North America and Europe.[20] In 1921 he embarked on his first field trip by sailing south on a United Fruit Company steamship to Panama. He initially described

Colón as a "beautiful paradise" created by the U.S. government, but otherwise his first impressions of the tropics, perhaps influenced by the environmental determinism still influential among geographers, were not auspicious for a budding Latin Americanist. After venturing into the "white light" district of Colón, he asserted: "Women solicit from the doorways, opium dens running without disguise—saloons and dance halls with mixtures of black, yellow and white men and women such as could only be found in the enervating, moral destroying Tropics. I cannot believe that the white man can ever be acclimated to this land."[21]

In Peru James visited Cuzco, Machu Picchu, and other sites, then travelled to Antofagasta, Chile, and with three companions crossed the Atacama Desert and the Andes into Argentina by train, automobile, and mule. This journey, along with library research, was the basis of his dissertation, "Geographic Factors in the Development of Transportation in South America" (1923). James was not overly concerned about his defense of the dissertation because no one on the examining committee had even been to Latin America.[22]

James later decided to concentrate on Brazil, then little studied by U.S. geographers. With the help of a grant from the National Research Council, he was able to spend a year (1930–31) studying land-use patterns in several Brazilian cities. This fieldwork established his reputation as a Brazilianist: "No American geographer had travelled so extensively in Brazil, or published so much as James. He had enjoyed *carioca* sambas, had dined in the same room as President [Getúlio] Vargas, had seen the *sertão*, and had become enchanted with the whole country and its hospitable inhabitants."[23]

At Michigan James taught courses on the geography of Middle America and South America, but he appears to have trained few if any graduate students in the Latin American field until after he moved to Syracuse University in 1945. He reached thousands of students, however, with his geography text, *Latin America*, which first appeared in 1942 and was revised for several subsequent editions. This massive work was the result of James's extensive field experiences throughout the region as well as two decades of reading and map study.[24]

In 1954, on the occasion of the fiftieth anniversary of the founding of the Association of American Geographers, James collaborated on a survey of the field with another geographer who specialized in Latin America: Clarence F. Jones.[25] An economic geographer, Jones received his doctorate from the University of Chicago in 1923. It was not until after he joined the faculty of Clark University that he evinced any interest in Latin America. He made two trips to South America (1925, 1928), which yielded data for two books: *Commerce of South America* (1925) and *South America* (1930), which emphasizes regional geography. In both volumes he noted the progress and prosperity of the Southern

Cone, especially southern Brazil, Argentina, and Uruguay, which had the advantages of fertile soils, good transportation facilities, and largely European populations. He was not sanguine about the future of the tropical lowland areas of South America: "They do not have favorable climatic conditions, a coal supply, an easily utilizable natural vegetation, any mineral resources, nor an energetic population."[26]

Robert S. Platt was another distinguished geographer who devoted most of his career to Latin America.[27] He received his doctorate from the University of Chicago in 1920 and spent his entire career on its faculty, teaching geography courses on the Caribbean and South America. Between 1922 and 1937 he made seven field trips to Latin America during which he made detailed studies of various kinds of basic economic units, mainly of haciendas, ranches, and farms. These studies were published as journal articles and brought together, with additional commentary, in *Latin America: Countrysides and United Regions* (1942). After 1950, however, Platt's interests shifted from Latin America to Europe.

By the end of the 1930s Latin American geography was firmly established in major institutions. Courses in the geography of Latin America were offered to both undergraduate and graduate students, and, with the appearance of the books by Jones, Platt, and James, students had access to authoritative texts. Most significant, the specialists discussed here were recognized as leaders in their discipline whose contributions transcended their regional specialization. They all received honors, such as election to high office in professional organizations, and Jefferson, Bowman, Sauer, James, Jones, and Platt each served as president of the Association of American Geographers. Thus, geography could take its place alongside anthropology and history as disciplines in which scholars of Latin America had earned distinction among their peers.

Political Science, Economics, and Sociology

In the other major well-established social sciences—political science, economics, and sociology—little attention was given to problems outside the United States or western Europe, nor did Latin America seem to be a fertile field for inquiry, as it did in the disciplines previously discussed. In the first place, the quantitative data that was the basis for much of the research in these disciplines was believed to be lacking for Latin America, and there was little rapport with practitioners in the region, who often followed theories and principles different from those used in the United States. Accordingly, in 1941 Frank W. Fetter, who had served as Edwin Kemmerer's secretary during his missions to Chile, Ecuador, and Bolivia in 1925–27, expressed the opinion that the bases for the study of economics in Latin America were nonexistent, except possibly in Argentina, because of the lack of adequate libraries and full-time faculty; neither professors nor students did any worthwhile research.[28] Moreover, the emphasis of social scientists on the development of theories and models that would be universally valid inhibited research outside of Europe and North America. As anthropologist Charles Wagley observed in the 1960s: "A Ph.D. candidate could contribute to economic, sociological, or political theory more easily by a study of New Haven, Connecticut, than by a laborious study of Mendoza, Argentina."[29]

As a result, the Spanish-American War and the projection of U.S. economic and military power in the region in the early twentieth century had little effect in stimulating interest among professionals in the social sciences. The principal exception was the appearance of books and articles relating to the territories acquired by the United States as a result of the war. For example, Bernard Moses was represented in the first volume (1904) of the *Proceedings of the American Political Science Association* with an article titled "Colonial Policy with Reference to the Philippines," a work undoubtedly inspired by his recent service in the islands (see chapter 5). In short, few political scientists, economists, or sociologists became Latin American specialists until well after World War II. Moreover, those who did frequently moved into other disciplines later on or left the academic world altogether for government service. Thus, they failed to train new cohorts of specialists to carry on their work in the classroom or in research.

The first article on a Latin American subject to appear in the *American Political Science Review* was "Parliamentary Government in Chile" by Paul S. Reinsch, a distinguished professor of political science at the University of Wisconsin.[30] The article, which gave a generally favorable view of Chile's political institutions and leadership, was probably a result of Reinsch's recent participation in the Pan-American Scientific Congress in Santiago. Reinsch, an expert in colonial government and international organization, was also part of the U.S. delegations to the third and fourth inter-American conferences, and published several other articles related to Latin America, but he never developed a permanent commitment to the region. In any event, he left the academic world in 1913 to serve as minister to China.

Reinsch was elected president of the APSA in 1919. His successor in this post was another eminent political scientist, Leo S. Rowe, who did become identified as a Latin Americanist during this period.[31] The son of German immigrants, Rowe earned a bachelor's degree at the University of Pennsylvania's Wharton School of Finance and Commerce and a doctorate at the University of Halle in Germany. After receiving a law degree from Pennsylvania, he joined the faculty there, becoming a professor of political science. In the early years of his career, Rowe was primarily a student of municipal government and of urbanization in general. He believed that "only under the conditions of city life can the possibility of human development be realized,"[32] but in accordance with Progressive thinking at the time, he hoped to make municipal government more efficient.

It was only after the Spanish-American War that Rowe would direct his attention to Latin America in a concentrated fashion. The origin of this new interest lay in his appointment (1900) to the Puerto Rican Code Commission at the suggestion of the provost of the University of Pennsylvania. As a member of the three-man commission, Rowe was assigned the task of studying the island's government, administrative departments, and tax system and to make recommendations that might be implemented by Puerto Rico's new rulers.

Rowe spent several months in Puerto Rico. His views appeared in the commissioners' report and in his book, *The United States and Porto Rico* (1904). That his interest in Latin America now went beyond the island is indicated by the book's subtitle: *With Special Reference to the Problems Arising Out of Our Contact with the Spanish-American Civilization.* In the book he stressed the differences between Puerto Rico and the United States in terms of their people, history, culture, and institutions. The island was suffering from "arrested development," the result of Spanish efforts to isolate the island and of the enervating effects of the tropical climate.[33] He believed that this "unprogressive" civilization would benefit by the introduction of American institutions and capital, but cautioned that these could not be imposed without taking into account the social and political environment. This attitude was evident in his disagreement with the two other members of the commission, who believed that both houses of the Puerto Rican legislature should be elected by popular vote. Rowe argued in a minority report that the upper house should continue to be appointive to reflect Spanish traditions of hierarchical authority and to ensure stability and the protection of property rights.

After 1902 Rowe deepened his knowledge of Latin America. He visited Mexico six times between 1903 and 1915. After serving as a delegate to the third inter-American conference in 1906, he spent more than a year in South America. In 1908–9 he returned to South America as head of the U.S. delegation to the scientific conference in Santiago, Chile. Meanwhile, he had introduced courses on Latin American government and on U.S.–Latin American relations at Pennsylvania. During this period he also wrote frequently on Latin American subjects, both in professional journals and in more popular periodicals, and published a book titled *The Federal System of Argentina* (1915). He constantly asserted that political institutions had to reflect the nature of the society for which they were created. In 1903, for example, he described the regime of Porfirio Díaz as an "enlightened despotism," but one that was necessary for the maintenance of law and order and national unity among a people wholly unfitted to implement the democratic provisions of the constitution of 1857.[34] After the ouster of Díaz, however, he described the Mexican Revolution as an "expression of a genuine popular feeling" and identified numerous failings of the regime, which had become overly centralized and dependent on the will of the aging dictator. He pointed to the problems confronting Francisco I. Madero, whose removal, he believed, "would be a national calamity, since it would inevitably bring the country to the verge of social disruption."[35]

By 1917 Rowe's reputation as a Latin American expert was such that he was briefly employed by the Commerce and State departments to deal with regional issues. In 1920 he became director of the Pan-American Union, a position he held until his death (see chapter 5). When he was elected president of the APSA, he returned to a favorite theme in his 1921 presidential address, in which he stressed the importance of bringing Latin America's social institutions into harmony with its republican political institutions.[36] The latter would not function smoothly so long as any considerable portion of the population lived in a state of "abject economic dependence." To correct this problem he recommended numerous reforms, including the establishment of a minimum wage scale for both agriculture and industry, the construction of public housing for workers, the gradual conversion of rural tenants into small landed proprietors, and the restriction and eventual elimination of intoxicating liquors.

During Rowe's relatively short service as a Latin Americanist in academia, his most distinguished student was Dana G. Munro.[37] The son of a prominent medievalist, Munro was an undergraduate at Brown and the University of Wisconsin and then spent a year studying in Germany before enrolling as a graduate student at the University of Pennsylvania in 1913. He was recruited to Latin America when Rowe, his adviser, suggested the political problems of Central America as a dissertation topic. Funding for such a proposal would be forthcoming from the Carnegie Endowment for International Peace, which was undertaking studies on the causes of war. As originally envisioned, the dissertation was to have compared the relatively stable Costa Rica with turbulent Nicaragua, where the U.S. government was deeply involved in the maintenance of fiscal and political order. Eventually, however, Munro decided to cover all five of the Central American republics.

With the support of the endowment, Munro spent more than a year (1914–16) in Central America, starting with a pleasant six-month stay in Costa Rica.[38] He later travelled to the other four republics, where he had an opportunity to meet U.S. diplomats and local leaders such as José María Moncada and Juan Bautista Sacasa, both future presidents of Nicaragua. By contrast, in Guatemala, which was ruled by the dictator Manuel Estrada Cabrera, he found little cooperation. The dissertation that resulted from his observations was published in 1918 as *The Five Republics of Central America*, a detailed examination of the political and economic conditions in each of the countries. Given the paucity of English-language writings on the region, which had clearly entered the U.S. sphere of influence, it is not surprising that Munro's volume won high praise at the time of its appearance and for many years was considered the standard work on the subject.

After receiving his doctorate, Munro embarked on a government career. Entering the foreign service in 1920, he served in the Division of Latin American Affairs and in the legations in Panama and Nicaragua before being named to the difficult post of minister to Haiti in 1930 (see chapter 5). On his retirement in 1932, he became affiliated with Princeton University, where he was a member of the History Department and for several years director of the Woodrow Wilson School of Public and International Affairs. His writings of this period were clearly historical, offering detailed accounts of the U.S. role in Central America and the Caribbean in the early twentieth century in which he emerged as an apologist for U.S. policies.

Munro's academic career illustrates the early fluidity between history and political science. The same situation in reverse can be seen in the career of John Lloyd Mecham, a student of Bolton and one of the early Native Sons of the Golden West scholars. His dissertation (1922) was on a historical subject—"Francisco de Ibarra and the Founding of Nueva Viscaya, 1554–1575"—and was published in 1927, but he became a member of the Department of Government at the University of Texas, where he had trained seven Latin Americanists by 1963. On receiving a doctorate in political science from Columbia University in 1916, W. W. Pierson was employed by the University of North Carolina as a history instructor, but he later headed the university's Political Science Department. Although not trained as a Latin Americanist, he moved into this field.

Another student of political science at Pennsylvania who became a specialist on Latin America was Chester Lloyd Jones. After graduating from the University of Wisconsin, he earned a doctorate (1906) at Pennsylvania with a dissertation on the U.S. consular service. In 1910 he returned to Wisconsin as a member of the Department of Political Science, which had recently been split off from the Department of History. He now moved into the Latin American field, producing *The Caribbean Interests of the United States* (1916), which placed heavy emphasis on economics and trade. After several years of employment with the federal government, he rejoined the Wisconsin faculty in 1928, now dividing his time between the Department of Political Science and the Department of Economics, which was located in the university's School of Commerce, of which he was director from 1929 to 1935. He continued writing about Latin America and shortly before his death published a detailed study titled *Guatemala: Past and Present* (1940), notable for its concluding chapter, "If I Were Dictator." Here he identified the economic and cultural obstacles a benevolent dictator might face as he sought to move a country such as Guatemala toward political democracy.

Jones trained Russell H. Fitzgibbon, one of the few early political scientists who devoted his entire career to Latin America. On receiving his doctorate from Wisconsin in 1934, Fitzgibbon published *Cuba and the United States, 1900–1935* (1935) and proved to be a prolific scholar, producing a monograph on Uruguay (1954) as well as many books and articles on Latin American constitutions and democracy. At UCLA from 1936 until 1964, he produced a "family" of Latin Americanists, which by 1963 included eight students of his own and their progeny.[39]

Academics who specialized in Latin American economics were exceedingly rare in the early decades of the twentieth century. One of the few Latin Americanists to earn a doctorate in economics during this period was Frank Tannenbaum, but he spent his academic career in the History Department of Columbia University.[40] Tannenbaum's background was more unconventional than that of any of his Latin Americanist contemporaries. Not only was he a Jewish immigrant from eastern Europe, but soon after he arrived in the United States with his family he ran away from home and never acquired a high school diploma. Working at a variety of menial jobs, he become involved in radical causes and in 1914 gained notoriety when he was arrested after leading an "army of the unemployed" into several churches in New York City and demanding food and work. He was convicted of participating in an unlawful assembly and spent a year in jail, but ironically the experience brought him to the attention of benefactors who made it possible for him to attend Columbia, from which he graduated in 1921. Tannenbaum now earned his living as a journalist and speaker on the Chautauqua circuit and published books and articles on the labor movement, prison conditions, and the U.S. South. By the mid-1920s he still considered himself a socialist though he was less doctrinaire than he had been a decade earlier. "In 1914 I was convinced I had the key to heaven and that no one else's key would fit the lock," he told an interviewer in 1925. "Now I know that others will."[41]

Tannenbaum made his initial acquaintance with Latin America when he went to Mexico in 1922 on behalf of *Survey* magazine. His encounter with Mexico's revolutionary process had a profound effect on him, but when he applied for admission to the Graduate School of Economics and Government (the future Brookings Institution) in 1924, he indicated that his chief interest lay in the study of the professional criminal. After a subsequent trip to Mexico, however, he decided to write a dissertation on that country's agricultural system. His largely statistical compilation, gathered during a long stay in Mexico in

1925–26, was published as *The Mexican Agrarian Revolution* (1929). He wrote a second book on contemporary Mexico, this one a work of synthesis, called *Peace by Revolution* (1933). In these two works, which established him as a leading academic expert on Mexico, he expressed sympathy with the goals of revolutionary leaders despite the limited accomplishments to date and emphasized the agrarian and popular roots of the upheaval of 1910.

After receiving his doctorate in 1927, Tannenbaum took part in a Brookings Institution study of Puerto Rico's economic problems, focusing on rural conditions, education, and public health. In 1933 he prepared a memorandum on research problems in Latin America for the Social Science Research Council, published the following year as *Whither Latin America?* Here he identified several topics that deserved investigation, among them the region's racial groups, agricultural structures, and household and village industries. Meanwhile, he had been awarded a Guggenheim Fellowship to study agricultural problems in Peru. Despite his concentration on contemporary economic and social issues, in 1935 Tannenbaum was offered what turned out to be permanent employment in Columbia's History Department, which presumably regarded him as the successor to the recently deceased William Shepherd. During his years at Columbia he was the mentor of several distinguished historians, among them Stanley R. Ross and Richard M. Morse, while his own writings continued to exhibit breadth of subject matter and treatment. This was illustrated by his *Slave and Citizen: The Negro in the Americas* (1946), a pioneering comparative study.

Only a few students of economics besides Tannenbaum can be mentioned. Frank W. Fetter, quoted earlier in this chapter, published *Monetary Inflation in Chile* (1932), based on his South American experience and his Harvard dissertation. The volume, which became a classic, was notable for Fetter's deployment of the argument that Chile's politically powerful landowning class had instigated the inflationary policies of the late nineteenth century. After World War II, however, Fetter concentrated on European problems.

Earl J. Hamilton's primary interest was the economic history of Spain, but his work was related to the New World, and he was justifiably regarded as a Latin Americanist. He received his doctorate from Harvard in 1929 and was a member of the Duke faculty from 1928 to 1944. His dissertation was the basis of his most important work, *American Treasure and the Price Revolution in Spain, 1501–1650* (1934). Called "one of the most important works of the last decade" by a reviewer in the *Journal of Political Economy*, Hamilton's study investigated the amount of silver shipped from the colonies to Spain in the sixteenth century and demonstrated that it was the primary cause of the rise in prices on the peninsula.[42]

Another young scholar who gradually emerged as a student of Latin American economic development was Sanford A. Mosk. Trained in U.S. and European economic history at Berkeley, Mosk received his doctorate in 1931 with a dissertation titled "Spanish Voyages and Pearl Fisheries in the Gulf of California." In 1935 Carl Sauer sent him to Spain, where he spent a year microfilming manuscripts related to the geography and economy of the colonies. He joined the Berkeley Economics Department in 1936, but it was not until 1945 that he was able to teach a course on the economic problems of Latin America.[43]

Harvard's Bureau for Economic Research also made a contribution to the field by publishing a pioneering work titled *The Economic Literature of Latin America: A Tentative Bibliography* (1936). Compiled by bureau staff under the supervision of historian Clarence H. Haring, this two-volume work contained more than 12,500 entries covering writings on the Latin American economies from pre-Columbian times through the postindependence era.

According to sociologist T. Lynn Smith, "Prior to 1935 anything dealing with Latin America on the part of a sociologist in the United States was conspicuous by its absence."[44] He did identify a few early titles in the field, including two books by Edward A. Ross, a well-known sociologist at the University of Wisconsin, but these were superficial works. The first, *South of Panama* (1915), was partly a travel account, but also a catalogue of the failings of the inhabitants of South America, which ranged from a lack of altruism to the "sex obsession" of males. He attributed these flaws not to race or to the personal qualities of the original settlers but to circumstances that gave a continent a bad start: "The masterful [Spanish] whites simply climbed upon the backs of the natives and exploited them. Thus, pride, contempt for labor, caste, social parasitism, and authoritativeness in Church and State fastened upon South American society and characterize it still."[45] Ross also wrote a study titled *The Social Revolution in Mexico* (1923), based on a stay there of eleven weeks. Although he questioned the intellectual capacity of Mexicans compared with that of Europeans, he found possibilities for gradual reform in current conditions. He also deprecated the fears of Mexican conservatives about radicalism in the Mexican Revolution. According to Ross, by the standards used in Mexico, where socialism was equated with social welfare for the working class, Theodore Roosevelt and Woodrow Wilson would have been considered socialists.[46]

Also singled out by Smith as a pioneering effort in the sociology of Latin America was *Problems of the New Cuba* (1935). The report was the work of a commission appointed by the Foreign Policy Association at the invitation of President Carlos Mendieta. Among the members of the commission were the sociologist Carle C. Zimmerman of Harvard and the economic historian Leland Hamilton Jenks of Wellesley College, the latter of whom had published *Our Cuban Colony* (1928), an indictment of U.S. investment on the island. The report examined the economy and fiscal condition of the island but also included chapters titled "Family Organization and Standard of Living" and "Social Aspects of the Sugar Industry." In Smith's view, the report was the first to show the "application of North American empirical research techniques in the sociological study of a part of the Latin American area."[47]

Eyler M. Simpson received a doctorate in sociology from the University of Chicago in 1926 with a dissertation called "Wishes: A Study in Social Psychology." From 1927 to 1935 he lived in Mexico as an expert observer for the Institute of Current World Affairs and as the representative there of the Guggenheim Foundation.[48] In 1937, after being named a professor at Princeton, he published *The Ejido: Mexico's Way Out*, an important study of rural conditions as of 1934, when his research was concluded. The volume identified many flaws in Mexico's land reform policies to date and, as the title implies, saw the communal landholding unit known as the *ejido* as the solution for Mexico's rural problems. The promise suggested by this book was never realized, for Simpson died in 1938 at the age of thirty-seven.

The works of Rowe, Munro, Jones, and other discussed here contributed to the expanding fund of information about Latin America in the United States. In these early decades of the twentieth century, however, the fields of economics, sociology, and political science—the last only recently divorced from history—tended to be focused on domestic problems and issues. Absent were the attractions that had led others to perceive Latin America as a worthwhile and potentially fruitful field of inquiry: the Spanish heritage of California and the Southwest for historians, for example, or the disciplinary emphasis on a regional specialization for geographers. To be sure, some did direct their attention to such places as Puerto Rico, Nicaragua, and, above all, Mexico, where U.S. interests seemed to be deeply involved, but these scholars were not sufficiently numerous—compared to historians, anthropologists, and geographers—to form a substantial bloc within their respective disciplines. It was not until after World War II that changes in external conditions and within the disciplines propelled political scientists, economists, and sociologists toward Latin America.

5

Latin Americanists and the World of Policy Making

Contemporary scholars often assert a linkage between Latin Americanists and U.S. political and economic ambitions in the region, especially during the first decades of the twentieth century. In fact, Mark T. Berger and others maintain that the development of academic expertise about Latin America was inextricably linked to the rise of U.S. hegemony in the region. According to Berger, "US emergence as an economic and politico-military power in Latin America was central to the constitution of 'Latin America' as an object of study and the rise of 'Latin American studies' as a series of professional discourses."[1] Concentrating primarily on historians and other academics who wrote about U.S.-Latin American relations (though not necessarily regional specialists), these analysts depict them as agents or instruments of American imperialism who shared the ethnocentric and racist assumptions of government policy makers and other elites. The fact that some scholars, such as Dana G. Munro, became policy makers, or "service intellectuals," further confirms the belief that Latin Americanists used their expertise to advance the political and economic hegemony of the United States in Latin America.[2]

This interpretation, although partly accurate, lacks nuance. As this chapter will show, some Latin Americanists did serve in the U.S. government for varying periods of time. On the other hand, if one considers the entire universe of Latin American academic specialists from 1895 to 1935, only a few were government employees at any given moment. A somewhat larger number had the opportunity to express their views regarding contemporary U.S.-Latin American relations in public lectures and in books and articles addressed to general readers as well as specialists. Given the ethnic and socioeconomic background of most Latin Americanists during this period, it is not surprising that they generally shared the values and attitudes of the country's political leaders. Even so, some questioned the prevailing wisdom about the region, and others dissented from specific government policies toward Latin America. Finally, a few seem to have been indifferent to the policy debates that swirled around them.

The foregoing is not meant to suggest that Latin American studies in the United States were unaffected by official interest in the region. On the contrary, the Spanish-American War and the territorial acquisitions made by the United States stirred curiosity about the Iberian world and offered employment opportunities to individuals who later became students of Latin America. Irving A. Leonard, who was born in 1896, traced his interest in the Spanish language to childhood reading about the campaigns in Cuba and the Philippines. "Scattered through these tales were Spanish words to give verisimilitude to the narrative," he recalled, "and, like a little scholar, I jotted them down in a notebook."[3] Leo Rowe's service on the Puerto Rican Code Commission has already been mentioned.

Bernard Moses of the University of California was already gaining a reputation as a student of Latin America when the war began. It was probably for this reason that in 1900 President McKinley appointed him to the Second Philippine Commission, which, according to Moses, took responsibility for eight million "disorganized Filipinos." As part of his work on the commission, Moses served as secretary of public instruction, and he later took satisfaction in having drafted the islands' school law, which, among other provisions, established English as the language of instruction and authorized the hiring of one thousand trained teachers in the United States. A modern commentator has noted that, like the other members of the commission, Moses had a low opinion of the Filipinos but thought them capable of improvement; he was, however, the least effective member and was eased out late in 1902. Ten years later Moses remained convinced of the necessity of continued American rule over the islands. The elements of civilization that existed there, he wrote, were due to their connection with Spain; now the U.S. presence provided peace and government attention to the needs of all Filipinos. If the United States were to withdraw, it would leave the islanders "either to become subject to a less liberal power or to drift backward toward barbarism."[4]

Several future scholars of Latin American history and culture were employed in the Philippines. From 1901 to 1904 Herbert I. Priestley was a teacher and superintendent of schools in Luzon. Charles H. Cunningham interrupted his graduate work at the University of California to teach in the Philippines, meanwhile working in the archives in Manila. He completed a dissertation (1915) under Bolton that was later published as *The Audiencia in the Spanish Colonies as Illustrated by the Audiencia of Manila* (1919). Irving A. Leonard improved his knowledge of Spanish as a Yale undergraduate but majored in science and pre-forestry. On graduation he was employed for three years in various places in the Philippines as the representative of an export-import company. Here too he worked to develop his Spanish skills, but he also realized that "language was only an instrument and that literature was a way to further knowledge of a culture."[5]

James A. Robertson's immersion in the history of the Philippines eventually led him to the ranks of Latin Americanists and to the editorship of the *Hispanic American Historical Review* in 1918. After graduating from Western Reserve University in 1896, he was employed as a proofreader for the seventy-three-volume *Jesuit Relations* being edited by Reuben G. Thwaites of the Wisconsin Historical Society.[6] The assistant editor was Emma Helen Blair, curator of the Manuscript Division of the society, with whom Robertson began to collaborate on a project to publish documents related to the Philippines. As a result, he spent the years 1902–7 searching for documents in the archives of Portugal, Spain, France, Italy, England, and the United States. The labors of Blair and Robertson culminated in the publication (1903–9) of fifty-five volumes of translated and annotated documents under the general title of *The Philippine Islands, 1493–1898*. This monumental work was intended not only to provide materials for a scholarly history of the islands but also to shed light on the "great problems" that confronted the American people there. Thus, it can be seen as an instrument of American imperialism. In recognition of Robertson's work on the project, Western Reserve conferred on him the degree of LHD in 1906. Four years later he was appointed superintendent of the newly established Philippine Library. He remained in this position for five years, during which he purchased for the library a large collection of manuscripts, books, and newspapers owned by the Compañía General de Tabacos de Filipinas.

E. G. Bourne's historical introduction to the Blair-Robertson collection was mentioned in chapter 2. Its generally positive assessment of Spanish rule, along with the editors' annotations, drew a letter of commendation from Adolph Bandelier, but a reproof from Paul S. Reinsch. In a review of the first ten volumes of the collection in the *Dial*, Reinsch questioned the "superlative and unqualified statements" made by Bourne and in particular the editors' favorable view of the missionary clergy, who, despite their bravery and dedication, treated the natives like children. Robertson was distressed by the review, which he called careless and contradictory.[7]

Bourne's introduction appears to have been conceived as part of his work on behalf of the Philippine Information Society, an organization founded in 1900 to collect and disseminate reliable information about the islands. The organization, whose officers included several prominent Boston intellectuals, claimed to be impartial in current debates about the Philippines but tended to lean toward the anti-imperialist position. The society issued several pamphlets before its dissolution in 1902. Earlier, in 1899, Bourne had anticipated U.S. retention of the Philippines, noting that conditions were different from those that had prevented the absorption of all of Mexico in 1847–48. At present, he said, expansionism "has no substantial hindrance save the conservative spirit, to whose objections our sanguine people are wont to pay little attention."[8]

The entry of the United States into World War I in April 1917 gave many scholars the opportunity to contribute to the war effort in one way or another. Some served in the armed forces, among them Hiram Bingham, who became an aviator at age forty-two and later commanded the Allies' largest flying school in France. Lesley Byrd Simpson and Dana G. Munro also served in the Army Air Service. Alfred M. Tozzer was a captain in the air service and presided over air force examining boards in Denver and San Francisco. Robert Redfield was an ambulance driver in France during the war, and Frank Tannenbaum served in the army despite his radical past. As a Harvard undergraduate, Preston James joined the Reserve Officers Training Corps in 1917 and volunteered for the army the following year. He had nearly completed the requirements for a commission when the war ended; later he was persuaded to obtain his commission and became a second lieutenant in the Military Intelligence Reserve. There is no evidence that any of the Latin American specialists were opposed to the war or to U.S. participation in it. One exception was Ralph Beals, the future anthropologist, who went to Mexico to avoid military service.[9]

Although Latin America was marginal in relation to the war, fears of German influence or espionage in the region led the government to make use of the expertise of specialists. In 1918 the youthful Irving A. Leonard was employed by the postal service to censor foreign letters because of his knowledge of Spanish. "We read mail taken off ships on the high seas," he recalled, "and looked to see which Latin American countries were dealing with the Germans, usually through Sweden."[10] The experience, though brief, gave Leonard insight into internal conditions in Latin America.

Several archaeologists served as secret agents for the Office of Naval Intelligence (ONI), conducting surveys of possible enemy threats in Mexico and Central America while claiming to be engaged in research for various institutions. The most prominent of these was Sylvanus G. Morley, a fervent supporter of the Allied cause, who considered Germany an outlaw nation. Upon the U.S. declaration of war, he was commissioned an ensign, nominally attached to the Naval Coast Defense Reserve of the Navy Yard, Washington, D.C.[11]

Using his affiliation with the Carnegie Institution of Washington as a cover, Morley spent thirteen months in Central America and Mexico, accompanied by the artist John Held, who was employed as a cartographer. During his months in the field Morley reconnoitered the Atlantic coasts of Nicaragua, Honduras, and the Yucatan Peninsula, gathering information about German activities in the region. He remained an intelligence officer for approximately nine months after the armistice, during which time he reported on political conditions in the Central American republics.[12]

Morley also recruited Samuel K. Lothrop, then a Harvard graduate student who had worked with him in Yucatan, to naval intelligence. Lothrop, assisted by his wife, worked in Bluefields, Nicaragua, and San José, Costa Rica, but accusations that he leveled at the American chargé in San José led to his resignation from ONI. He then served briefly as an intelligence officer for the army.[13]

Herbert J. Spinden was another naval intelligence agent during World War I. Spinden, whose Harvard doctoral dissertation (1909) was a pioneering study of Maya art, was a curator at the American Museum of Natural History when the United States entered the war. Like Morley, he was hostile to Germans, whom he described after the *Lusitania* sinking as a people "who scorn the laws of God and man." Spinden was active in Honduras, El Salvador, and Nicaragua, ostensibly on behalf of the museum, but in reality collecting mahogany wood for use in airplane propellers. Later he was sent to Colombia to study platinum deposits.[14]

J. Alden Mason, in 1917 an assistant curator at Chicago's Field Museum of Natural History, was employed briefly in Mexico. He was dismissed from the ONI for reasons that are unclear, though he is later reported to have described himself as "the worst spy in the world."[15]

Reports of Mason's activities reached Franz Boas in 1917. Boas, a pacifist and opponent of U.S. participation in the war, was indignant that Mason, who had been a fellow of the International School, would engage in espionage in Mexico while pretending to work as an archaeologist. In 1919 he vented his feelings in a letter published in the *Nation* in which he claimed to have proof that at least four (unnamed) anthropologists had passed themselves off as representatives of scientific institutions while secretly working for the U.S. government. Anticipating issues raised by the Camelot episode of the 1960s (see chapter 8), Boas argued that such behavior would seriously compromise scholars in the future. The secret agents "have not only shaken the belief in the truthfulness of science," he wrote, "but they have also done the greatest possible disservice to scientific inquiry. In consequence of their acts, every nation will look with distrust upon the visiting foreign investigator who wants to do honest work, suspecting sinister designs."[16]

The publication of Boas's letter generated controversy among anthropologists, though the uproar may have been due as much to hostility to Boas on religious and other grounds and to quarrels within the discipline as to the issues he raised. As a result, at a meeting on December 30, 1919, the council of the

American Anthropological Association adopted, by a vote of twenty to ten, a resolution stating that Boas's statements in the letter were unjustified and did not represent the views of the association. Morley and Spinden were among those who voted for the resolution; Kroeber and Tozzer were among those in the minority.[17]

Latin Americanists, especially geographers, contributed to the peace process through their participation in the Inquiry, a commission organized in 1917 to gather information and draft reports on various parts of the world that would be relevant to the postwar settlement.[18] Made up mainly of academics, the Inquiry was housed in the headquarters of the American Geographical Society, which Bowman put at the disposal of the government. The director of the Inquiry was Sidney E. Mezes, president of the College of the City of New York, but Bowman, who had the title of chief territorial specialist, became increasingly influential within the organization. On his return to the United States in September 1918 from his South American expedition, Mark Jefferson was named chief cartographer of the Inquiry. Both he and Bowman attended the peace conference at Versailles.

The Inquiry had a Latin American Division, which employed several specialists, including the geographer George M. McBride and the historian Osgood Hardy, to prepare maps and reports on the region, especially related to boundaries and the economy. Despite the limited role that Latin American issues could be expected to have at the peace conference, the Inquiry devoted large sums to research on the region. The historian of the Inquiry, Lawrence E. Gelfand, was critical of the situation: "Though the Inquiry was in constant need of funds, the available money went into projects mainly concerned with Latin America, projects which could have only the most remote relationship to the peace settlement."[19] He attributed this anomaly to Bowman's influence. Gelfand's account suggests that Bowman made use of the Inquiry to carry out favored Latin American projects of the American Geographical Society. Jefferson's investigation of colonization in South America appears to fit into this category. Some analysts have surmised that because the emphasis was on German colonization, Jefferson may have been gathering information on behalf of the Inquiry, but his biographer insists that he did not even know of the Inquiry's existence until after his return from South America. On the other hand, a tribute to Jefferson's assistant, Alfred Coester, asserts that during the expedition he was collecting data for the State Department.[20]

Although Latin America may have been marginal to the principal issues related to World War I, the conflict had an impact on the region, and in 1921 historian Percy A. Martin devoted a series of lectures, later expanded into a book, to that topic.[21] Martin emphasized the waning of European influence and a new attitude of friendliness toward the United States in the region, as well as increased commercial and financial relations.

These trends undoubtedly contributed to the entry of several Latin Americanists into the State and Commerce departments for periods of varying length during the war years and those immediately following the armistice. The State Department grew substantially in size and influence during the war, but the Commerce Department had expanded even earlier to promote American exports throughout the world. In 1912 Congress established the Board of Foreign and Domestic Commerce within the department. Although the bureau was assigned various responsibilities, its primary task was encouraging the export trade, particularly with Latin America, for which purpose Congress appropriated a special fund of $50,000 in 1914. The same legislation created the position of commercial attaché under the jurisdiction of the department. By the end of 1923 commercial attachés were stationed in eighteen foreign cities, including Buenos Aires, Havana, Mexico City, and Rio de Janeiro.[22]

In 1917 Julius Klein became chief of the Latin American Division of the Bureau of Foreign and Domestic Commerce. A native of California, Klein had received his bachelor's degree at Berkeley, where he studied Latin American history and came under the influence of Bernard Moses. He went on to earn a doctorate at Harvard with a dissertation (1915) on the Spanish *mesta*, or herdsmen's board, and taught Latin American history and economics there. After serving as commercial attaché in Buenos Aires, he was named director of the bureau in 1921. In this post he gained a reputation as the "right-hand assistant" to Secretary of Commerce Herbert Hoover, whose views on economics and government he shared and who appointed him assistant secretary of commerce in 1929. Both Klein and Hoover have been described as leading exponents of progressive Pan-Americanism, "a United States program primarily aimed at expanding trade, building investment opportunities, and tapping sources of agricultural and mineral raw materials in Latin America." They also believed that the federal government had a limited role to play in advancing these goals and in reconciling conflicting economic interests. Klein did not return to the academic world; after he left the Commerce Department in 1933, he acted as a private consultant and headed economic missions to Peru, Bolivia, and Chile in the 1950s.[23]

The Commerce Department employed several other Latin Americanists during this period. After leaving the Philippine Library in 1915, James A. Robertson joined the Bureau of Foreign and Domestic Commerce in 1917, serving as head of the Research Division and later of the Near Eastern Division. Charles H. Cunningham joined the Commerce Department in 1920 after two years of teaching at the University of Texas. He served as commercial attaché in Havana, Madrid, and several other posts. Also employed by the Commerce Department was William Lytle Schurz, a contemporary of Cunningham's at Berkeley, who wrote a dissertation published in 1939 as *The Manila Galleon*. From 1920 to 1926 he was commercial attaché in Rio de Janeiro and headed a team that studied the prospects for rubber cultivation in Brazil. Chester Lloyd Jones was director of the Bureau of Foreign Agents of the Trade Board during the war and then spent a decade as a commercial attaché in Madrid and Paris. Preston James, by contrast, refused the post of chief of the Latin American section of the Bureau of Foreign and Domestic Commerce in 1926. He turned it down because it promised few opportunities for fieldwork and required concentration on commercial rather than regional topics.[24]

During the World War I era, Leo S. Rowe became an important adviser on Latin American affairs to the Wilson administration. In 1915 he served as secretary-general of the Pan-American Financial Conference, which was convened by the administration to consider the economic dislocation caused by the war and to promote economic integration of the United States and Latin America. The principal result of the conference was the creation of the International High Commission, with sections for each participating nation, which encouraged uniformity in legislation pertaining to trade and finance. Secretary of the Treasury William Gibbs McAdoo was chairman of the U.S. section, and Rowe was secretary-general. Rowe so impressed McAdoo by his work in these positions that he was appointed assistant secretary of the treasury.[25] In 1919 he became chief of the State Department's Latin American Division, moving on in 1920 to head the Pan-American Union. Another academic who joined the State Department was William R. Manning. In 1918 he left the University of Texas to join the office of the trade adviser in the department. He remained in the State Department after the war, mainly in the Division of Latin American Affairs.

The Treasury Department sponsored a second Pan-American Financial Conference in Washington in January 1920. In the opinion of Percy A. Martin, "One of the most striking features of the Conference was the tacit recognition of the importance of Hispanic American studies in the United States at the present time." He went on to point out that half of the secretaries of the national committees at the conference were either teachers of Latin American history or individuals noted for their research and writing in the field, among them Charles H. Cunningham and C. H. Haring.[26]

Another one of the group secretaries was Dana G. Munro, who was already embarked on a long and successful State Department career. After his military service during the war, he was encouraged to join the department by his mentor,

Rowe. By 1919 Munro was known as an expert on Central America and therefore a valuable recruit at a time when professionalism and regional expertise were assuming greater importance within the department.

Munro's initial appointment in 1919 was as an analyst in the Office of the Foreign Trade Advisor, but he rose rapidly after passing the foreign service examination and spending a year in the legation in Santiago, Chile.[27] In 1921 he was assigned to the Division of Latin American Affairs, where he gave often unheeded policy recommendations. In a memorandum of November 1921, for example, he stressed the importance of encouraging American bankers to provide loans to the capital-starved Caribbean states and urged the State Department to give guarantees to the bankers, who might be reluctant otherwise to invest in that volatile region.

In 1927 Munro was sent to Managua, Nicaragua, in effect to substitute for the ineffectual minister. While there, he performed ably in a difficult situation, overseeing the U.S.-supervised election of 1928 and negotiating an agreement for the establishment of a national guard. He was promoted to chief of the Latin American Division, but in 1930 he was given another delicate assignment: that of minister to Haiti, where the Hoover administration was attempting to extricate itself from its deep but controversial involvement in that country's affairs. While in Port-au-Prince, Munro oversaw the negotiation of agreements providing for the withdrawal of U.S. marines and for the Haitianization of services controlled by American personnel since 1915.

Before he accepted the Haitian assignment, Munro had been offered a position in the History Department at Princeton University. On his return from Haiti, he retired from the State Department and began a new and lengthy career as an academic specialist on Latin America. His numerous books, articles, and lectures were devoted mainly to the Central American and Caribbean region where he had served. In general he defended interventionist American policies there in the early twentieth century, arguing that they were needed to protect U.S. security and had brought benefits to the countries affected.

Roscoe R. Hill was also employed in the Office of the Foreign Trade Advisor after World War I, but he soon had an opportunity to move to Nicaragua, where from 1921 to 1928 he served as a member of the High Commission that supervised part of the country's financial affairs. A graduate of Eureka College, Hill had been director of an American school in Matanzas, Cuba, and had done graduate work in Latin American history at Chicago and Columbia, experiences that presumably qualified him for the assignment in Nicaragua.[28] While there, Hill came into conflict on several occasions with Nicaraguan officials who wished him to loosen the purse strings and may have been offended by his "somewhat brusque manner." He successfully escaped removal in 1924–

25, but the axe fell in 1928 after an American consultant, W. W. Cumberland, reported: "[Hill] has little competence in finance, is contentious, interests himself in questions of local politics and does not properly represent the United States. He enjoys neither the respect nor the confidence of the Nicaraguan government."[29] By this time, too, the High Commission had little work to do, and Hill's duties were assigned to the Collector of Customs. After receiving his doctorate from Columbia with a dissertation published as *Fiscal Intervention in Nicaragua* (1933), Hill was employed by the National Archives until his retirement in 1946. During this period he visited nearly all the national archives of Latin America, about which he published a book in 1945.

Latin Americanists on U.S. Policy

Scholars of Latin America often publicly expressed their views on U.S. government policy toward the region in the years after 1900, an era of armed intervention and intensified projection of American influence in the region. Moreover, because scholarly activity was not so compartmentalized as it would later become, historians and others had the opportunity to weigh in on contemporary U.S.–Latin American relations in print or in public lectures regardless of their discipline or specialization. Only archaeologists generally refrained from commenting on current issues.

In these writings a few common themes emerge. First, the scholars tended to regard the South American nations, especially Brazil, Argentina, and Chile, differently from the nations of the Caribbean Basin, a distinction current at least as early as 1906, the year of Secretary of State Elihu Root's attendance at the inter-American conference in Rio de Janeiro.[30] As Chester Lloyd Jones put it, by 1900 a "group of South American states had developed stability of government and national strength to a degree which differentiated them from the other independent states of the continent." Writing a decade later, Charles W. Hackett maintained that the United States had pursued three distinctive sets of policies for Latin America since 1898: one for the Caribbean area, another for Mexico, and a third for South America. For the last of these, the United States had tried to allay fears of imperialism, for example, by signing arbitration agreements and ratifying the Thomson-Urrutia Treaty (1921) with Colombia.[31]

Hiram Bingham also emphasized the rise of South America in his influential 1913 article, "The Monroe Doctrine: An Obsolete Shibboleth," and a book with the same title. "We seem to be blind," he wrote, "to actual conditions in the largest and most important parts of South America, such as Brazil, Argentina, and Chile."[32] Bingham went on to point out the economic growth of the three countries, which accounted for more than half of the population of South America and four-fifths of the continent's foreign commerce. Bingham's principal argument was that the Monroe Doctrine was extremely offensive to the people of these countries and had in fact outlived its usefulness. Clarence H. Haring made a similar point in a 1928 volume when he wrote: "There is no question but that [the Monroe Doctrine] is regarded by great numbers in these southern countries as a sinister menace to their national sovereignty and dignity."[33]

What Bingham proposed in 1913 was that the Monroe Doctrine be gradually replaced by a multilateral alliance of the leading South American powers and the United States. He acknowledged that it might be sometimes necessary to intervene by force to crush rebellions in Central America, but he asked: "Why not let these forces consist not solely of American marines, but of the marines of Argentina, Brazil, and Chile as well?" Thus, even Bingham, who was prepared to scrap the Monroe Doctrine, conceded like other scholars that certain states—the Central American and Caribbean nations, with the latter occasionally defined to include Venezuela and Colombia—presented problems that might require intervention under the doctrine. Charles E. Chapman made a somewhat similar proposal in a 1922 article in which he noted Latin American dislike of the Monroe Doctrine. He believed that it should be upheld only with respect to those countries nearest to the United States and the Panama Canal. In addition, the United States might refashion the doctrine as a multilateral instrument for defense of the aforementioned region through treaties with Argentina, Brazil, Chile, and other South American countries that could be extended to the Caribbean Basin later on.[34]

In a book published three years after Bingham's, Chester Lloyd Jones asserted that the weak nations of the Caribbean Basin were still vulnerable to the extension of European control. He was also convinced that the more stable countries of South America would see an advance by Europe in the Caribbean as inimical to their own interests and would give "zealous support" to the principle of the Monroe Doctrine.[35] Jones believed that it was the political instability and resulting weakness of the Caribbean states that created the potential for European intervention, which they would be unable to resist unaided. For strategic and commercial reasons it fell to the United States to assume a commanding role in the region, as had occurred during the administrations of Roosevelt, Taft, and Wilson despite their otherwise divergent positions. Indeed, Jones suggested, had it not been for U.S. intervention, some of the Caribbean countries might have lost their independence to non-American powers.

In explaining the instability of the Caribbean Basin, Jones found a positive correlation between dark skin color and political incapacity, expecting greater progress in places such as Cuba, where whites were numerous or at least influential. Writing from the perspective of the State Department after World War I,

Dana G. Munro attributed Caribbean instability not to race but to the ignorance of the populace and to the lack of self-government and other evils associated with the Spanish heritage. Like Jones, he justified intervention as a temporary expedient that would end when these nations could manage their own
affairs satisfactorily. As the dominant power in the region, the United States
could not adopt a policy of noninterference, for it would lead to intervention
by other nations. After serving as an official observer of the elections of 1920 in
Cuba, Herbert J. Spinden was distressed by the irregularities he had witnessed.
He concluded that Cubans lacked the ability to govern themselves without pe-
riodically resorting to revolution. In such a situation, the United States had a
"moral obligation" to intervene to prevent chaos.[36]

Scholars examining U.S. relations with Mexico during the revolutionary era
that began in 1910 saw the latter as a source of difficulties but offered more nu-
anced or at least more variegated explanations for Mexican problems and pre-
scriptions for the American government than was the case when they dealt with
the Caribbean Basin nations. In a 1926 publication Charles W. Hackett attributed the 1910 revolution almost entirely to the miserable condition of Mexico's
rural masses, "worse by far than any form of Southern slavery against which
William Lloyd Garrison and Harriet Beecher Stowe raised their voices." In general, scholars viewed past and present Mexican leaders as incompetent, venal, or
dictatorial, though some, such as Isaac J. Cox, a historian at Northwestern University, identified both positive and negative features in the regimes of Porfirio
Díaz and Venustiano Carranza. In a set of 1926 lectures, Herbert I. Priestley
pointed to other factors besides poor leadership that hindered Mexico's development, among them inadequate water resources for agriculture and the preva-
lence of tuberculosis and other diseases. By contrast, in a book published in
1926, J. Fred Rippy stressed the importance of Mexico's "fabulous natural resources" as a factor in shaping its relations with the United States, as well as its
proximity, the enterprise and aggressiveness of the American people, and the
fact that during most of its independent existence Mexico had been a "very dis-
orderly and bankrupt nation."[37]

Rippy wondered whether the United States might establish a protectorate
over Mexico as it had done for several nations in the Caribbean Basin, but neither he nor other scholars advocated such a step or armed intervention of any
sort. Rather, the tendency was support for the pacific resolution of disputes. In
a foreword to a 1919 volume, William R. Shepherd warned of the dangers of intervention, which was supported mainly by European investors threatened by
the new constitution. If their assets were in fact confiscated, would that "justify
us in conquering Mexico, with all the expenditure of blood and treasure which
war involves? . . . 'Intervention' . . . would be nothing other than the entry of an

army of invasion. History tells us what that signifies for both invaded and invader." After reviewing U.S. relations with Mexico in the early 1920s, Hackett counseled patience and greater efforts by Americans to understand what Mexico was trying to accomplish. "The Anglo-Saxon people secured their human liberties and rights centuries ago, and for that reason it is hard for us to appreciate the fact that the Mexicans have begun to secure their human rights and liberties only since 1910."[38]

In a 1919 address before the Council of Foreign Relations, of which he was a founding member, Shepherd expressed a hope for improved news coverage on both sides of the border, with more emphasis on important developments and less on the sensational. He also wished that movies might show the positive features of Mexican life instead of focusing on the villainy of Mexicans. Priestley made a similar point: "There is a deep resentment against our film plots which represent the villain as a Mexican, overcome at last by a virtuous Westerner. Our newspapers too frequently reflect the active petroleum propaganda of a few years ago, and articles whose main distinction is distortion of the truth through search for 'news' values probably do more to keep up Mexican distrust of us than does our expansive commercial policy."[39]

In his 1926 volume Rippy recounted recent conflicts between the United States and Mexico and observed that American "vested interests" had felt "implacable enmity" toward Carranza and the 1917 constitution and had later prevented the early recognition of the Obregón government, impelling the United States "along the path of economic imperialism." Priestley also identified problems caused by American investment in Mexico. U.S. investors had brought Mexico and most of the Latin American countries into a state of "economic dependence," causing some of them to become "virtual protectorates." In many cases, especially with respect to petroleum production and mining, foreign investors drained the host country of its natural resources and sent their profits abroad.[40]

Rippy found a counterweight to the imperialists in the clashing sectoral and economic interests of the United States and in the activities of laborers, churchmen, and liberal educators and journalists. Nevertheless, he could foresee a day when American business interests, driven by the "aggressive" Anglo-Saxon nature and faced with continued disorder in Mexico, might unite to force the U.S. government to adopt a coercive policy toward Mexico. Priestley agreed that it would be "disingenuous to aver that large vested interests avoid imposing their political will to secure conditions favorable to themselves." He added that although critics of this situation had concepts of national sovereignty and international law on their side, neither could resist the "expansive force" of American capital. Somewhat contradictorily, he also asserted that the differing conditions of Mexico and the United States were the inevitable result of their divergent historical experiences, but he faulted Mexican and Latin American capitalists for failing to develop their own countries, which thus fell to daring American investors by default.[41]

In making observations such as these, Rippy and Priestley expressed what is now called a realist interpretation of U.S.– Latin American relations. This point of view was common among scholars who addressed the issue, whether to praise or criticize U.S. policy, especially in relation to the Caribbean Basin and Mexico. In rejecting such arguments as Bingham's for modification of the Monroe Doctrine, Chester Lloyd Jones asserted that in the Western Hemisphere, "as in all the world, strong nations will lead the weak." In South America the "better governed" states would play a predominant role, but in the northern part of the hemisphere the United States would "inevitably hold a position of primacy." In a 1922 essay titled "Literary Yankeephobia" in Latin America, Rippy wondered whether the small nations of the region would really be able to act as sovereign states in the present world order. He asked, "If the absolute sovereignty of small states should prove to be an international fiction, is it to them a matter of indifference who acts as their mandatory and perhaps their champion?" Which countries would they choose as "godfathers" in preference to the United States?[42]

Even those who were somewhat critical appeared to accept U.S. hegemony as an expected and unalterable condition. In 1916 Shepherd questioned the relevance of the Monroe Doctrine to American policy in Latin America, which had been "dictated, instead, by a desire to uphold our political preponderance and promote our commercial aggrandizement in the western hemisphere." In a 1927 article in the *New Republic,* he linked American infringements on the sovereignty of Caribbean Basin nations to the growth of U.S. financial interests in the region. Despite the criticism of Latin American and European states, he suggested that further expansion of U.S. political and economic power was inevitable: "Business is business. And Southward the course of empire takes its way."[43]

The chief argument made by those who were critical of U.S. policy in Latin America was that it evoked intense opposition in the region, especially in South America. As regional experts, the scholars cited here had had opportunities to travel in South America or at least to become aware of opinion there. After a year of travel in Brazil, Argentina, and other South American countries on the conclusion of the 1906 inter-American conference in Rio de Janeiro, Leo Rowe published an article identifying U.S. misconceptions about the continent and asserting that these emerging nations could no longer be the object of the "condescending sympathy" of Americans.[44] Bingham's broadside against the Monroe Doctrine was inspired at least in part by his impressions at the 1908 First Pan-American Scientific Congress in Chile, where he heard fellow scholars inveigh against U.S. policies. It should be noted, however, that less-happy experiences in South America—his problems in Peru in 1912 and 1916—contributed to an about-face by 1917, as did his renewed fear of European ambitions in the Western Hemisphere and Latin American neutrality during World War I.[45]

Clarence Haring devoted a whole volume to analyzing South American perceptions of the United States. The book was based on a year's residence and travel in South America (1925–26), his first extended visit to Latin America, which was funded by Harvard's Bureau for Economic Research. Haring indicated that there was continuing distrust of the United States in South America as a result of its policies in the Caribbean Basin, which infringed on the political independence of the countries affected and violated the principle of the legal equality of states. In addition, he criticized Americans living or working in South America for their arrogance and crudeness and for failing to learn Spanish or Portuguese. In Haring's opinion, "Americans in South America do not as a whole represent the best that the United States has to offer in intelligence, breeding or personality." To improve relations he offered numerous recommendations: "If we are to retain or increase the friendship of South American peoples, we must carefully watch our step, not only in our relations with Mexico and the smaller republics, but in our conduct at Pan-American conferences, . . . in our negotiation of international loans, and in our efforts at the mediation of South American disputes. American consular and diplomatic representatives in Latin America must possess tact and understanding, speak the Spanish language (except in Brazil), and have a reasonable appreciation of the racial sensibilities and cultural achievements of Latin-American countries."[46]

Somewhat stronger criticism of U.S. policy in Latin America, especially the extension of American economic power in the region, emerged in a series of books sponsored by the American Fund for Public Service. Under the general editorship of historian Harry Elmer Barnes, the series was intended to provide "concrete studies of [economic] imperialism." Of the five studies dealing with Latin America, only two were written by Latin American specialists. *The Capitalists and Colombia* (1931) by J. Fred Rippy is a detailed and judicious work that found advantages in recent American investment there but was cognizant of the dangers of heavy-handedness on the part of the U.S. government in supporting and promoting the economic interests of its nationals. The authors of *Porto Rico: A Broken Pledge* (1931) were Bailey W. Diffie and Justine Whitfield Diffie, the former of whom would become well known as a historian of early modern Portugal and colonial Brazil. As the subtitle indicates, the authors argued that American control had meant American exploitation of the island. Another book in the series, Leland H. Jenks's *Our Cuban Colony* (1928), drew a scathing review from Charles E. Chapman, who asserted that "the author, or the association he represents, is not capable of an unbiased presentation of facts."[47]

It is ironic that just the year before, Chapman himself had come under intense criticism from Cubans because of a book he had written, one of the most controversial of the period. The book, *A History of the Cuban Republic: A Study in Hispanic American Politics* (1927), also chagrined its chief backer, General Enoch Crowder, because its denunciation of Cuban politicians ran counter to the U.S. policy of the moment. The idea for the book originated with Crowder, who had been deeply involved in Cuban affairs since 1921 and appointed ambassador in 1923. Crowder, who had failed in his efforts to control the administration of Alfredo Zayas, apparently hoped that an exposure of Cuban corruption and misrule would allow him to exert pressure on Cuban authorities. Chapman was invited to write the book on behalf of the Carnegie Endowment, which became the sponsor of the project, for which he was initially to receive $2,500.[48]

Chapman made two trips to Cuba in 1924 to conduct research for the book. During his visits he renewed his friendship with Charles H. Cunningham, once a fellow graduate student at Berkeley and now commercial attaché in Havana, and met frequently with Crowder, with whom he believed he got along very well, though the two men differed on methods and points to be emphasized in the book. Chapman travelled extensively throughout the island and observed the presidential election of November 1, 1924, in Sancti Spiritus; he also made time to go to the races and the jai alai fronton and to play the lottery.

After Chapman had completed the manuscript, Crowder wanted him to soften his strictures against the Cuban government because the president elected in 1924, Gerardo Machado, was proving more cooperative than Zayas. Chapman refused to alter the content and agreed only to insert an optimistic conclusion and to indicate that his criticisms applied to administrations prior to Machado's. An agreement was eventually reached with the publisher and the Carnegie Endowment, but the latter's name appeared nowhere in the printed text.

The book is a narrative of Cuba's political history from 1902 to 1924, followed by several topical chapters on political institutions and social and economic conditions. Overall, the book is a scathing indictment of the Cuban political system, whose most salient characteristics, according to Chapman, were colossal corruption, violence, and disregard for the law. He described Cuba's first president, Tomás Estrada Palma, as honest and perhaps too virtuous for the Cuban milieu, but his successors had surpassed each other in looting the national coffers. The worst had been Zayas, who could almost be said to symbolize evil in contrast to Crowder, whom Chapman called the epitome of good, in this case ultimately bested by evil. Chapman indicated by his subtitle and in his preface that he considered Cuba's political deficiencies to be common to all the Spanish-speaking republics, the result of the region's Hispanic heritage. Cuba, however, was in a more advantageous position than others because of its relative wealth, lack of racial problems, and other favorable conditions. Therefore, "it may confidently be asserted that Cuba already has the elements within her own body politic that could make government attain to the level of decency that most other factors in Cuban life have already reached."[49]

Not only was Crowder unhappy with the book; there was also an avalanche of criticism in Cuba, where it was denounced as an imperialist libel. The historian Ramiro Guerra called the book tendentious and one-sided, a compilation of the most extreme criticism directed against each Cuban president. Using Chapman's methods, Guerra said, one could easily prepare a similar attack against the United States: "We could simply emphasize the vices and hide the virtues of [Chapman's] compatriots. But one does not produce history that way, but shameful and bare-faced imperialism."[50]

Some Cubans were more positive, at least in private. José Estrada Palma y Guardiola, son of Cuba's first president, found Chapman's account on the whole extremely accurate, and the writer Fernando Ortiz expressed the opinion that Chapman's censures against "openly delinquent regimes" were well merited.[51] Chapman also received praise from some of his academic colleagues in the United States, such as Mary W. Williams, who called his account truthful and refreshing: "I am enjoying your frank exposures of the stinking political methods of Cuba, for I feel that it is high time that the truth were told." W. W. Pierson wrote in a similar vein: "A book like yours is a good antidote for the stuff that Hispanic-American sentimentalists and boosters have been getting off—to the great injury of historical truth and, I believe, to the people of the countries in question."[52] William R. Shepherd, on the other hand, expressed reservations in a published review, observing that a country such as Cuba, with a heritage so different from that of the United States, could hardly be expected to govern itself in a manner likely to win American approval. He was also skeptical about the value of exposing Cuba's political ills: "Criticism of this sort, no matter how justified from the standpoint of the foreigner, may not stir the Cubans to clean their official house but heighten rather their resentment over the amount of external supervision already exercised." He wondered whether the powerful American influence might not have retarded Cuba's political development.[53]

Chapman's book and the reactions to it exemplify themes developed in this chapter. The early Latin Americanists as a group cannot be considered as architects of instruments of U.S. government policy. Only a relative handful served in government or even commented publicly on contemporary U.S.–Latin

American relations. Yet they were often supportive of U.S. actions in the region; indeed, Chapman apparently had no qualms about undertaking a book suggested by Crowder, the American ambassador in Havana. At the same time, the Latin Americanists' expertise and their experiences in Latin America enabled them to regard the region from a perspective often unavailable to businessmen and government representatives and occasionally to speak as advocates for a Latin American point of view. The Latin Americanists were by no means rebels; neither were they unthinking mouthpieces for official U.S. policy.

PART II

MATURITY AND INSTITUTIONALIZATION

6

A Decade of Expansion, 1935–1945

The study of Latin America experienced what has been called "unprecedented expansion" during World War II. In reality the upsurge began in the mid-1930s largely as the result of initiatives by private and public agencies that provided support for more intensive study of the region. These initiatives seemed all the more pressing as the international situation deteriorated and a second global conflict seemed increasingly likely. During the war years, Latin America, although peripheral to the main theaters of operations, was nevertheless perceived, to a greater extent than in 1917–18, as an area vital to U.S. security. The emphasis was on developing Western Hemisphere solidarity to better confront the dangers emanating from Europe and Asia. Accordingly, the cultivation of friendly relations with people and institutions in the region became a high priority, as did efforts to create a favorable image of the United States. Private philanthropies and organizations now expanded projects related to Latin America while the federal government created agencies and programs to encourage Latin American cooperation and goodwill during the immediate emergency and presumably in subsequent years as well. Indeed, a veritable "craze" for Latin America seemed to grip the nation.[1]

During this period many Latin Americanists served in government agencies, apparently eager to further the war effort, while others took advantage of new programs to advance their own scholarly goals. As a result of the initiatives of the decade, both private and public, additions were made to the fund of scholarly knowledge of Latin America, and collaboration and other contacts with the region were intensified. With the return of peace and the start of the cold war, however, Latin America was again marginalized, and wartime support for research and scholarship about the region dwindled.

Early Initiatives

An early impetus for the upsurge in interest in Latin American scholarship came from the U.S. government. In 1935 Assistant Secretary of State Sumner Welles asserted the importance of cultural relations as an element of foreign policy, and at the Inter-American Conference for the Maintenance of Peace in 1936 in Buenos Aires, the United States introduced a convention for the annual exchange of graduate students and professors among the American republics. The final act of the conference also contained numerous recommendations for closer cultural and intellectual cooperation, including the compilation of quarterly bibliographical bulletins to be distributed among the member states. To carry out its responsibilities under the Buenos Aires convention and in general to promote cultural understanding and counteract Fascist propaganda in Latin America, the State Department created the Division of Cultural Relations on July 27, 1938. The new division directed its efforts exclusively toward Latin America until 1942, when its activities were extended to China and later to other parts of the world. Although funds were appropriated to enable the division to support the academic exchanges and other programs called for at the Buenos Aires meeting, its primary goal was to encourage the work of private institutions in carrying out exchanges that would contribute to inter-American understanding.[2]

A second important source of support for Latin American scholarship during this period was the Rockefeller Foundation, which in the 1930s increased its commitment to the humanities and social sciences in addition to its work in the natural sciences, medicine, and public health. It had been the primary financial benefactor of the Social Science Research Council since the latter's establishment in 1923 and was a major supporter of the American Council of Learned Societies, on which the principal associations of humanities scholars were represented.[3] During the 1930s and 1940s the ACLS served as the main vehicle for the transmission of Rockefeller Foundation funds for Latin American projects, though the SSRC also gave modest support. By the late 1930s, however, the SSRC had decided not to deal with groups that focused on a single geographical area, though it awarded fellowships to individuals for study and research in Latin America.

The Rockefeller Foundation became a significant supporter of the humanities after 1928, when it took over projects in this area from two other Rockefeller philanthropies, the General Education Board and the International Education Board. A new Division of the Humanities was created, whose first director, Edward Capps, continued a traditional Rockefeller emphasis on the archaeology, history, and languages of classical antiquity. After his retirement, his successor, David H. Stevens, gradually moved the division in a new direction with the support of the foundation's trustees. The goal was a less elitist policy that would support humanistic expression in the arts and make it available to larger numbers. The trustees set another goal in 1933: "Beyond . . . benefits to the individual, the humanities should exert national and international influence for a reduction of racial prejudice. Ignorance of the cultural background of another people is at the root of many misunderstandings that are as harmful internationally as political and economic differences. That ignorance can be steadily lessened by an interchange of cultural values, by discovery of common origins for diversified national ideas and ideals and by the interpretation of one cultural group to another."[4] Later in the decade the foundation decided to expand its Latin American (and Far Eastern) activities in furtherance of the international objectives of the Humanities Program: "(1) to improve our means of transmitting and of organizing knowledge for scholarly or popular use; and (2) to aid with plans to promote understanding of other peoples through appreciation of their culture."[5] To provide advice, the foundation added Irving A. Leonard to its staff in 1937; he was succeeded in 1940 by William L. Berrien, a professor of romance languages at Northwestern.

Leonard's first task for the Rockefeller Foundation was a four-month tour of South America, mainly of Peru and Chile, to report on institutions likely to benefit from the foundation's largesse. Having won a Guggenheim Fellowship to do research in these countries, he kept his Rockefeller connection sub rosa. He did reveal it to historian Jorge Basadre, who was then head of the library of the University of San Marcos in Lima and with whom he was very favorably impressed. On the whole, however, Leonard was baffled by the apathy he found in Peru: "The general . . . inertia as well as politics affects all public and especially cultural establishments while those in charge usually have their energies dispersed among various offices in an effort to get a living." The institutions he visited in Chile seemed much better developed than those in Peru, in particular the University of Concepción, which he considered a "triumph of private initiative."[6] During this period the foundation made several relatively small awards to Latin American institutions; its largest grant was a $20,000 award in 1939 to the recently established National Institute of Anthropology and History in Mexico City.

A third source of support for Latin American studies was the American Council of Learned Societies, and especially its permanent secretary, Waldo G. Leland, who had previously been associated for many years with the historical research department of the Carnegie Institution of Washington. In 1932 he persuaded the ACLS to authorize the formation of a provisional committee on Latin American studies to encourage the humanities in a region he believed had been neglected in the United States. He later recalled that he had encountered opposition to his proposal, especially from modern language scholars, and had been told that "nobody read Latin American literature anyhow, and that there was no field of study in Latin American subjects."[7]

The members of the new committee were Harvard historian C. H. Haring, Alfred V. Kidder of the Carnegie Institution, and Sturgis E. Leavitt, a professor of Spanish at the University of North Carolina. At its first meeting, which took place on February 24–25, 1933, the members agreed to focus their energies on the promotion of scholarship on Latin American literature, for which a foundation had already been laid. Among their recommendations was the provision of grants to enable graduate students to travel to Latin America, aid that universities were unable to supply. They also took cognizance of the fine arts in Latin America, but the field was so neglected in the United States that they felt incompetent to make recommendations.[8]

Complementing the work of Haring's committee were the efforts of a group of Latin Americanists in the social sciences at the universities of Michigan and Chicago. Leland brought the two groups together, with the support of the SSRC, for a conference in New York in April 1935. Haring chaired the meeting, which was attended by Leavitt and by other prominent Latin Americanists, including the historian Arthur S. Aiton and geographer Preston E. James, both of the University of Michigan, and economist Chester L. Jones. Those attending voted to constitute themselves as a permanent but informal group loosely linked to the ACLS committee, but their most important decision was to devote their energies to the publication of an annual critical bibliography of research related to Latin America.[9]

This goal was realized with the appearance in 1936 of the first volume of the *Handbook of Latin American Studies*. It was edited by Lewis U. Hanke, an energetic young historian who completed his doctorate under Haring's direction at Harvard that year and is regarded as the originator of the project. The first volume contained only critical annotations of selected titles in the various disciplines, but essays on scholarly trends were promised for subsequent volumes. The purpose of the *Handbook*, according to Hanke, was "to make it easier for the specialists to keep abreast of current literature in their own corners of the field and to give them the opportunity to peer over the fences which set them off from their fellows and to observe each other's movements."[10]

Funding for the *Handbook*, which was published by Harvard University Press, was limited and uncertain. For the first two volumes the ACLS contributed approximately $2,000 from a Rockefeller Foundation grant for the promotion of work in new fields of scholarship. The Carnegie Endowment for International Peace also spent approximately $1,900 to purchase copies of the second volume of the *Handbook* at a discount for distribution in Latin America. These contributions and the sums generated by sales in the United States did not, however, cover the costs of production. In 1938, the Rockefeller Foundation came to the temporary rescue of the *Handbook*, with the appropriation of $15,000 for its support for a period of five years, ending on February 28, 1943. In addition, the Carnegie Endowment continued its purchases of the *Handbook*.[11]

By July 1939 it had become evident that the informal group, eventually consisting of twenty-five members, was too large and unwieldy to function effectively. Accordingly, it gave way to a new Committee on Latin American Studies that was formally associated with the ACLS. Chaired by Haring, the committee was made up of seven members, all but one of whom (Robert Redfield) had been members of the disbanded group. Three others—Lewis Hanke, who had continued as editor of the *Handbook*, historian Charles W. Hackett of the University of Texas, and geographer Carl O. Sauer—were associate members of the group, which embraced the social sciences as well as the humanities. At the committee's organizational meeting, Waldo Leland of the ACLS set forth the principal activities that it should pursue:

(1) Stimulating interest in Latin-American study through the organization of national or regional conferences and by other means; (2) Providing tools of research . . . ; (3) Developing the personnel engaged in the study of Latin America through the attraction and financial support of young scholars intending to specialize in some phase of the Latin-American field; (4) The sponsoring of the publication of important manuscripts; (5) Possibly at a later date the securing of grants-in-aid for research projects by mature scholars.[12]

In 1940 the Rockefeller Foundation gave the ACLS the sum of $52,000 for the support of the Committee on Latin American Studies and related activities over a three-year period. These activities included several bibliographical projects besides the *Handbook*, such as *A Bibliographical Guide to Materials on American Spanish* (1940) by Madaline W. Nichols. In addition, the committee was a sponsor of Latin American institutes at the University of Michigan (1939) and the University of Texas (1940), both of which also received direct financial assistance from the Rockefeller Foundation. The institutes were held concurrently with regular summer sessions at each institution but featured instruction by visiting professors as well as special lectures and conferences. The Texas proceedings were designed to be an introduction to a permanent Institute of Latin-American Studies, which was established on the Austin campus in September 1940. In addition to its support of the committee, the Rockefeller Foundation provided funding for numerous other projects, many of them intended to increase U.S. library holdings of Latin American materials. In 1940 Duke, North Carolina, and Tulane were awarded a total of $68,000 for the purchase of books and documents on Latin America over a five-year period. Each institution was to concentrate on acquisitions related to a specific region: Central America and the Caribbean for Tulane, the Southern Cone for North Carolina, and Brazil and the Andean states for Duke.[13]

The Rockefeller Foundation provided financial assistance to another important institution created at this time, the Hispanic Foundation (now Division) of the Library of Congress. With the help of the endowment provided by Archer M. Huntington in 1927, the library's Hispanic and Portuguese collections had grown to number more than 100,000 monographic volumes by 1939. Perceiving a need for a special Hispanic division, Huntington provided funds for "a center for the pursuit of studies in Spanish, Portuguese, and Hispanic culture" based in a reading room designed in the style of the Spanish renaissance. The vestibule of the reading room was decorated with a mural in fresco created by the Brazilian artist Cândido Portinari. Completed in 1942 and financed by the Brazilian and American governments, the four panels depict various aspects of the arrival of the Spaniards and Portuguese in the New World.[14] Lewis Hanke, who after receiving his "depression doctorate" in 1936 had travelled in Latin America thanks to a SSRC fellowship, was named the first director of the foundation, a position he considered "an opportunity that ordinarily comes once in a lifetime."[15] In 1939–41 the Rockefeller Foundation awarded the Hispanic Foundation $33,000 for assistance in cataloguing its collection of books and serials. In 1943 a second Rockefeller grant of $17,650 was awarded to the foundation to expand its Archive of Hispanic Culture over a two-year period. The archive was established in 1940 as a repository of photographs, slides, and other visual materials relating to Latin American art. The archive was the brainchild of Robert C. Smith, a specialist in Luso-Brazilian art and architecture who was named assistant director of the foundation in 1940. His appointment reflected Hanke's desire to develop Brazilian studies in the United States.[16]

Latin Americanists in Wartime

As the United States moved closer to entering the war in 1940 and 1941 and especially after Pearl Harbor, the interest in Latin America grew apace. This was due partly to an expansion of federal government initiatives related to the region. During the years 1940–45 many Latin Americanists were employed directly by the government; others carried out projects financed by federal funds. The Rockefeller Foundation also remained active in its support of Latin American activities. The war brought immense disruption to normal university life, but Latin Americanists were confident that with the restoration of peace they would be able to build on the achievements of the war years both in their research and in the classroom.

After Pearl Harbor an important vehicle for advising the government and private institutions on hemispheric projects was the Joint Committee on Latin American Studies, which was launched on March 29, 1942. An outgrowth of the ACLS committee organized in 1939, the new body also had the somewhat ambivalent support of the SSRC and of the science-oriented National Research Council, which had formed its own committees on Latin American psychology, anthropology, and geography and geology. The ten original members included three who had served on the older committee—Haring, Preston James, and Redfield, who was its first chairman—but others were dropped to accommodate the new sponsors. The archaeologist Wendell C. Bennett was its executive secretary. Subcommittees on personnel, research, and publications were also established.[17]

The Joint Committee had two sometimes contradictory responsibilities: it was to offer advice on programs being considered by public and private agencies and to promote Latin American studies in all fields of knowledge. In the latter capacity it sponsored the *Handbook of Latin American Studies* as well as bibliographical projects begun under the ACLS committee. The Joint Committee also established what it hoped would become a permanent periodical publication, *Notes on Latin American Studies*. It was unable to attract a sufficient number of subscriptions, however, and was discontinued after only two issues had appeared, both in 1943.

Despite its tripartite sponsorship, the primary financial backer of the Joint Committee was the ACLS, which continued to rely on the Rockefeller Foundation for this purpose. In 1944 the foundation awarded the committee a two-year grant of $12,500 for support of the secretariat and other purposes, as well as $7,500 for publication of the *Handbook*. The foundation continued to support Latin American projects in other ways, too. In 1941 its Social Science Division allocated $50,000 to enable scholars to travel to Latin America to study problems in which they were interested. At the same time they were to explore the possibilities for social science research in the region and develop ties with Latin American institutions. Four social scientists received awards of $10,000: economic historian Earl J. Hamilton of Duke University, who was to travel to South America to study the economic background of the Monroe Doctrine; anthropologist Melville Herskowits of Northwestern, who was to study the Negro population of Brazil; Carl O. Sauer, who was to conduct research on agricultural geography and culture history in western South America; and Robert

Hall, a geographer and Japanese specialist at Michigan, who was to study Asian settlements in the Western Hemisphere. Hall also reported his findings to the U.S. government.[18]

Sauer, whose reports to the foundation have been published and who had not been to South America before, spent more than five months there. In addition to describing his own work, he commented on institutions and scholars in the region that might be deserving of foundation aid. He was especially complimentary of the Peruvian Julio C. Tello, whom he called "the greatest archaeologist in the New World." He was also impressed by two private universities, the University of Concepción, Chile, and the Bolivarian Catholic University in Medellín, Colombia. "At the opposite ends of our route," he wrote, "we have found two centers of special interest, Concepción and Medellín. Unfavored by central authority, in isolated situation, each is going ahead fashioning out of its own resources, a distinctive center of civilization."[19] As it turned out, the principal Latin American beneficiary of Rockefeller funding during this period was the Center of Historical Research of the Colegio de México, which received nearly $86,000 for the period 1942–48. The Colegio de México had won high praise from Waldo Leland and from Earl Hamilton, who described it as "one of the most promising institutions for higher education and research in Latin America. . . . Without exception its staff is able, earnest, and distinguished." In 1943 the foundation awarded Mexico's National Institute of Anthropology and History a grant of $70,000, to be spent over five years.[20]

One of the federal agencies for which the Joint Committee served in an advisory capacity was the Office of the Coordinator of Inter-American Affairs (CIAA). Founded in 1940 with an initial budget of $3.5 million and headed by Nelson A. Rockefeller, the office financed many cultural and educational projects aimed at fostering a favorable image of the United States in Latin America and stimulating American interest in the region. At first, Rockefeller's ambitious agenda clashed with that of the State Department's Division of Cultural Relations. In 1941 the differences were resolved with a statement of the responsibilities to be assigned to each body, and a Joint Committee on Cultural Relations was established to consider proposals in the field. Both the CIAA and State were represented on the committee; Waldo Leland of the ACLS was also a member. In 1943 most of the CIAA's cultural programs were transferred to the State Department.[21]

American academic specialists on Latin America participated in many of the programs financed by the CIAA, which did not execute projects itself but rather operated on the basis of contracts with private groups. Among them was the Inter-American Training Center, a program sponsored by the ACLS and the Joint Committee on Latin American Studies. Offices were set up in both

Washington, D.C., and Philadelphia. Wendell Bennett was general director of the program; sociologist W. Rex Crawford of the University of Pennsylvania was in charge of the Philadelphia center, and Henry Grattan Doyle, a professor of Spanish at George Washington University, headed the Washington, D.C., center. The program was designed to offer government personnel, including army and navy officers, intensive language instruction during an eight-week cycle as well as background information on the history, culture, and society of Latin America. The Philadelphia center attracted little interest and was closed in 1943, but more than ten thousand government employees received instruction at the Washington center during the two years of its existence (1942–44).[22]

Other programs funded by the CIAA included a three-volume travel guide (1943) to Latin America, which contained several sections by such scholars as Robert C. Smith, who wrote on art and architecture. The editor of the guide, Earl P. Hanson, also oversaw another project funded by the CIAA: preparation of an index to the Millionth Map of Hispanic America described in chapter 4. The CIAA also helped finance *A Handbook on the Teaching of Spanish and Portuguese* (1945), edited by Henry Grattan Doyle and intended to be of assistance to language instructors. Still another project, devised by the National Planning Association, aimed to "analyze the human and natural resources of selected Latin American regions, and to suggest desirable readjustments in the economy of the regions that would bring about a more efficient use of the resources and improve the standards of living of the people in those areas." This effort, under the general direction of geographer Clarence F. Jones, resulted in the publication of studies of the Laguna district of Mexico and of the Upper Huallaga Valley of Peru, among others. At Yale the CIAA supported compilation of the "Strategic Index of Latin America" under the auspices of the university's Institute of Human Relations. With a staff of twenty-five in 1942, it gathered, classified, and cross-referenced data on society and culture in contemporary Latin America and issued several bibliographies, including one on Colombia and one on Paraguay, both in 1943.[23]

The CIAA also sponsored numerous workshops and lectures at American colleges and universities in its campaign to advance knowledge of Latin America in the United States. It gave the new Institute of Latin American Studies at the University of Texas a grant of $37,500 that was to be expended over a period of sixteen months starting on March 1, 1941, on a visiting professorship, postdoctoral fellowships, and library and research materials. In 1943 and 1944 the University of Texas received funding from the CIAA and the State Department to help support an Extension Field School at the University of Mexico. Carlos E. Castañeda, Charles W. Hackett, John Lloyd Mecham, and other Latin Americanists took part.[24]

A major beneficiary of funding from the CIAA was the Institute of Andean Research, which had been founded in 1937 to promote and coordinate anthropological research in Andean South America and related regions. With a grant of $114,000 from the CIAA, the institute sponsored ten programs in 1941–42, most of them in the Andean area but others in Mexico, El Salvador, and Cuba. Participants included George C. Vaillant, Alfred Kidder, Wendell Bennett, and the Peruvian archaeologist Julio C. Tello. As part of the institute's program, for example, in 1941 William Duncan Strong of Columbia University directed stratigraphic excavations at Pachacamac with two of his graduate students, Gordon Willey and John Corbett, who went on to work in the Chancay Valley, Supe, and Ancón. During this period Junius B. Bird of the American Museum of Natural History excavated in northern Chile as part of his ongoing study of early man in the Americas.[25]

The development of inter-American intellectual ties was a secondary goal of institute projects, but, according to Sauer, little was accomplished in this regard. "These fellows have come down supplied with money for field work, automobiles, living conditions, demonstrating that the U.S. is the land of incredible wealth," he wrote during his 1942 visit to Peru. "They have done almost nothing in picking up potential native archaeologists or ethnologists and giving them a year's experience, and they have hardly blocked out or tied into a feasible local program of investigation. It has been a great year for the American youngsters, but that is about all."[26] Alfred Kroeber, who was invited by the CIAA's Committee on Inter-American Artistic and Cultural Relations to review the Peruvian archaeological situation in 1942, also recommended that in the future Peruvians be given a larger role. During his eight weeks in Peru, his first visit since 1926, Kroeber met with Tello and Luis Valcárcel and toured the country with two younger scholars, Manuel Escobar and Jorge C. Muelle. Kroeber lectured in Spanish on archaeological methods to a packed house at Lima's University of San Marcos and published the results of his reconnaissance as *Peruvian Archaeology in 1942* (1944).[27]

Official interest in the promotion of inter-American intellectual interchange brought State Department funding for several major programs that were to engage anthropologists and archaeologists in the United States and Latin America during the war years and beyond. These projects were carried out under the aegis of the Smithsonian Institution's Bureau of American Ethnology and directed by Julian H. Steward, a staff member there. Steward was an ethnologist and archaeologist who had specialized in research regarding North American Indians, but had done some fieldwork in Ecuador and Peru. This experience gave him the background to undertake the general editorship of the first project, the *Handbook of South American Indians*, which appeared in six volumes between 1946 and 1959. Steward was assisted by Alfred Métraux, whose experience in South America far exceeded his.[28]

Discussion of the need for such a compilation began in 1932, but it was not until 1940 that funding became available and work got under way. A *Handbook of American Indians North of Mexico* had been published in 1907–10, but that work had been organized alphabetically by tribes and topics. The South American *Handbook* would be not only larger but also organized by culture area, with articles on the archaeology as well as the "historical present" of the native peoples of the continent; three volumes contained topical articles. Nearly one hundred scholars, half of them Latin Americans, contributed to the project. The Smithsonian Institution, at Steward's initiative, also sponsored an organization called the Inter-American Society of Anthropology and Geography, which published a short-lived journal, *Acta Americana*.

A third collaborative enterprise with which Steward was closely associated was the Institute of Social Anthropology, established in 1943 with financial support from the State Department and housed in the Smithsonian Institution.[29] What Steward envisioned was the dispatch of American anthropologists, geographers, and other social scientists to Latin America, upon agreement with the host countries, to teach and to conduct research on contemporary rural communities expected to undergo modernizing social change. At a time when "applied anthropology" was in vogue, Steward hoped that institute studies might be of future value to policy makers.

During the nine and one-half years of its existence the institute worked in five countries—Mexico, Guatemala, Brazil, Colombia, and Peru—to which seventeen social scientists were sent for varying periods of time. Among them was George M. Foster, who had received a doctorate in 1941 from the University of California with a dissertation on the Popoluca of Veracruz. Arriving in Mexico City in May 1944, Foster taught at the National School of Anthropology and in 1945–46 took a group of students to the Lake Pátzcuaro area, where they studied the community of Tzintzintzan. When Foster left Mexico in 1946 to become director of the institute, his successor at the School of Anthropology was Isabel Kelly, another Berkeley PhD, who also did fieldwork among the Tajín Totonac. The institute published studies by Foster and Kelly, as well as by others, but he later regretted that none of these publications were translated into Spanish.

In Peru the institute was represented by several young anthropologists, including John P. Gillin (1944–45) and Harry Tschopik, Jr. (1945–46). In accordance with Steward's plan, geographers such as F. Webster McBryde, Donald D. Brand, and Robert C. West participated in the program, but Steward later concluded that he had erred in believing that geographers "would supply crucial information about land potentials and land use among agrarian societies."[30] In

Brazil the work of the institute was directed by Donald Pierson, a former student of Robert E. Park at the University of Chicago, in cooperation with the Escola Livre de Sociologia e Politica of São Paulo, where Pierson had also been teaching for several years.

Looking back on the institute's record, Foster asserted that its programs unfolded most successfully in Mexico and Brazil, where an anthropological infrastructure was already in place. The uncertainty and timing of U.S. financial support presented additional difficulties. Despite these problems, Foster's assessment of the program, at least from the U.S. perspective, was positive. The seventeen American scholars who participated "had an unparalleled opportunity to be intimately associated with teaching and research" in five countries, and all of them remained committed to Latin America afterward. "To teach, and to be an organic part of a Latin American institution, promotes a depth of understanding of, and sympathy for, the countries concerned in a way that goes far beyond the level of comprehension one achieves when independent research is the sole interest."[31] He also believed that the institute's fieldwork and publications contributed significantly to the emergence of the peasant community (as opposed to folk culture) as a unit of study.

Inter-American cooperation also occurred after a fire on May 10, 1943, that destroyed the National Library of Peru and many of its holdings (as well as the headquarters of the Geographical Society of Lima). Lewis Hanke spearheaded U.S. efforts to assist in the collection of books and other materials for the library and was named secretary of a twelve-man committee appointed by the secretary of state for this purpose. Hanke believed that the crisis offered an opportunity for the replacement of the library's eighty-year-old director, "amiable but deaf and indifferent," with Jorge Basadre, who had been trained in librarianship in the United States and was in fact appointed to the position. The aid program also included the dispatch of librarians from the United States and Cuba to assist in the organization of a new library school in Lima.[32]

Many American academics had an opportunity to lecture or teach in Latin America under State Department auspices, among them some who were specialists in the region. One of the first exchange professors under the Buenos Aires convention was Charles C. Griffin of Vassar College, who lectured on U.S. history at the Pedagogical Institute in Caracas, Venezuela, in 1940–41. Rex Crawford spent a year at the University of Chile. Herbert E. Bolton and Arthur Aiton taught shorter courses in Mexico and Costa Rica, respectively. The State Department also helped support a year's stay in Honduras by William S. Stokes, a graduate student in political science. In a letter to the department, Stokes explained, rather boastfully, that he had done his utmost to advance its program of cultural relations, for example by offering English classes to university students. He had also "made a careful historical and first-hand study of Nazi activities in Honduras."[33]

There also occurred what Lewis Hanke called "an extraordinary mingling of scholars" as distinguished Latin Americans came to the United States on visits sponsored by the State Department. Among such visitors was the Brazilian novelist Erico Verissimo, who lectured at the University of California and other institutions. Others included the Peruvian archaeologist Luis Valcárcel and numerous historians, such as Jorge Basadre and the Argentine Enrique de Gandía.[34]

An important aspect of the enhanced attention to Latin America during this period, both by the government and by private foundations, was a new awareness of the significance of Brazil and a corresponding awakening of scholarly interest in that vast country, a valued ally of the United States because of its size, resources, and propinquity to West Africa. The increased interest was evident even before the war, as seen in Lewis Hanke's employment of Robert C. Smith as his assistant at the Hispanic Foundation. From the beginning the *Handbook of Latin American Studies* allotted separate sections to Brazilian art, literature, history, and other fields; its third volume, dedicated to the Instituto Histórico e Geográphico Brasileiro in honor of its centenary, contained several special articles on Brazil, including a guide to the country's principal cultural institutions and their publications. The *Hispanic American Historical Review* devoted its August 1940 and August 1942 issues to articles on Brazil. Numerous monographs were published, including Karl Loewenstein's *Brazil under Vargas* (1942), Donald Pierson's *Negroes in Brazil: A Study of Race Contact at Bahia* (1942), and Alexander Marchant's *From Barter to Slavery: The Economic Relations of Portuguese and Indians in the Settlement of Brazil, 1500–1580* (1942).

During this period Samuel Putnam, a journalist and critic, contributed substantially to knowledge of Brazilian letters in the United States. He prepared the section on Brazilian literature for the first thirteen volumes of the *Handbook of Latin American Studies* and translated Jorge Amado's novel *Terras do sem fin* (*The Violent Land*, 1945), as well as two nonfiction classics: Euclides da Cunha's *Os Sertões* (*Rebellion in the Backlands*, 1944) and Gilberto Freyre's *Casa Grande e Senzala* (*The Masters and the Slaves*, 1946). In 1948 he published *Marvelous Journey: A Survey of Four Centuries of Brazilian Writing*. The new interest in Brazil's language and literature was also reflected in an increase in the number of Portuguese courses taught in colleges and universities and in the change in the name of the Spanish instructors' professional organization. In 1944 it became the Association of Teachers of Spanish and Portuguese.[35]

Even as some Latin Americanists were able to teach or conduct research in the region with federal funding during the war years, others proffered their services directly to the government. Many, both established scholars and relative newcomers, interrupted their careers to serve in the armed forces or in federal agencies, such as the State Department or the Office of Strategic Services (OSS).

The Research and Analysis Branch (R&A) of the OSS employed geographers, historians, and many other academics in its various divisions, one of which was devoted to Latin America. Preston James, still a reserve officer in military intelligence, was an early consultant for the new agency and was named head of the Latin American Division in R&A. He later stated that his job was difficult at first "since nobody knew what the devil a Latin American section should do."[36] The division devoted much attention to the assessment of the possible dangers posed by Axis sympathizers in the region, evaluated threats to the Panama Canal, and prepared strategic surveys for the War Department.

In 1943 James was made chief of the Geography Section of the Europe-North Africa Division of the Research and Analysis Branch. The biographer of Maurice Halperin, James's chief assistant and successor as head of the Latin American Division, attributed the transfer to his involvement in an extramarital affair. James is also described as a poor administrator, though elsewhere he has been called abrasive but highly effective in his position.[37] Halperin had received a doctorate in French literature from the Sorbonne but had travelled in Mexico and written about contemporary politics there. In *Current History* (November 1936), for example, he spoke glowingly of the Cárdenas administration in Mexico, where, despite continuing problems, "standards of living definitely have improved." Moreover, "Mexico is more nearly a free, democratic country than it has ever been."[38]

Halperin was also a secret member of the Communist Party, and his assessments of political events in Latin America often echoed the party line. On one occasion he clashed bitterly with Arthur M. Schlesinger, Jr., employed by R&A as editor of a weekly intelligence report, over Halperin's insistence that the coup in Bolivia in 1943 was part of a pro-Nazi hemispheric conspiracy hatched in Argentina. In addition, according to the Venona records of Soviet espionage, Halperin transmitted to Russian agents diplomatic material that came across his desk while he was at the OSS.[39] Halperin's chief research assistant at R&A was Woodrow Borah, a young historian who had recently received his doctorate from the University of California.

After Pearl Harbor, Edwin M. Shook, an archaeologist employed by the Carnegie Institution of Washington, was briefly an agent for the FBI. He had little to do, he recalled, as the Guatemalan government shipped most Germans out of the country. His assignment ended after the FBI was able to place its own agents in the field. Later the Board of Economic Warfare put Shook in charge of a large quinine-planting program on an estate near the Mexican border. John Gillin was also employed by the Board of Economic Warfare in the field, both in Guatemala and Peru.[40]

Many other Latin Americanists were employed in the State Department or in other Washington agencies, sometimes serving in several of them during the war years. For example, historians Harold E. Davis and A. Curtis Wilgus were both employed in the CIAA's Division of Education and Teacher Aids. After returning from his year in Venezuela, Charles Griffin served in the State Department's Office of American Republics. Roland D. Hussey, a colonial historian and faculty member at UCLA since 1926, held various posts in the State Department from 1944 to 1947, including that of chief of the Office of Intelligence Research. F. Webster McBryde, who completed a dissertation on the native economy of southwestern Guatemala in 1940, served as a senior geographer in the Military Intelligence Division of the War Department from 1942 to 1945; Lesley Byrd Simpson was in air force intelligence, rising to the rank of lieutenant colonel. Sanford Mosk was an economic analyst for the Board of Economic Warfare and for the CIAA. In addition to directing the National Planning Association project mentioned earlier, Clarence F. Jones served on the Board of Economic Warfare and in 1944 became Preston James's assistant at the OSS. Harvard archaeologist Alfred M. Tozzer was director of the Honolulu office of the OSS from January 1943 to July 1945. George Blanksten, who would receive his doctorate from UCLA in 1949 with a dissertation on the constitutional problems of Ecuador, was a political analyst in the CIAA and the State Department from 1943 to 1946.

After his work with the Institute of Andean Research, the anthropologist William Duncan Strong took a leave from Columbia University to serve as director of the Ethnogeographic Board from 1942 to 1944. The principal mission of the board, which was financed primarily by the Smithsonian Institution, was to provide the military and war agencies with data about regions that might be of use to the war effort. The Joint Committee was one of the groups listed as cooperating with the board, but given the latter's mandate, few of its activities were related to Latin America. The board's projects included a compilation of a roster of area specialists, including Latin Americanists, and a survey of area programs in U.S. universities.[41]

The veteran geographer George M. McBride performed an especially lengthy and important assignment for the State Department during the 1940s. On the recommendation of Isaiah Bowman, he was appointed to the post of U.S. technical adviser to the Ecuador-Peru Boundary Demarcation Commission. Created by the Rio Protocol of 1942, the commission was to define the border between the two nations as part of the recent settlement of their long-standing territorial dispute. Each of the nations that had mediated the dispute—the United States, Argentina, Brazil, and Chile—was to name a technical adviser to assist the commission as needed. When he was appointed in 1942, McBride expected that the assignment would last a year or two at most. As it turned out, McBride's State Department appointment did not end until September 30, 1948, and he spent another nine months writing his report on the boundary settlement. Not only was McBride the only official of the six nations involved to remain in his post during the entire demarcation process, but he also distinguished himself for his mastery of the issues at stake, his impartiality, and his work as a mediator and liaison among all the interested parties.[42]

When the State Department created the position of cultural attaché in 1941, several Latin Americanists were among the first appointees. Some, such as John T. Reid of Duke University, were specialists in literature, but other fields were also represented. Robert S. Chamberlain, the historian formerly employed by the Carnegie Institution of Washington, was in Guatemala from 1941 to 1945. The archaeologist George Vaillant served in the Lima embassy in 1943–44 while Rex Crawford served in Rio de Janeiro during the same period.[43]

In some instances government-employed scholars who had not been Latin American specialists became dedicated to that area after the war. The interest of Bryce Wood in Latin America is said to have been sparked by a year of travel in the region and by his service as an administrative assistant in the State Department in 1942–43. Wood, who had earned a doctorate in political science at Columbia in 1940, spent most of his postwar career with the SSRC, where he was active in issues related to Latin America, and produced several volumes on U.S.–Latin American relations. The anthropologist Oscar Lewis, who received his doctorate from Columbia in 1940 with a dissertation on the culture of the Blackfoot Indians, became a Latin American specialist on the basis of language instruction at the Inter-American Training Center in Philadelphia and a stint with the Strategic Index of Latin America. In 1943 he spent seven months with the Justice Department studying Hispanic organizations in the United States to determine whether they presented security threats. The same year he was sent to Mexico City to act as a liaison between the U.S. Office of Indian Affairs and the recently created Interamerican Indian Institute, which was based in the Mexican capital. With his wife, Ruth, a trained psychologist, he took part in research on the personality of Mexican Indians, which was to parallel contemporary studies of native North Americans. After approximately ten months in Mexico, he returned to the United States, where he was assigned to the Bureau of Agricultural Economics.[44]

Five rural sociologists became students of Latin America during the war as a result of assignments they received from the State Department and the Agriculture Department's Office of Foreign Agricultural Relations. The purpose was to acquire information about rural societies in hemispheric nations that might become sources of critical wartime materials, such as rubber and quinine. In 1942 T. Lynn Smith, Carl C. Taylor, and Nathan Whetten were sent to Brazil, Argentina, and Mexico, respectively, to study patterns of rural life. Attached to the U.S. embassies in their respective countries for about a year, they traveled widely, interacted with local officials and academics, and produced reports for the U.S. government as well as important studies: Smith's *Brazil: People and Institutions* (1946), Taylor's *Rural Life in Argentina* (1948), and Whetten's *Rural Mexico* (1948). Whetten also spent five months in Guatemala in 1944. In 1945 Lowry Nelson, a professor at the University of Minnesota and a mentor to fellow Mormons Smith and Whetten, was given a similar assignment in Cuba. After the war he published *Rural Cuba* (1950) and was frequently called on to serve as a consultant on problems related to Latin American agriculture and land tenure.[45]

T. Lynn Smith was also dispatched to Colombia as an adviser on colonization and settlement as part of a collaborative program of technical assistance conducted by the Office of Foreign Agricultural Relations and the State Department. Another sociologist participating in the program was Olen E. Leonard, who was director of a cooperative agricultural station in Bolivia as well as a researcher. He produced monographs on Bolivian regions as well as a comprehensive survey of the country in 1952.

Lewis Hanke believed that on the whole the wartime experiences of Latin Americanists had been enriching:

Many now had their first real taste of life in the countries whose cultures they had been studying. As economic analysts, cultural officers, or special assistants of one kind or another, anthropologists, historians, economists, and professors of literature found their horizons suddenly broadened, their understanding deepened by intimate contact with life in Latin America. Other specialists who found themselves drawn into wartime research in Washington or administering some government program in the field also discovered new and interesting aspects of Latin American affairs hitherto unfamiliar to them.[46]

Hanke predicted that the teaching and research of these specialists would benefit from their wartime experiences. This was assuredly the case, but with the end of the war and the emergence of new preoccupations for policy makers, intellectuals, and the public in general, the interest in Latin America that had characterized the decade 1935–45 tapered off. In fact, even before the United

States entered the war, Hanke himself expressed concern about the instrumental nature of contemporary American interest in Latin American culture, which seemed intended mainly to counteract Nazi ambitions. He also wondered about its staying power: "Once the crisis is over, this political interest in their culture, if it is shallowly rooted, will topple over. Such a crash would raise an echo to be heard throughout the Americas very unpleasantly for many years to come."[47]

Toward the end of the conflict, several other scholars expressed awareness of impending change in the close and relatively harmonious inter-American relationship of those years. Although he hoped that this change would not occur, Dana G. Munro feared that the Latin American economies would be disrupted by a decline in American expenditures in the region and that tensions would arise over trade. Writing after the Chapultepec Conference of March 1945, Arthur P. Whitaker observed that a "clear-cut rift" had been evident there over trade policy and U.S. aid for postwar reconversion in Latin America. In *Foreign Affairs* Frank Tannenbaum agreed that the end of the U.S. financial outflow would leave Latin American ambitions unfulfilled. In the absence of a strong peasantry and middle class (except in Mexico and Costa Rica), he was not sanguine about prospects for economic and political stability in the region.[48] The forebodings of these scholars were borne out in the years immediately following the war, as Latin America seemed to be a secondary concern in Washington and in universities throughout the United States. Nevertheless, the academic stalwarts who had devoted themselves to the region remained faithful and even attracted new adepts.

7

Marking Time, 1945–1958

During the fifteen years following the end of World War II, the perception arose that Latin American studies were in a state of stasis if not decline. Lewis Hanke recalled this period as comprising "long years of drought"; Howard F. Cline described it more dramatically as a "cataclysmic, catastrophic tumble from 1942–1945 heights."[1] In reality, drastic retrogression did not occur: professors continued to teach and conduct research and new graduate students continued to appear.

The malaise that emerged was due in part to a sense of relative deprivation. Amid the rising cold-war concerns of the immediate postwar era, policy makers in Washington and the foundations relegated Latin America to a status even more peripheral than it had occupied during the war. The resulting decline in financial support seemed all the more galling because of the relative generosity of the war years. Meanwhile, programs and scholarship related to other areas of the world seemed to be faring much better. Also contributing to the malaise was a belief, held even within the Latin Americanist community, that the field offered few intellectual challenges, was marginal to the mainstream of most social science research, and failed to attract first-rate practitioners.

As is well known, this "bust" was soon followed by a "boom," usually seen as a result of Fidel Castro's rise to power in Cuba in 1959 and his efforts to export his socialist revolution to other countries in the hemisphere. Even before these events had occurred, however, there were signs of an impending revival of interest in Latin America.

The State of the Disciplines in the Late 1940s

The state of Latin American studies in the various disciplines during the 1940s can be gleaned from two surveys undertaken at the time. The first took place

in 1942 when, at the behest of the Joint Committee on Latin American Studies, Irving A. Leonard spent five months examining personnel, programs, and
library facilities at twenty universities, primarily to assess their potential for
training graduate students and doing research in Latin America. Although the
war disrupted his work, especially because of the departure of university personnel for military service or other war-related work, Leonard nonetheless prepared an incisive assessment of the state of the field.[2]

He found that in general the universities of the West, Southwest, and South—
that is, those located in the old Spanish borderlands—had the strongest commitment to Latin American studies and had "long accepted them as equal or
nearly equal in importance to the more traditional studies of the curriculum."
He singled out the University of California at Berkeley, his own alma mater, as
the "leading graduate center" in the field, but also spoke favorably of Stanford
and Texas. At the older private universities of the Northeast, by contrast, he detected a "slightly snobbish attitude or one of condescending indifference" to
Latin American studies.[3]

As might be expected, offerings were strongest in language and literature,
history, geography, and anthropology and archaeology. "Other disciplines are
but slightly or incidentally developed," he wrote, "and in many institutions are
entirely neglected." He found numerous faults with personnel, asserting that
"with notable exceptions, Latin American studies do not seem to have attracted
scholars of first rate ability and equipment." Moreover, when the distinguished
scholars who did exist retired or died, the universities lacked men of comparable stature to replace them. In the field as a whole, there was a shortage of faculty adequately trained in language and in the tools of their discipline as well
as sufficient firsthand experience in Latin America.[4]

In the late 1940s the Pan-American Union (PAU) conducted a more extensive survey of courses with Latin American content and accompanied the publication of its findings with a lengthy assessment of the field by the Peruvian
historian Jorge Basadre, who was then the director of the PAU's Department
of Cultural Affairs. The PAU examined curricula at approximately 1,500 institutions of all kinds (including universities, liberal arts colleges, teachers' colleges, and junior colleges) and found that in 1948–49, 875 of them offered one
or more courses with Latin American content, for a total of 3,346 courses (see
table 7.1).[5]

This figure compared favorably with the results of a PAU survey in 1938–
39, which revealed that 383 colleges and universities offered 981 courses dealing with Latin America.[6] Basadre noted that the later survey was probably more
painstaking than its predecessor and that large increases in college and university enrollment had occurred over the past decade. He wondered about the

Table 7.1
Number of Courses with Latin American Content, 1938–39 and 1948–49

Field	1938–39	1948–49
Literature	193	877
History	476	1,097
Anthropology	38	129
Geography	165	361
Political Science*	62	254
Economics	31	130
Sociology	2	52
Brazilian Portuguese	—	13
Total of Latin Americanist courses	981	3,346
Number of institutions surveyed	383	875

*Fifty-eight of the 1938–39 courses were in international relations, as was an unknown number of those in this category for 1948–49.
Source: *Courses on Latin America in Institutions of Higher Learning in the United States, 1948–1949*, comp. Estellita Hart (Washington, DC: Department of Cultural Affairs, Division of Education, Pan American Union, 1949), v–vi, xxxi. Other fields covered in the two surveys but omitted from this table include art, biology, education, music, and others.

quality of the courses offered and the degree of institutional support for them, but overall he was highly impressed with the academic commitment to Latin America in the United States.

One area that both Leonard and Basadre found to be flourishing was Spanish language and literature. At the institutions visited by Leonard in 1942, Spanish was the most widely studied foreign language, and a 1944 survey of 679 colleges showed that the number of students enrolled in Spanish classes nearly equaled enrollments in French and German combined. The PAU survey of 1948–49 did not even include Spanish language courses (though it identified forty-nine courses in commercial Spanish). It seemed, therefore, that the condescending attitude toward Spanish evident earlier in the century had disappeared, at least where undergraduate education was concerned. Basadre did comment, however, that the intensive, conversation-based method used by the army during the war had revolutionized the field, making the traditional emphasis on reading "outmoded."[7]

In 1942, courses in Spanish American literature were "practically universal" at Leonard's institutions. Growth in the area was indeed impressive, as shown by the PAU surveys of 1938–39 and 1948–49. In the former, 193 courses in Latin

American literature represented 19.7 percent of the total; by 1948–49 the number of courses had risen to 877, which represented 26.2 percent of the total (see table 7.1).

The vast majority of these courses dealt with Spanish American literature, but Brazil was not completely neglected. The 1948–49 PAU survey indicated that about a dozen institutions offered courses in Brazilian Portuguese, a situation that led Basadre to conclude: "The battle for Portuguese has not yet been won."[8] He held the same belief about Brazilian literature. Even so, courses in this subject were offered at California (Berkeley), UCLA, Columbia, Harvard, Florida State, New Mexico, North Carolina, and others.

History

In both 1938–39 and 1948–49 history led the list of Latin American courses, accounting for nearly one-half the courses identified in the former survey and nearly one-third of those listed in the latter (see table 7.1). Leonard, too, defined history as one of the most widely taught subjects. Concentrating as he did on institutions capable of offering graduate work, Leonard expressed concern about the programs at Berkeley and Stanford, where the outstanding figures had died (Chapman, Priestley, Martin) or had reached retirement age (Bolton). He was also distressed by the fact that Yale, where he had done his undergraduate work, had the "unflattering distinction" of lacking a Latin American specialist. Wisconsin and North Carolina were also underserved.[9]

By 1948 Leonard might have viewed the situation more positively. Berkeley had engaged three of its own graduates—James F. King, Engel Sluiter, and George P. Hammond—to handle its Latin American offerings; Hammond, a borderland specialist, also served as the director of the Bancroft Library. John J. Johnson, another Berkeley PhD, had joined the Stanford faculty in 1946. Yale was beginning to atone for its long neglect of Latin American history by engaging Howard Cline as an instructor. Though Wisconsin remained underserved, North Carolina had employed Harold A. Bierck, who had received his doctorate at UCLA. Even so, as Cline observed in 1948, the number of positions available to teachers of Latin American history, was limited: "Considering the fact that there are only about half a dozen top jobs in universities toward which the neophyte may aspire, it is surprising that as many as do put in a considerable time in qualifying themselves as well as they do."[10]

A 1943 study of college textbooks on Latin American history showed a total of eleven on the market. The authors of the study, James F. King and Samuel Everett, faulted the texts for an excessive emphasis on the political history of individual nations to the neglect of synthetic treatment of social, economic, and cultural topics, such as race relations, labor, literature, and science. They did, however, find in them "scholarly disinterestedness" and an absence of the "invidious comparison or the superiority complex" often seen in other writings that referred to Latin America.[11]

These texts reflected perhaps the most significant trend in Latin American historiography of the 1930s and 1940s: the erosion if not the demolition of the Black Legend, the name given to traditional assertions of Spanish rapacity, cruelty to the Indian population, religious fanaticism, and intellectual obscurantism. Scholars in Latin America and Spain played a major role in this trend, but American historians, building on the precedent set by E. G. Bourne, made important contributions as well. Various works by Lewis Hanke, for example, explicated the legal underpinnings of Spanish colonial policies and demonstrated official Spanish interest in the spiritual and material welfare of the Indians, and Irving A. Leonard in a series of monographs and articles provided convincing evidence that colonials had ready access to ancient and contemporary works of literature despite the vigilance of the Inquisition. A collection of essays edited by Arthur P. Whitaker, *Latin America and the Enlightenment* (1942), showed that the great intellectual movement of the eighteenth century had reverberated in the Spanish colonies and Brazil.[12]

During the 1930s and 1940s, the *Hispanic American Historical Review* remained the primary outlet for scholarly articles on Latin America, but in 1944 it was joined by a new quarterly journal, *The Americas*. The journal was the organ of the Academy of American Franciscan History, which had been founded in Washington in April 1944 to promote research on the order in the New World and to make its contributions better known.[13] Both the academy and the journal also proclaimed interest in "inter-American cultural history," and the latter from the beginning published articles unrelated to the work of the Franciscans.

Another new journal was the *Revista de Historia de América*, founded in 1938 as an organ of the Pan American Institute of Geography and History (PAIGH) and intended to serve all the Western Hemisphere republics. According to Lewis Hanke, it was he and the Mexican historian Silvio Zavala who persuaded the director of the PAIGH to establish the periodical. Hanke and Zavala also played a key role in organizing the First Congress of Historians of Mexico and the United States, which took place in Monterrey and Saltillo in 1949. Attended by 141 delegates representing institutions from Maine to Oaxaca, this high-profile affair attracted both the governor of Coahuila and the U.S. ambassador and ended with a luncheon offered by Cervecería Cuauhtémoc.[14]

The late 1930s had brought a more elaborate structure to the Conference on Hispanic American History. Still concerned about its nebulous relationship with the American Historical Association, which did not list it among its affiliated organizations, the conference appointed a committee in 1937 to consider drafting an improved constitution for the group. At the annual meeting the following year the committee, which was chaired by Charles W. Hackett, presented a draft constitution for a proposed Conference on Latin American History. Only committee member Charles E. Chapman refused to sign the draft because he disapproved of the substitution of "Latin American" for "Hispanic American" in the proposed name of the group.[15] A founder of the HAHR in 1916, he still adhered to the now-outmoded view that "Hispanic" embraced all things pertaining to Spain and Portugal.

As stated in the constitution, which was approved in 1938, the primary purposes of the conference were to assist the AHA program committee in organizing a Latin American session and to hold a luncheon or dinner during the meeting. Despite the new charter, the organization's ties with the AHA remained tenuous, and when the latter was sounded out about providing financial assistance, it refused, whereupon those present at the 1938 meeting collected $7.10 for secretarial expenses for the following year.

Anthropology

Anthropology in all its aspects received great impetus during the war, and, as the previous chapter showed, programs and publications related to Latin America benefited from federal spending. Thus, anthropology with a Latin Americanist slant, traditionally a vigorous area, emerged from the conflict stronger than ever.

Leonard gave a positive assessment of Latin Americanist anthropology and archaeology in the institutions he visited: "Training and research personnel and graduate students in these disciplines seem, on the average, better equipped by foreign experience and adequate language command than in most of the other disciplines; they tend to be more realistic in their understanding of actual conditions existing in Latin America." For his part, Basadre agreed with Leonard, noting the "remarkable" progress of recent years and the emergence of a new generation of scholars with experience in Latin America to join the old guard.[16]

Basadre's optimism seems belied by the figures for anthropology courses related to Latin America in the two surveys. Both in 1938–39 and in 1948–49, less than 4 percent of the courses dealt with anthropology (including archaeology), though it should be kept in mind that many scholars in the field were employed in nonteaching institutions, such as museums (see table 7.1). A tendency noted by Leonard was still in evidence: most of the courses emphasized Mexico and Central America while South America lagged. During this period the regions of Mexico and Central America where archaeological work was concentrated came to be known as "Mesoamerica" after a classic 1943 article by Paul Kirchhoff defined it as a unique culture area.[17]

The 1948–49 survey listed Alfred M. Tozzer as the professor in charge of courses on the ancient civilizations of Mexico and Central America at Harvard, but he retired shortly afterward. The years following the war saw the retirement or death of several prominent scholars and the emergence of a new generation. Alfred L. Kroeber, for example, retired from the University of California in 1946, though he remained professionally active for many years afterward. George C. Vaillant died by his own hand in 1945 as he was about to leave for Madrid to serve as chief representative there of the Office of War Information. Sylvanus G. Morley died in 1948 and Wendell C. Bennett in 1953. Younger scholars gaining distinction in the immediate postwar years included Robert Wauchope, who followed Frans Blom at Tulane in 1942; John Howland Rowe, formerly of the Institute of Andean Research and the Institute of Social Anthropology, who joined the Berkeley faculty in 1948; and Gordon R. Willey, who succeeded Tozzer as Bowditch Professor at Harvard in 1950.

The postwar years also brought the demise of the Maya project of the Carnegie Institution of Washington. Not only was its "panscientific" study of Maya history, society, and culture disrupted by the war, but its accomplishments were belittled by Clyde Kluckhohn, as noted in chapter 3, and by Walter W. Taylor. In *A Study of Archaeology* (1948), based on his 1943 dissertation, Taylor minimized the value of Carnegie contributions, arguing that Alfred V. Kidder and his colleagues had done little to elucidate the nature of prehistoric Maya culture, especially that of nonelites:

> Both the field work and the publications of the Carnegie are weighted overwhelmingly toward the hierarchal. They have hardly . . . touched the cultural remains of the common Maya. But even within the hierarchal culture, the emphasis has not been to construct a picture of how the Maya hierarchy lived. . . . Such intensive excavations as have been made [have been directed] toward the finding of material for comparative and chronological studies or, many times, just to excavate a structure which appeared to be of rare or unknown type or was prominent or artistically beautiful.[18]

The decisive blow was the determination of Carnegie's new director, Vannevar Bush, to devote the institution's efforts entirely to the physical sciences. At the urging of some of the Carnegie trustees, the Maya program was given a temporary reprieve and was allowed an additional project before it was terminated.

The place chosen for investigation was Mayapán, a Late Postclassic site in northern Yucatan. Fieldwork began in 1949 under the direction of Harry E. D. Pollock, a twenty-year Carnegie veteran, and continued through 1955. Though carried on with reduced funding, the work at Mayapán was notable for several reasons, including the extensive use of graduate students; the efforts to link archaeological findings with historical works, such as native accounts and Spanish writings; and detailed investigation of domestic structures.[19]

In 1958 the Carnegie's Maya project came to an end. Among the Carnegie staff members who now found employment at Harvard's Peabody Museum was the Russian-born Tatiana Proskouriakoff. Already known for her *Album of Maya Architecture* (1946) and *Study of Classic Maya Sculpture* (1950), she would soon revolutionize the interpretation of Maya writing by demonstrating in a 1960 article that inscriptions at Piedras Negras, Guatemala, recorded historical events instead of calendrical and astronomical data alone.[20] Meanwhile, the Peabody and other institutions undertook archaeological projects in the Maya zone, often with the participation of former Carnegie scholars. The Peabody returned to Mesoamerica in 1953 with the investigation of settlement patterns at Barton Ramie, British Honduras (now Belize), in a project directed by Gordon Willey and funded by the National Science Foundation, which began to support archaeological research in the 1950s. In 1959 Willey and Ledyard Smith, who had joined the Peabody staff after the Carnegie work was terminated, launched another major project at the Altar de Sacrificios site in Guatemala. In 1956 Tulane's Middle American Research Institute began fieldwork at Dzibilchaltún and other sites in Yucatan under the direction of E. Willys Andrews IV, another Carnegie veteran.[21]

The most important archaeological project undertaken by Americans in the Maya zone in the postwar era was at Tikal in the Petén region of Guatemala. In the 1930s Edwin M. Shook and other Carnegie staffers had envisioned investigation of this large and influential Classic era site as a CIW project, but once this was no longer possible, the University Museum of the University of Pennsylvania stepped in, hoping to receive financial support from the United Fruit Company and other American firms operating in Guatemala. The tensions between the United Fruit Company and Guatemala's revolutionary governments of the late 1940s and early 1950s prevented the realization of the museum's goals. Not until after the fall of President Jacobo Arbenz in 1954 was a contract signed with the government. That agreement called for a ten-year commitment by the University Museum, which pledged to spend $100,000 annually. For its part the government was to use its air force to supply Tikal at a nearby airstrip.[22]

Fieldwork began in 1956 with a scant $20,000 in initial funding from the American Philosophical Society and the Rockefeller Foundation. Shook was the first director and was succeeded by William R. Coe in 1964. Continuing until 1969, the project was significant for several reasons. The methods it devised for excavating, mapping, and recording became standard in the field. The mapping of Tikal not only indicated a substantial population but also called into question many traditional assumptions about the function of Maya sites, their class system, and the nature of the agricultural production needed to support the population. Much attention was paid to the description and preservation of monuments, and hieroglyphs on carved structures were carefully analyzed. In part the emphasis on excavation reflected the desire of the Guatemalan government for the development of Tikal as a tourist destination. To this end it declared the site and the contiguous area of 576 square kilometers a national park.

Another ambitious project initiated in the mid-1950s was the preparation of a Mesoamerican counterpart to the *Handbook of South American Indians*. Funded primarily by the National Science Foundation, the *Handbook of Middle American Indians* appeared in sixteen volumes between 1964 and 1976 under the general editorship of Robert Wauchope of Tulane. Topics covered included archaeology, ethnology, cultural and physical anthropology, linguistics, and ethnohistory.[23]

As before, American archaeological investigations in South America were more limited than in Mesoamerica and continued to focus on the Andean area, especially Peru. In 1946–47 the Virú Valley of Peru's northern coast was the site of an ambitious project sponsored by the Institute of Andean Research. Conceived by Wendell Bennett, the project aimed at an integrated archaeological and environmental study of the valley, including investigation of preceramic remains, settlement patterns, and stratigraphic sequences by Junius B. Bird, Gordon Willey, William Duncan Strong, and others. Geographer F. Webster McBryde studied physical and hydrographic features and present-day land use. The project was considered a landmark in Andean archaeology because of its multidisciplinary nature and because of Willey's analysis of settlement patterns in the valley. Findings generated by the project were reviewed in 1946 and 1947 at conferences at the Hacienda Chiclín near Trujillo, which was owned by Rafael Larco Hoyle, an archaeology enthusiast, and in New York. Bennett edited the proceedings of the latter meeting, *A Reappraisal of Peruvian Archaeology* (1948) and, with Bird, published *Andean Culture History* (1949), considered a groundbreaking work at the time.[24]

Several public and private institutions provided funding for the Virú Valley project. One of them was the Viking Fund, established in 1941 by the controversial Swedish industrialist Axel Wenner-Gren. It was the first such institution founded in the United States specifically for the support of anthropology in the broadest sense: ethnology, physical anthropology, linguistics, and archaeology.[25]

The fund supported fieldwork and research in all parts of the world, subsidized conferences and the publication of manuscripts, and brought scholars together in its New York headquarters. In 1946 it created the Viking Fund Medal and Viking Fund Prize ($1,000), to be awarded annually to outstanding scholars in archaeology, cultural anthropology, and physical anthropology. Alfred Kidder was the first Viking medalist in archaeology. In 1950 the American Anthropological Association created an award in his honor, to be given every other year for achievement in American archaeology. Alfred Tozzer was the first recipient of the Kidder Award.

Among ethnologists or cultural anthropologists the postwar years brought continued activity by veteran researchers who were joined by younger colleagues. Ralph Beals, who received his doctorate from Berkeley in 1930, became the first anthropologist to be hired by UCLA, where he stayed for his entire career. Robert Redfield remained at the University of Chicago and the Carnegie Maya program until 1946. He published *The Folk Culture of Yucatan* (1941) and *A Village That Chose Progress: Chan Kom Revisited* (1951) but in the 1950s became increasingly interested in the comparative study of world civilizations. Sol Tax, Redfield's former student and Carnegie colleague, joined him at Chicago in 1944 after serving for a year (1942–43) as a visiting professor at the National School of Anthropology in Mexico City with financial support from the CIW and the Rockefeller Foundation. As mentioned in chapter 6, George M. Foster taught at the National School of Anthropology on behalf of the Institute of Social Anthropology from 1944 to 1945; he later headed the institute and after its demise in 1952 went to Berkeley. Richard N. Adams did his doctoral research in Peru. After receiving his doctorate from Yale in 1950, he was reluctant to undertake an academic career and instead found employment with the Institute of Social Anthropology in Guatemala, where he was able to observe a social revolution in progress.[26] Oscar Lewis joined the faculty of the University of Illinois while another recent Columbia PhD, Charles Wagley, remained at his alma mater. Wagley's dissertation dealt with a Mam-speaking village in northwestern Guatemala, but unlike most of his contemporaries he left the Middle American field to concentrate on Brazilian peoples and society.

The prevailing trends in anthropological projects related to Latin America remained consistent with prewar concerns. Projects involving several researchers, including representatives from the host country, and often extending over several years were favored. Another theme was the desirability of undertaking research that would be of use or relevance in improving the lives of the people studied. Finally, concentration on groups that were primarily indigenous in culture waned somewhat as anthropologists increasingly began to focus on groups more directly affected by modern Latin American society.[27]

An early cooperative enterprise was the Tarascan project, begun in 1940 by Mexico's Department of Indian Affairs, National Polytechnic Institute, and UCLA. Led by Beals and Daniel Rubín de la Borbolla, the project envisioned fieldwork among the Tarascans of Michoacán, a relatively compact tribal group experiencing substantial change. The researchers hoped that the findings would be helpful in the administration of the region, which was the birthplace of President Lázaro Cárdenas. In 1944 George Foster and others associated with the Institute of Social Anthropology began to work on the project as well.

The Tarascan project yielded several community studies, including Foster's on Tzintzunztán and Beals's *Cherán: A Sierra Tarascan Village* (1946). Reviewing the project in 1949, Julian Steward found several weaknesses. Despite the recognized need for a multidisciplinary approach, because of budgetary constraints, investigators in only two disciplines—anthropology and geography—took part. In addition, according to Steward, the project treated the communities in isolation, failing to integrate them into larger functional units, including the nation.[28]

During his year in Mexico (1943–44), Oscar Lewis began a study of "the effects of government administration policies upon the democratic sentiment and personality of the Mexican Indian." Financed mainly by the Viking Fund, Lewis chose Tepoztlán as his primary focus and, with a team of Mexican aides, considerably broadened the scope of the study before the funding ran out. According to Lewis, the project came to combine "a practical program of aid to the people with a scientific study. . . . These practical measures have been of great help in establishing rapport, but even more important, it has given us an opportunity to observe behavior in a more or less controlled experimental situation." Lewis returned to Tepoztlán for additional fieldwork in 1947 and 1948 and later published *Life in a Mexican Village: Tepoztlán Restudied* (1951), notable as the first reassessment of an earlier ethnographic study. The book was also notable for the fact that it portrayed Tepoztlán as less harmonious, and the villagers as less contented, than in the account offered by Robert Redfield twenty years earlier. Lewis also disagreed with Redfield's implicit assumption that "folk societies are good and urban societies bad."[29]

Julian Steward, who moved to Columbia University in 1946, directed one of the largest anthropological projects of the immediate postwar era: a study of the rural population of Puerto Rico. Initially proposed by Clarence Senior, a sociologist at the University of Puerto Rico, the project reflected the desire of the university and the government to apply the insights of social science to the island's problems. Steward also hoped to elaborate hypotheses regarding cultural functions and change that might be valid for similar rural areas elsewhere and thereby enhance the predictive value of social science. Participants in the study, which was supported mainly by the University of Puerto Rico and the Rockefeller Foundation, included Sidney Mintz, Eric Wolf, and other Columbia graduate students in anthropology, as well as several individuals associated with the university, notably the Rumanian-born John Murra, then on the faculty, who was the project's first field director.[30]

The project began with a graduate seminar at Columbia, during which the existing social science literature was reviewed. Fieldwork took place over a period of eighteen months in 1948–49 and entailed a survey of the island, selection and ethnographic study of several rural communities, and analysis of the communities with reference to each other and to Puerto Rico as a whole. The principal study resulting from the project, written by Steward, Wolf, Mintz, and others, was *The People of Puerto Rico* (1956). Gordon Willey described the project as "one of the most thorough-going social anthropological studies of a nation and its institutions that has ever been carried out." Mintz and his fellow students, however, thought that Steward showed insufficient interest in Puerto Rico's status as a U.S. possession.[31]

One of the best-known, long-term anthropological projects in Latin America during this period was undertaken by Cornell University and the Indigenous Institute of Peru at Vicos, a hacienda in the central highlands about 250 miles north of Lima. The hacienda, about forty-four thousand acres in size, belonged to the Public Benefit Society of nearby Huaraz, which leased it to an enterprise called the Santa Corporation that grew flax for a small linen factory. The residents of the hacienda, approximately 1,750 Quechua-speaking Indians, were expected to work the fields and perform other chores in exchange for a plot of land. Although better off than others in the region, the Vicosinos were illiterate, impoverished, and victims of exploitation.

Allan R. Holmberg, an anthropologist who had earned his doctorate from Yale and had been employed by the Institute of Social Anthropology in Peru (1946–48), is considered the originator of the project, which was part of a larger undertaking at Cornell called the Culture and Applied Social Science Program. After a chance visit to the area in 1949, he devised a plan to combine research and action in Vicos to study the processes of modernization, improve the lives of its residents, and extend the insights derived therefrom to similar communities elsewhere. In 1951, with the support of the Peruvian government and its Institute of Indian Affairs, Holmberg, who was now chairman of the Anthropology Department at Cornell, arranged for the transfer of the hacienda lease to the university, which now became the *patrón*. Under the new dispensation the worst abuses in the labor system were ended, steps were taken to increase crop yields, and improvements were made in schooling and health care. In 1957 the lease was transferred to the Vicos community, and in 1962 the hacienda was expropriated and turned over to the Vicosinos.

Supported with funds from various sources, including the Carnegie Corporation of New York and the Wenner-Gren Foundation for Anthropological Research (as the Viking Fund was renamed in 1951), the project yielded numerous research papers by Peruvians and Americans and caused some controversy in both countries. For his part Holmberg remained convinced that the Vicos experience proved that "contrary to a widely held opinion in Peru and elsewhere, the indigenous population of the *sierra* have a great potential for development and for becoming a dynamic and progressive part of the Peruvian nation." Moreover, this could be accomplished without the loss of the positive values of indigenous society, that is, "respect for work, frugality, cooperation." He also stressed the new empowerment of the Vicosinos in their dealings with the outside world.[32]

The Other Social Sciences

In the other social sciences—geography, political science, economics, and sociology—trends followed the pattern set in the early decades of the twentieth century, with the first of these seemingly the strongest in classroom offerings, quality of scholars, and professional esteem. As table 7.1 shows, all the disciplines except geography made gains during the decade 1938–48.

Geography experienced internal dissension in the immediate postwar period over the definition of the field, its academic respectability, and accusations of elitism directed at the Association of American Geographers by younger non-academic geographers. A major blow was the decision of Harvard to terminate its geography program in 1948. Amid the turmoil, scholars who focused on Latin America held their own, and Jorge Basadre described the U.S. contribution to the field as "impressive."[33]

Several of the early practitioners retired or died, but others remained active. Mark Jefferson retired from teaching in 1939, and George M. McBride did the same in 1947. Isaiah Bowman, who had been president of Johns Hopkins since 1935, died in 1950. Carl Sauer still dominated geography at Berkeley, which was "still less a department than an individual."[34] He continued to work in Mexico until 1950, several of his trips being funded by the Berkeley Associates in Tropical Biogeography, an interdisciplinary group founded at the university in 1946 that concentrated on Latin America. By now Sauer's research interests had turned to plant domestication and aboriginal agriculture in the Western Hemisphere. He pursued these interests not only in Mexico but also in South America during his 1942 trip and in the Caribbean, which he first visited in 1950.

In 1951 he was awarded a contract from the Geography Branch of the U.S. Office of Naval Research for studies in the Caribbean and spent the summer of 1952 there, mainly in the Dominican Republic, which became the base for the naval research program. The program offered opportunities for students to do field-work and yielded numerous mimeographed reports, dissertations, theses, and journal articles. Sauer's Caribbean fieldwork, coupled with archival research, formed the basis of his monograph titled *The Early Spanish Main* (1966).[35]

Preston James began his postwar career by moving from Michigan to Syracuse University in 1945. He remained at Syracuse until his retirement in 1970, building up the Geography Department and attempting to promote the study of Latin America at the university. He maintained his ties with Brazil, spending eight months there (1949–50) as an adviser to Brazilian geographers at the invitation of the National Council of Geographers. Several young Brazilians went to Syracuse to study geography with James. He was also actively involved for many years with the Geography Commission of the PAIGH.[36]

Clarence F. Jones also moved in 1945, from Clark University to Northwestern. In 1949 he launched a large-scale survey and mapping of land use in Puerto Rico, a project that he regarded as a contribution to solving the problem of population pressure on the island. Funded mainly by the federal government, the project generated approximately ten doctoral dissertations by students of Jones during the 1950s as well as several publications to which he contributed. Among the project's consultants was a former student of Jones, Rafael Picó, who had received his doctorate in 1938 and had served as chairman of Puerto Rico's Planning Board (1942–45).[37]

Many younger scholars oriented toward Latin America attained prominence during this period. Several were students of Sauer. These included Donald D. Brand, who established the Geography Department at Texas; Dan Stanislawski, who taught at the University of Arizona; Robert C. West, who taught at Louisiana State University; and James J. Parsons, who became Sauer's colleague at Berkeley. John P. Augelli, one of the last geography PhDs to be produced at Harvard, was on the faculty of the University of Maryland during the 1950s. Perhaps the most unusual background was that of Raymond E. Crist. He had worked as a geological surveyor for oil companies in Mexico and Venezuela from 1926 to 1931 and received a doctorate from the University of Grenoble in 1937. During World War II he was employed as a field technician in Brazil and Bolivia by the Rubber Development Corporation. After teaching at the University of Puerto Rico and the University of Maryland, in 1952 he went to the University of Florida, which was launching a doctoral program in geography. In his twenty-three years at Florida he directed twenty-eight doctoral dissertations, all but two of them related to Latin America.[38]

Despite the apparent increase during the 1940s in the number of college courses with Latin American content classified as political science, the field remained undeveloped. Much of what was taught and written under the rubric of political science with respect to Latin America related to diplomacy or inter-American relations. Research in the area of politics and government tended to be "narrowly focused, ethnocentric, atheoretical, and noncomparative."[39] These traits were evident in the first textbook in the field, Austin F. Macdonald's *Latin American Politics and Government* (1949). The author of studies of U.S. city and state government as well as a book titled *Government of the Argentine Republic* (1942), Macdonald described the governmental machinery and recent political history of each of the Latin American countries, but there was little analysis, and he showed a tendency to compare Latin America to the United States to the former's disadvantage.

What was perhaps most noteworthy about the period was the emergence for the first time of scholars whose entire career was devoted to the study of Latin American politics and government. Several of these political scientists were trained by Russell H. Fitzgibbon, who remained at UCLA until 1964. Among them were William S. Stokes, George I. Blanksten, and Harry Kantor, who joined the faculties at Wisconsin, Northwestern, and Florida, respectively. Robert S. Scott, who studied under Stokes, became a professor at Illinois in 1949. Philip B. Taylor, Jr., completed his doctorate at Berkeley in 1950 with a dissertation on the executive power in Uruguay; during the 1950s he was employed by the University of Michigan. The Cuban-born Federico Gil was a professor of political science at the University of North Carolina from the 1940s until the 1980s. Two of the most influential political scientists of the postwar era were Bryce Wood and Kalman H. Silvert, not only because of their own scholarship but also because of their future affiliation with the Social Science Research Council and the Ford Foundation, respectively. After leaving the State Department, Wood taught at Swarthmore College before joining the SSRC staff in 1950. Silvert received his doctorate from Pennsylvania in 1948 with a dissertation on the Chilean Development Corporation and joined the Tulane faculty the same year. In 1962 he moved to Dartmouth and began his association with the Ford Foundation.

By 1941 the number of political scientists who considered themselves Latin Americanists was sufficiently large that a group called the Latin-American Conference was established within the American Political Science Association. At the 1945 meeting of the group, discussion revolved around ways of promoting studies of Latin America within the discipline. What were needed, some members asserted, were "dynamic studies of Latin American politics," not "merely formal descriptions of constitutional machinery."[40]

In 1946 John Lloyd Mecham identified another problem facing political scientists with a Latin American specialty: the lack of publication outlets for scholarly articles in the field. Because the number of "high class" manuscripts on Latin American government was so small, he proposed creation of a journal that would include economics and sociology. He contrasted scholars in these disciplines with historians, who had their own journal and a group identity: "We in the other social sciences are working without cohesion and without the enthusiasm which our subjects of interest should inspire." The Joint Committee on Latin American Studies discussed the proposed journal at its May 1946 meeting but decided not to pursue the matter.[41]

According to Miron Burgin, an economic historian who received his doctorate from Harvard in 1941, World War II created a demand for specialists in Latin American economics that exceeded the supply of credible experts. As a result, historians, geographers, and others were recruited to fill the demand, along with a few others who were brought into the Latin American field in "shot-gun weddings or marriages of convenience."[42]

In Burgin's estimation, wartime interest in the Latin American economies had quickly faded, an assessment with which Earl Hamilton would surely have concurred. At the meeting of the Joint Committee in 1946, Hamilton observed that the field did not attract promising students. He also noted that the American Economics Association had declined to include a Latin American session on the program of its forthcoming conference, even though the conference was to be devoted entirely to the subject of public debt.[43]

Despite Hamilton's gloomy observations, in reality the field exhibited modest growth, as can be seen in the expansion of course offerings. The postwar period also saw the appearance of *Inter-American Economic Affairs*, a quarterly journal published in Washington under the direction of Simon G. Hanson. After receiving a doctorate from Harvard in 1938 with a dissertation on the Argentine meat industry, Hanson had served in various federal agencies during the war and was the author of several books, including *Utopia in Uruguay* (1938).

In addition, during the fifteen years after 1935, several economists who received doctorates became and remained Latin Americanists. Some held positions with the federal government for many years. George Wythe, for example, who earned a doctorate from George Washington University in 1938 and published an influential study titled *Industry in Latin America* (1945), spent his entire career in the employ of the Commerce and State departments. The same was true of Burgin, who was employed by various agencies, including the Library of Congress and the State Department. From 1949 until his death in 1957 he was head of the Division of Research for American Republics in the State Department's Office of Intelligence Research. Burgin also served as editor-in-chief of the *Handbook of Latin American Studies* from 1941 to 1948. His dissertation, published with the title *Economic Aspects of Argentine Federalism* in 1946, was a major contribution to the early nineteenth-century history of that country.

Other young economists with a Latin American specialization remained in academe. Among them was Wendell C. Gordon (PhD, New York University, 1940), who was on the faculty of the University of Texas and published *The Economy of Latin America* (1950), which became a basic text for college courses. Another younger scholar in the field, Robert J. Alexander, wrote a dissertation (1950) on organized labor in Chile. Although he was a member of the Economics Department at Rutgers for his entire career, Alexander also taught courses in political science and labor studies, his primary research fields. In the 1950s he made annual visits to Latin America under the sponsorship of U.S. labor unions, with funding from government and CIA sources.[44]

Alexander received his doctorate from Columbia, where he studied under Frank Tannenbaum, still a member of the History Department. In 1950 Tannenbaum published his *Mexico: The Struggle for Peace and Bread*, in which he questioned that country's seemingly headlong drive to industrialize and indicated that it would do better to strengthen its agricultural sector, especially that segment of it rooted in the small rural community. Sanford A. Mosk, who had returned to Berkeley after his wartime service, raised questions similar to Tannenbaum's in his *Industrial Revolution in Mexico* (1950) and suggested that Mexico should pause to take stock of the pace and nature of its efforts to industrialize.

Mosk reviewed the state of Latin Americanist economics in a 1949 article. Despite some signs of progress, he said, he did not anticipate substantial increases in the ranks of economists with a Latin American specialization. Not only was a regional orientation foreign to the training of economists, but also the prospects for those who did work in the subfield where the need was greatest—the internal dimensions of Latin American economies as opposed to their international economic relations—were not inviting: "a small audience, limited teaching opportunities, the need to do much collateral work in other social sciences and in history, the assurance that most of this work cannot bear fruit in immediate publication, and meager sources of quantitative and other economic data." Only in economic history did Latin America offer fertile ground for economists: "The economic historian is prepared for fruitful work in Latin American economics by his interest in institutions and by his academic training, and psychologically, too, he is prepared to work in a marginal, inter-disciplinary field."[45]

In his 1942 survey Leonard called sociology "one of the most neglected disciplines, while one of the most essential for an understanding of Latin America in the United States." In 1948 Basadre saw some advances, as sociology gradually moved forward "to riper maturity and a better coordinated effectiveness."[46] In fact, sociology had made very limited gains. Like economics, the field was organized on the basis of nonregional specializations, and in the postwar years only a handful of sociologists claimed to be Latin Americanists. Even so, productivity in the field had advanced to the point that sociology was allotted its own section in the *Handbook of Latin American Studies* in 1951.

The most senior of the group, W. Rex Crawford, was mainly a student of social thought. Donald Pierson, Lowry Nelson, Nathan Whetten, and T. Lynn Smith continued their work on Latin America during the postwar years. At the University of Florida, where he moved in 1949, Smith was able to train younger scholars, such as John V. Saunders, who received his doctorate in 1955 and became a Brazilian specialist like his mentor.

Merely a Wartime Fad?

The 1948–49 Pan-American Union survey showed that numerous institutions offered multidisciplinary majors or programs in Latin American studies. A few, such as the University of Texas, maintained an Institute of Latin American Studies. The concept of area studies—at its most basic, an academic program that combined language training with courses in the history, society, and culture of a geographic region—antedated World War II but gained great impetus as a result of wartime experiences with such programs. The Inter-American Training Center was mentioned in chapter 6, but the U.S. Army sponsored much larger programs for its personnel (which excluded Latin America). The Army Specialized Training Program–Foreign Area and Language Study and the Civil Affairs Training School, for enlisted men and commissioned officers, respectively, were established in 1943 at universities that could offer the required languages and related courses in short, intensive sessions. At its peak in December 1943 the Army Specialized Training Program–Foreign Area and Language Study enrolled more than thirteen thousand students in fifty-five institutions. The Ethnogeographic Board has also been cited as a precursor of postwar area studies programs because of its accumulation of information on area specialists and the reports and conferences it sponsored on regions important in the war effort.[47]

After the war, interest in area studies remained keen among some scholars and the Social Science Research Council, which sponsored a conference on the study of world areas in November 1947. Charles Wagley, who wrote the conference report, stressed that area studies were even more important in the postwar era when international understanding was the objective. "Thus," he wrote, "area studies are not to be regarded as military preparation for war, and the fact that some knowledge so gained can be useful in war is not pertinent to this discussion. Such knowledge is just as necessary for international cooperation between peoples of very diverse values, ideologies, and objectives as it is for effective international competition."[48]

The conference report made it clear that the participants conceived of area studies as heavily weighted in favor of the social sciences. Participants envisioned integrated research projects involving area specialists from various disciplines; the Tarascan and Virú Valley projects were mentioned as possible models.[49] Discussion of instruction in area studies emphasized the training of graduate students who should have knowledge of the language(s) of their chosen area as well as field experience there. Area studies were seen as complementing, not replacing, training in a discipline, and there was no support for granting doctorates in the field. Areas represented at the conference were Latin America, Europe, the Soviet Union, the Near East, the Far East, and Southeast Asia and India.

The report of the Latin American panel at the conference exuded a bit of complacency. It noted that Latin America had long been the focus of interdisciplinary study and that Latin Americanists had already addressed many of the problems that faced other area specialists.[50] Indeed, a survey by Wendell Bennett for the Social Science Research Council in 1951 showed that six universities offered what were called integrated area programs in Latin American studies— California, North Carolina, Stanford, Texas, Tulane, and Vanderbilt—and another nine had significant offerings.[51] Moreover, in 1947 the Carnegie Corporation of New York had made grants of approximately $60,000 each to North Carolina, Texas, Tulane, and Vanderbilt for a five-year cooperative program to develop centers for Latin American studies. Each of the institutions was to concentrate on a specific subregion: Mexico, in the case of Texas; Brazil, Vanderbilt; Central America, Tulane; and the Southern Cone of South America, North Carolina.[52]

Despite the apparent vitality of Latin America in the universe of area studies, in reality in the 1950s the field suffered a substantial decline relative to other regions. In part, this trend can be attributed to the cold war and the emergence of conflicts in other parts of the world that created interest in them as well as a demand for specialists, especially the Soviet Union, the Near East, and the Far East. During the decade following the end of World War II, Latin America, except for the case of Guatemala, seemed remote from the main arenas of cold war contention and therefore peripheral to the concerns of policy makers, social scientists, and other scholars who had no prior interest in the region. As the geographer Preston James observed, "After the invasion of Africa attention to Latin America sharply decreased; and between that time and Mr. Nixon's visit to South America in 1958, Latin American problems were given the lowest priority, and public interest in that part of the world all but disappeared."[53]

There may also have been vestiges of the old belief held by some that Latin America was not worthy of sustained academic study. William N. Fenton suggested as much in reviewing area studies programs before and just after the war: "Whether Latin America offers the depth of other areas is questionable. That the preoccupation with Latin America was a wartime fad—'a notion and not a spinal interest,' as one professor put it—may be demonstrated by the reluctance of administrators to sponsor programs in this area after the war."[54]

Bennett's findings bore out the latter assertion. The six integrated area programs in Latin American studies that he identified in 1951 were the same that had existed in 1946. Meanwhile, the number of programs in other areas had increased during the five-year period: those dealing with Russia from three to five, for example, and with the Far East, from four to eight. Moreover, Latin America seemed to be falling behind these areas in the production of new researchers. Bennett's survey showed that in the spring of 1951 there were fifty-eight third-year doctoral students in Russian programs, fifty in Far Eastern programs, and only fifteen in Latin American programs.[55]

Another sign of the declining interest in Latin America was the demise of the Joint Committee on Latin American Studies in 1947. By late 1943 Lewis Hanke sensed a lack of enthusiasm for the committee and wrote to Haring: "My own feeling . . . is that unless the S.S.R.C. decides to take an active interest and support the Joint Committee with its ideas and with funds, the Joint Committee ought to be abandoned."[56] No such interest or support was forthcoming, and the three sponsoring councils decided to terminate it as of July 1, 1947, citing financial and personnel considerations and uncertainty over its future role now that the war was over. The councils formed a small committee to investigate future needs in the field. In April 1948 this group, which was chaired by anthropologist John Gillin, recommended the formation of a new committee, which "could be most useful in continuing the momentum already acquired in Latin America if its purpose were one of stimulating thought on current problems and of affording scientists of all disciplines a means of exchanging views."[57] These recommendations went unheeded, and no new committee was formed. Meanwhile, the Social Science Research Council and the American Council of Learned Societies established a Joint Committee on Slavic Studies in 1948, and the SSRC sponsored a Committee on the Near and Middle East in 1950.

Latin American studies also fared relatively poorly in external funding by private agencies. After its previously mentioned 1947 grants, the Carnegie Corporation in subsequent years awarded an additional $85,000 to Tulane for the support of Latin American studies and $25,000 to North Carolina for the study of the Latin American political process. Meanwhile, it awarded much larger sums for area studies in other regions, for example, $155,000 in 1947 to the University of Pennsylvania for studies on India; $875,000 between 1947 and 1957 to Harvard for its new Russian Research Center; $250,000 in 1954 to Columbia for East European studies; and $200,000 in 1956 to Columbia to enable U.S. Russian specialists to visit the Soviet Union.

During these lean years, of course, new and established scholars of Latin America continued their teaching and research and tried to maintain contact with each other. As Howard Cline observed, "Several individual Latin Americanists persisted in their seemingly futile efforts to prevent their chosen specialization from degenerating into a shabby genteel academic slum. Singly, in pairs, or in small groups, they worked at the thankless task of rebuilding."[58] In the absence of the Joint Committee on Latin American Studies or any national organization, Latin Americanists, supported by the Pan-American Union, took steps to form regionally based, multidisciplinary associations. After meetings at Columbia and the University of Delaware in 1953, the Northeastern Council for Latin American and Inter-American Studies was chartered. Supported by the dues of individual members and institutions, the group, renamed the Council for Latin American Affairs in 1957, held annual conferences on different themes during the 1950s.[59] Over the same period regional councils were established to cover other sections of the country: the Southeast, the Pacific Coast, Rocky Mountains, and Middle Atlantic. There were other bright spots. Despite perennial funding problems, the *Handbook of Latin American Studies* continued to appear, the editorial costs now being borne by the Library of Congress. In the late 1940s the new Henry L. and Grace Doherty Foundation began to provide fellowships to American graduates students to conduct research in Latin America. Between 1947 and 1957 the foundation awarded fellowships worth nearly $300,000 to seventy-four Americans, more than half of them in history and anthropology.[60]

Starting in 1958, an interested observer might have discerned some evidence of rising concern with Latin America on the part of the foundations and the learned societies. An important figure in encouraging this tendency was Howard Cline, who had succeeded Lewis Hanke as director of the Hispanic Foundation in 1952. Cline had experienced in his own career the effects of the relative indifference to Latin American studies. A student of C. H. Haring at Harvard, Cline received his PhD with a dissertation on nineteenth-century Yucatan that remained unpublished. Like Haring, he was employed by Yale but found little support for Latin America. "Unfortunately my experience at Yale has tended to parallel yours," he wrote to Haring in 1948. "After a considerable initial optimism about the Latin American field, the administration and the department rather visibly cooled." In 1948 he moved to Northwestern, where there was a cohort of Latin Americanists in various departments and where "the Latin American field ıs ñôt only respectable but a central interest of the administration and the student body." He soon became disillusioned, however, about the extent of Northwestern's commitment to Latin America and decided to move to Washington. When Northwestern's History Department planned to hire a specialist on the Far East instead of replacing him with another Latin Americanist, he wrote to the chairman to express his belief that a mistake had been made, given Northwestern's "weak resources ... material and human" in the Asian field. It grieved him, he added, "to see one of the last ... strongholds of Hispanic studies succumb to the headline hunters."[61]

Cline himself identified a one-day conference convened by the American Council of Learned Societies in April 1958 as the beginning of a "general renovative movement in Latin American studies." The conference stemmed from the concern of the ACLS about the "many gaps and shortcomings in the Latin American fields in American institutions of higher learning." Chaired by Cline, the conference was attended by about fifteen scholars and representatives of foundations and learned societies and was intended, among other objectives, to consider whether there was a need for a national body to coordinate the activities of practitioners in the field. Cline prepared a working paper for the conference in which he indicated that the various disciplines had advanced little beyond the state in which Leonard had found them in 1942. In discussing individual institutions, he did not mince words about the quality of their programs. He considered that Tulane was emerging as an outstanding Latin American center and that the University of Arizona was a "sleeper" whose work had been improving steadily in quality and quantity. By contrast, "the earlier promise that Vanderbilt would become a great Brazilian center has completely collapsed," he said, and training and research programs at Florida had yet to prove themselves: "This institution has the unfortunate tendency to confuse activity with progress."[62]

A survey of Latin Americanist courses commissioned by Cline in 1957–58 and paid for in part by the United Fruit Company also revealed slight progress since the 1940s. The survey of 821 institutions showed that the number of such courses had risen to 3,854, an increase of about 15 percent from the total of 3,346 at the larger group of institutions surveyed in 1948. The increases came mainly in a few fields, however: commercial Spanish (247 percent), anthropology (43.4 percent), and literature (25 percent). The number of courses in history rose by only 4.6 percent while there were slight decreases in geography and political science/international relations. In other fields the decline was more substantial: sociology, 34.6 percent; economics, 37.7 percent; and Brazilian Portuguese, 61.6 percent (see table 7.2).

The April 1958 conference yielded few concrete results, but it led to the con-

Table 7.2
Changes in Distribution of Disciplines, By Courses, 1957 vs. 1948

	1957	1948	% Change
Disciplines showing increase			
History	1,147	1,097	+ 4.6
Literature	1,096	877	+ 25.0
Anthropology	185	129	+ 43.4
Commercial Spanish	170	49	+247.0
Disciplines showing decrease*			
Geography	358	361	<1.0
Political Science	246	254	–3.0
Economics	81	130	–37.7
Sociology	34	52	–34.6
Brazilian Portuguese	5	13	–61.6
Number of institutions surveyed	821	875	

*Other fields showing decreases were civilization, music, religion, education, and philosophy. Source: *Latin American Fields and Disciplines at Major and Lesser Institutions of Higher Learning: A Statistical Panorama, Hispanic Foundation Survey Reports,* No. 5 (Washington, 1958).

vocation of a larger gathering at the Newberry Library in Chicago in November 1958. Sponsored by the library and the American Council of Learned Societies, the conference was chaired by Frederick Burkhardt, president of the ACLS, who noted the apparent decline in teaching and research related to Latin America. There was, however, the possibility of increased federal funding to support projects with a Latin American orientation.[63] Thus, the moment seemed propitious for the formulation of long-term plans. Cline, Charles Wagley, Miron Burgin, John Lloyd Mecham, and others reviewed the state of each discipline, pointing out how Latin Americanists were faring and what research problems needed to be addressed. Working papers showed, in accordance with the above-mentioned survey, that Latin American anthropology was flourishing, along with the study of the Spanish language and Spanish American literature. Latin American history, by contrast, seemed to be marginalized within the profession, and the percentage of doctoral dissertations within the field had declined from 10.1 percent of the total in 1947–51 to 5.6 percent of the total in 1952–56. In the case of geography, courses related to Latin America were numerous, accounting for about 22 percent of all geography courses on major world areas in 1957, but the number of significant graduate programs was small, and only a handful of geographers were actively engaged in research and writing about the area.[64]

The conference did not adopt a five-year program for the improvement of Latin Americanist scholarship in the United States, as was originally intended, but it did reach several conclusions. Among them was the need for fellowships and grants for fieldwork in the region: "It was the view of the group that students and scholars interested in Latin America were offered fewer opportunities for field research, either through university or national programs than were enjoyed by their colleagues who specialized in any other of the principal regions of the world."[65] In addition, the conference emphasized the importance of stimulating Luso-Brazilian studies through special fellowships and greater attention to Portuguese language training. The conference also endorsed the idea of creating a new joint committee on Latin American studies.

No such committee was formed immediately, but the signs were clearly evident—in references to federal funding, for example—that positive changes were on the way that would alter the long years of academic and public indifference to Latin America. In the changed environment the preliminary work done at the 1958 conferences would serve as a basis for the explosive growth in Latin American studies that would soon occur.

8

The Boom Years, 1958–1975

Reviewing the 1958 Newberry Library conference, Bryce Wood of the Social Science Research Council attributed the relative decline of scholarly interest in Latin America over the past fifteen years to the "tepid climate of opinion about the significance of Latin America that prevailed until recently in the United States." He believed, however, that a change was in the air: "Stirrings of concern and calls to action are now replacing plaints of 'neglect' of Latin America and of inter-American relationships. The new atmosphere may originate in political clouds, and it may not be of long duration, but one of its accompanying phenomena is a fresh look at area studies in the United States concerned with the other American republics."[1] Wood's comments were prescient, for in the subsequent fifteen years the academic study of Latin America would experience an era of growth that far eclipsed the expansion of 1935–45. He erred in speculating that the new atmosphere might be short-lived, for although there was a contraction starting in the early 1970s, the study of Latin America remained more firmly embedded in academe than ever before. As in earlier periods, the advance of Latin American studies was linked to international trends and governmental concerns. These in turn produced increased federal spending, more intense attention, and a stronger financial commitment from foundations, the learned societies, and the universities themselves.

Directly or indirectly the cold war provided the impetus for much of the renewed interest in Latin America. Except for a few incidents, notably the Guatemalan episode of the early 1950s, the region was not initially perceived as a major arena for East-West confrontation. This perception began to change in the late 1950s. The hostility directed at Vice President Richard Nixon in Lima and Caracas during his Latin American tour in May 1958 gave evidence of frayed relationships and a rising Communist threat and contributed to the Eisenhower administration's decision to modify its economic policies for the region, in particular by agreeing to support the proposed Inter-American Development Bank. With the triumph of the Cuban Revolution in 1959, Latin America became a focal point of the cold war struggle as Fidel Castro established commercial and diplomatic ties with the Soviet Union, proclaimed his adherence to Marxism-Leninism, and vowed to export his revolutionary model throughout the hemisphere.

In response, the U.S. government adopted a variety of policies to contain and reduce the Communist threat to the region: overt and covert efforts to destroy the Castro regime, isolation of Cuba within the hemisphere, and counter-insurgency assistance to Latin American armed forces. The Kennedy administration also expanded economic aid to Latin America and launched the Alliance for Progress in 1961 with the stated hope of encouraging economic and social reform within the region to ameliorate the poverty and inequities that had presumably contributed to Castro's rise and that might foster radical revolutions elsewhere. The Peace Corps, also created in 1961, sent many young volunteers to Latin America, including the very first contingent, which went to Colombia; some returned to take up postgraduate studies of the region.[2]

While heightening U.S. awareness of hemispheric problems, these developments also helped transform Latin America from a region with unique historical and cultural ties to the United States to a part of the Third World, that is, underdeveloped and non-Western. Indeed, a government publication of 1964 included Latin America as well as Eastern Europe in the non-Western world "because these areas share the contemporary problems of social and economic development of the geographically non-Western world and because they have resided outside the mainstream of American academic attention."[3] Accordingly, Latin America could be seen as a suitable laboratory for studying problems of development affecting other regions with similar characteristics. Bryce Wood expressed this perspective in his review of the 1958 conference:

> Latin America shares with other under-developed areas throughout the world the problems and turmoil of economic growth by forced draft. In this respect, Latin America equals other regions in offering interesting data to research-minded social scientists concerned with the contemporary scene and its trends. As a field for comparative studies of urbanization, ethnic relationships, and educational policy, to mention only a few, Latin America may be on the way to recognition as being no less promising than other continents previously regarded as more appealing because more exotic or more exposed.[4]

Wood's recommendations were in keeping with the dominant social science paradigm of the late 1950s and 1960s—modernization theory—which suggested that developing nations throughout the world might follow a similar path to Western-style economic development. As envisioned by the chief architects of the model, economic modernization would be accompanied by social change (especially the expansion of the middle class) and political democratization. Thus, the study of modernization could offer a fertile field for all kinds of social scientists. In addition, as Latin America gained prominence in national discourse, scholars who had not been specialists in the area might retool themselves as Latin Americanists. An official of the Ford Foundation observed in 1964: "Many senior U.S. scholars who have begun to work on . . . problems in Africa, Asia, and the Middle East having quite recently discovered Latin America, they have encouraged an expanding stream of lively pre- and post-doctoral research work on Latin America. Latin America has quite suddenly been discovered to be relatively accessible to North American professors and their students for depth research on social, economic, and political problems of societies involved in revolutionary change."[5]

"That Halcyon Period . . ."[6]

The cold war as reflected in the anxieties generated by the successful launch of the Soviet satellite Sputnik in 1957 played a significant role in the most important direct federal contribution to the expansion of Latin American studies in the 1960s, namely, the National Defense Education Act (NDEA) of 1958. Although the need to overcome the apparent Soviet advantage in science provided impetus for passage of the legislation, in reality the Sputnik crisis afforded an opportunity for those who had long sought, without success, a larger federal role in education to achieve their goals. Among these proponents were the Modern Language Association and other advocates of improved and expanded training in foreign languages and associated area studies.[7]

It was this feature of the NDEA that would be most beneficial to Latin American studies. As originally enacted, Title VI, section 601a, of the NDEA authorized the commissioner of education to enter into contracts with institutions of higher learning for the establishment and operation of centers for the teaching of modern foreign languages in which instruction was deemed inadequate. In addition, centers might offer instruction in fields such as history, geography, and political science needed to obtain a "full understanding" of the region in which a given language was spoken. Under the terms of the NDEA, the federal government would provide up to 50 percent of the cost of the centers, and a maximum of $8 million might be appropriated in any given year. By July 1961 forty-six centers were in operation throughout the country, but because the NDEA had specified support for neglected languages, Spanish was excluded. Portuguese was not, and it was the focus of language and area centers established at New York University and the University of Wisconsin.

On June 1, 1961, the commissioner of education announced that Spanish as spoken in Latin America would henceforth be designated as a language in which adequate advanced instruction was not then available. The commissioner attributed the decision to the fact that even as the United States was embarking on "sustained and varied efforts to assist Latin American peoples in social, economic, educational, and cultural development," the field of Latin American studies was seriously deficient in the "kind of advanced educational resources for which the NDEA language and area center authorization was created." Accordingly, a small number of Latin American language and area centers would be funded to strengthen advanced language instruction and the relevant disciplines. Five universities were selected in December 1961: Columbia, Florida, Texas, Tulane, and UCLA. By 1963–64 the language and area centers at these institutions and those at NYU and Wisconsin accounted for 12.5 percent ($312,700) of NDEA support for all centers.[8] Nahuatl and Quechua had also become targeted languages. Over the next few years additional universities received NDEA center funding, among them Stanford, Miami, Illinois, Cornell, and New Mexico.

Under Title IV, section 601b, of the NDEA, stipends for advanced training in the designated languages and fields were to be awarded to graduate students enrolled at area centers and other American institutions of higher education. In 1961 students of Spanish America as well as Brazilianists became eligible for a new Latin American National Defense Fellowship Program (Program B).[9] This program provided for the awarding of fellowships to graduate students preparing (1) to teach Spanish, Portuguese, or other Latin American languages at the college level, (2) to teach in another field for which competence in one of the aforementioned languages was highly desirable, or (3) for other employment in which command of a Latin American language was desirable. Stipends for nonmatriculating advanced study by professors and others were also available under the program.

While NDEA fellowships were intended primarily for study in the United States, several other federal programs provided support for research and study overseas. The Fulbright-Hays Act of 1961 aided mainly predoctoral students, and the National Endowment for the Humanities, established in 1965, awarded nearly $315,000 in postdoctoral grants for Latin America in 1967–71, primarily in history, language and literature, and anthropology. The National Science Foundation supported dissertation and postdoctoral research in Latin America by anthropologists and other social scientists. The Agency for International Development and the Department of Defense expended substantial amounts as well, but mainly for contract research on topics selected by them.[10]

Supplementing the role of the federal government were the foundations, especially the Carnegie Corporation of New York and the Ford Foundation. As mentioned in chapter 7, during the postwar years the Carnegie Corporation had generously supported area studies and programs involving non-Western areas and had provided limited funding for several Latin American programs. As early as 1954, its officials had concluded that Latin America was not receiving adequate attention from U.S. scholars. In that year William W. Marvel, an executive assistant at the Carnegie Corporation, invited Howard F. Cline to a meeting to discuss the state of social science research pertaining to Latin America. "In numbers, scope and variety," Marvel wrote, "the studies and investigation by American scholars are not . . . fully commensurate with the vast potentialities of the Latin American area as a source of additions to our store of knowledge of human behavior and social problems."[11] Even so, substantial funding for Latin America did not come until 1959, when the Carnegie Corporation awarded Cornell $250,000 for a five-year program of training and research in Andean South America. Even more significant, it awarded $190,000 to the American Council of Learned Societies and the Social Science Research Council to advance research on Latin America. The grant was to be expended over a three-year period; in 1962 an additional $50,000 was authorized.

The Carnegie Corporation grant came in response to a request from Frederick Burkhardt and Pendleton Herring, presidents of the ACLS and SSRC, respectively. In a letter dated April 29, 1959, they pointed out that Latin American studies in the United States had remained "largely dormant" during the past fifteen years: "Except in a few fields, notably archaeology and anthropology, leading scholars in the United States have not viewed Latin America as offering significant research opportunities, and aside from one or two institutions, the university area centers for Latin American studies have not matched the initiative and energy shown by specialists on other areas." The presidents considered the moment propitious for a "freshening" of the field, partly because of the "restiveness" of established practitioners. In addition, "Latin America itself is in process of rapid change; it is becoming politically more important, and more intellectually challenging than it was before 1939. Latin America has joined the modern world; its social manifestations are interesting in themselves and they offer opportunities for refining generalizations in a number of fields, such as urbanization, comparative politics, demography, and economic growth."[12]

In accordance with the recommendations of the 1958 Newberry Library conference, the presidents proposed in their letter of April 29, 1959, the creation of a new Joint Committee on Latin American Studies. The committee would use Carnegie Corporation funding to advance research in a variety of ways, such as the holding of seminars and conferences and the awarding of grants to scholars holding the PhD who were interested in engaging in research on contemporary Latin America, especially "in the badly neglected field of Brazilian studies." The presidents hoped that the various programs envisioned would attract scholars who had not previously conducted research on Latin America. Two of the members suggested for the proposed seven-man committee had only a "peripheral interest" in the region, but it was thought that their participation would bring "significant external stimulus and knowledge to bear on the formulation of plans."[13]

The Joint Committee was duly organized in 1959 along the lines proposed by the presidents. Sanford Mosk was the first chairman, but after his death in 1960 he was succeeded by Robert N. Burr, a historian on the UCLA faculty. As intended, the committee used the bulk of the Carnegie Corporation funds on grants to individuals for field research in Latin America. During the four years 1959–63 the committee assisted fifty-five individuals (four of whom were women) in the following fields: history, 18; language and literature, 10; government and politics, 9; sociology, 5; economics, 5; anthropology, 4; geography, 2; psychology, 2.[14]

Another goal of the Joint Committee and its sponsors was to enhance communication among Latin Americanists in the United States and between them and their Latin American counterparts. To further these ends, it organized or sponsored several conferences between 1959 and 1963, either alone or in cooperation with other groups. The first of these was the Inter-American Conference on Research and Training in Sociology, held at the Center for Advanced Study in the Behavioral Sciences at Palo Alto, California, in August 1961. Funded by the Council for Higher Education in the American Republics, the conference brought together sociologists from the United States and five Latin American countries (Argentina, Brazil, Chile, Colombia, and Costa Rica).[15] Formal papers were not presented; instead, the participants discussed the history and current status of sociology in their respective areas and mulled over prospects for scholarly communication and collaboration. The committee organized a similar meeting—the Inter-American Conference on Research and Training in Economics—in Santiago, Chile, in 1962 under the cosponsorship of the Council for Higher Education in the American Republics and the Instituto de Economía of the University of Chile.

The next major conference organized by the committee was based on the theme "Continuity and Change in Latin America." Held in Scottsdale, Arizona, in early 1963, it featured papers by several scholars that were published in 1964 in a volume of the same name edited by John J. Johnson of Stanford. In the introduction Johnson argued that social and political change in Latin America, either through reform or through revolution, was inevitable. "Latin America has a new sense of purpose," he wrote, and "modernization has top priority on the list of attainable goals." The bulk of the volume was made up of essays on important groups, such as peasants, industrial workers, and the military. R. P. Dore, a sociologist and Japan specialist, contributed the concluding essay, which compared Latin America with Japan as well as the issues that confronted foreign students of the two areas. He suggested that Latin America aroused sharper divisions of opinion than Japan among their respective students because of the great political, social, and economic problems in the former, "the competing solutions for which evoke strong political emotions." By contrast, contemporary Japan seemed to have fewer problems and therefore was less of "a society about which something should be done."[16]

Another result of the Scottsdale conference was the decision to convene a seven-week seminar in the summer of 1963 to assess the state of knowledge of Latin America in the various disciplines and to identify opportunities for research in the region. The members of the Joint Committee were to act as continuing members of the seminar, along with several others, including Raymond Carr of St. Antony's College, Oxford, and representatives of the Ford Foundation. Ralph W. Tyler, director of the Center for Study in the Behavioral Sciences at Palo Alto, where the seminar took place, served as chairman.

During the seminar, specialists discussed the major disciplines, mainly emphasizing American contributions, at sessions of several days each. For each discipline a paper was prepared beforehand, and the revised papers were published as *Social Science Research on Latin America* (1964), under the editorship of Charles Wagley.[17] In addition to history and the social sciences, law was represented in a chapter by Kenneth L. Karst of Ohio State University, who noted a "surge of law school interest in Latin America," which he called "part of our general national response to the region's social revolution."[18] Among the areas that he identified as offering good research opportunities were those related to land reform, an issue of intense contemporary interest, as shown by the fact that one of the seminar sessions was devoted to land tenure and legal institutions.

Funding for the seminar was provided by the Ford Foundation. The event thus underscored the increasing prominence of the Ford Foundation in providing support for programs to advance Latin American studies by scholars from the United States and within Latin America itself. Possessed of resources substantially larger than those of the Carnegie Corporation, the Ford Foundation had devoted large sums since the mid-1950s to its International Training and Re-

search program, which sought to "strengthen American knowledge and competence in international affairs through support for the study of international relations and foreign areas at colleges and universities." In the 1950s it emphasized
Asia, Africa, the Near East, the Soviet Union, and Eastern Europe, "areas about
which American research and teaching have been seriously deficient."[19] Thus, in
1959–60 it awarded Columbia $5.5 million and Harvard $5.6 million to develop
their programs in these non-Western areas. The aforementioned regions were
also the focus of the foundation's Foreign Area Fellowship Program (FAFP), begun in 1952, which provided grants to advanced graduate students. In the early
1960s the foundation added Latin America to the targeted areas of both programs in an effort to correct deficiencies noted by foundation officials:

> By comparison with other area fields, Latin American studies in the United
> States have not attracted the most capable scholars or produced commit-
> ments by the stronger universities. There is a dearth of contemporary and
> "problem" research, particularly in the social sciences; the supply of senior
> and middle-rank scholars is not adequate; research, teaching, and refer-
> ence materials for the full range of academic, government, and commer-
> cial and other uses are deficient. Although an increase in the numbers and
> quality of junior people can be noted, the field as a whole suffers by com-
> parison with Soviet, East Asian, and African studies.[20]

The foundation received guidance on Latin American projects from Carl B.
Spaeth, whom it engaged as a consultant in June 1962. Spaeth, a former dean of
the Stanford Law School and former director of the foundation's overseas activities, had extensive experience in the region. He now traveled widely in the
United States and Latin America, conferred with academics and officials, and
made a series of recommendations to the foundation, including the initial suggestion that led to the Palo Alto seminar. He also stressed the importance of re-
cruiting established scholars who were not Latin American specialists to the
field.[21]

In keeping with Spaeth's recommendations and its concerns as stated above,
the Ford Foundation adopted a multifaceted approach toward Latin America,
which can be described only briefly here.[22] In 1962 it awarded $1 million to the
SSRC for a three-year program of faculty interchange between Latin American institutions and selected U.S. universities, including California-Berkeley,
UCLA, Columbia, Harvard, Minnesota, and Texas. The following year it authorized the expenditure of $1.5 million for "experimental and exploratory"
grants: $400,000 for postdoctoral fellowships to promising Latin American-
ists and scholars who wished to develop expertise in the Latin American field;

$250,000 to the Hispanic Foundation of the Library of Congress for bibliographies and other research aids and for a program to coordinate the acquisition of Latin American materials nationally; $275,000 to universities in the New York and Chicago areas for faculty research and graduate student training; and $575,000 to the University of Texas for research and training in various disciplines related to Middle America and for training of library specialists. Cornell University also received $550,000.

In 1965 the foundation made grants totalling $2.65 million to Florida, New Mexico, Stanford, Tulane, and Wisconsin to support programs in Latin American studies. The University of Kansas and Pennsylvania State University were among later beneficiaries of Ford Foundation funds. By the early 1970s, however, budgetary constraints and bureaucratic problems in dealing with the universities led the foundation to end its direct support of Latin American centers.[23] Meanwhile, other organizations had received substantial Ford grants, among them the Brookings Institution and the Conference on Latin American History.

The Joint Committee was another beneficiary of the Ford Foundation's increased interest in Latin America. In the 1960s the foundation replaced the Carnegie Corporation as the committee's primary benefactor with a three-year grant of $300,000 (1963–66) and a five-year grant of $1 million (1966–71). Indeed, as an internal 1996 Ford Foundation review asserted: "Increasingly, over time, the JCLAS evolved into the primary Foundation vehicle for channeling assistance targeted toward the continued growth and development of Latin American studies in the United States."[24] The committee continued to devote the larger part of its funds to grants to individuals for postdoctoral research and lesser amounts for conferences, such as a gathering in Rio de Janeiro in 1965 that assessed the state of social science research in Latin America, much as the 1963 Scottsdale meeting had done with respect to American scholarship.

One result of the Rio meeting was a new emphasis by the Joint Committee on collaborative projects involving Latin American scholars in the expectation that they would encourage research relevant to contemporary problems in the region. As Manuel Diégues stated in his introduction to the conference papers, the problems studied by American social scientists "are not those which have the most direct bearing on the needs or aspirations of our peoples; nor are they problems or subjects of importance for the regional development process."[25] Accordingly, in 1966 the committee began to encourage interregional collaboration by offering grants to senior scholars—one from the United States or Canada and one from Latin America—who proposed joint projects, with resulting publications to appear in the two appropriate languages. In addition, Latin Americans began to be appointed to the committee, starting with the Colombian sociologist Orlando Fals Borda in 1966. There were some reservations about the emphasis on collaboration. Kalman Silvert later recalled that he had been opposed from the outset: "The reasons had not alone to do with my habitual distrust of faddism, but also with my feeling that North American scholars should not be constrained by Latin American definitions of what it is right and proper to investigate in Latin America."[26]

In the 1970s the Ford Foundation remained the primary financial backer of the Joint Committee, which assumed responsibility for a wider array of predoctoral and postdoctoral programs. For a time, research training fellowships were awarded, and seminars held in Latin America, for North American and Latin American graduate students. Internships in Latin America were offered to recent graduates of schools of business, engineering, and agronomy. Finally, in 1973 the Joint Committee assumed responsibility for the Latin America sector of the FAFP, which had previously been administered by a separate joint committee of the SSRC and ACLS.[27]

During the mid-1960s the Joint Committee and the Ford Foundation contributed significantly to the realization of two goals long sought by Latin Americanists: the creation of a multidisciplinary journal and the establishment of a national organization of regional specialists. As noted earlier, the desirability of a journal for Latin Americanists, particularly one that would serve as a publishing outlet for research in the social sciences, had been discussed at a meeting of the first Joint Committee in 1946. The matter was raised again in 1964 at a meeting in Cuernavaca of representatives of the FAFP, the Title VI language and area centers, and other universities with Latin American programs. The Institute of Latin American Studies of the University of Texas had drafted a proposal for a journal and, with the endorsement of the Cuernavaca group, obtained pledges from twenty universities and the Hispanic Foundation that each would contribute $1,000 a year for two years to support such a publication. In addition, the Ford Foundation awarded a three-year grant of $40,000 to the fledgling journal, which appeared in 1965 as the *Latin American Research Review (LARR)*.[28]

Meanwhile, initiatives leading to the organization of a national association of Latin Americanists were taking a parallel course. Proposals for the creation of such a group dated at least as far back as the 1940s and were reiterated at the 1958 meeting in New York sponsored by the American Council of Learned Societies. As a result of the latter meeting, a conference was held at Sagamore, New York, near Syracuse, in August 1959 to discuss the objectives and structure of what was intended to be a permanent national council. The thirty-two persons who attended the Sagamore conference unanimously agreed to form a body to be called the Association of Latin American Studies (ALAS) and to appoint an organizing committee.[29]

The new association had a constitution and an interim executive committee and council before the end of 1959, but it soon became evident that the ALAS was not fulfilling expectations. In part the difficulties arose because of the inaction of the officers and the lack of funds. According to Howard Cline, a major structural problem stemmed from the uncertainty about the relationship of the ALAS to the regional councils of Latin American studies, each of which was represented on the council. By the early 1960s the ALAS was "clearly moribund," Cline wrote later, and its "spectacular failure . . . cast a dark shadow on any subsequent attempts to replace [it] with a better designed instrument."[30]

Despite this recent failure, participants at the 1964 Cuernavaca meeting took steps to launch a national organization of Latin Americanists. At the request of the Cuernavaca group, in February 1965 the Joint Committee created a subcommittee to look into the matter. Later that year scholars associated with the *LARR* and its supporting institutions took steps in the same direction. As a result of these initiatives, a Constitutional Committee was appointed and prepared a draft charter that was discussed, modified, and approved at an assembly of approximately seventy-five Latin Americanists and observers held on May 6–7, 1966, at the Library of Congress.[31]

Thus the Latin American Studies Association (LASA) was born. The assembly also elected Kalman Silvert as the first president of the new organization. Its purpose, according to the constitution, was to "provide a professional organization that will foster the concerns of all scholars interested in Latin American studies and will encourage more effective training, teaching, and research in connection with such studies, and will provide both a forum and an instrument for dealing with matters of common interest to the scholarly professions and to individuals concerned with Latin American studies." The new organization assumed responsibility for the *LARR*, which became its organ, and in 1967 it received a $100,000 grant from the Ford Foundation for support of its activities. Initially housed at the Hispanic Foundation, the LASA secretariat was moved to the University of Florida in 1972.[32]

Internal Tensions

The insertion of Latin America into the cold war during the 1960s created an unprecedented situation for Latin Americanists. Although there had been fears of European intervention in weak Caribbean Basin states before World War I and of Fascist penetration before and during World War II, the close military

and economic ties between Cuba and the Soviet Union after 1959 seemed to
pose a far greater threat to American security. As government and private funding stimulated academic study of the region, Latin Americanists would be called
on to examine their views on policy matters as never before. Initially, there was
consensus about the proper course to be followed both by scholars and by the
American government, but it broke down as the decade of the 1960s wore on, a
casualty of developments within Latin America and the United States and of
the emergence of a new generation of Latin Americanists.

During the 1950s the cold war had touched Latin Americanists only lightly.
Just a handful of academic Latin Americanists had been targets of the domestic anti-Communist crusade. The most notorious case was that of Maurice Halperin, who had been with the Office of Strategic Services during World War II.
Having retooled himself as a Latin Americanist with interdisciplinary expertise,
Halperin became director of the Latin American Regional Studies Department
at Boston University in 1949. Named by Elizabeth Bentley, a Soviet courier, as a
Soviet agent, he was called before the Senate Internal Security Subcommittee in
1953. Halperin invoked the Fifth Amendment but on one occasion denied any
involvement in espionage. Boston University was in the process of investigat-
ing his case when he fled to Mexico with his wife in the fall of 1953. In another
case, the ethnohistorian John V. Murra had come under scrutiny because of his
service in the International Brigade during the Spanish Civil War and other associations. His application for U.S. citizenship was initially blocked, and even
after a federal court ordered his naturalization in 1950, he was denied a passport
until 1956. The historian Benjamin Keen was barred from teaching for several
years because of his political views.[33]

During this era Latin Americanists who commented publicly on events in
the region or on U.S. policy usually assumed a posture in accordance with contemporary liberalism. Although hostile toward Communism, they faulted the
U.S. government for its neglect of the region and for excessive support of
right-wing dictatorships. These were among the criticisms made by economist
Robert J. Alexander in the April 1953 edition of *Foreign Policy Bulletin*. In a series
of recommendations to the new Eisenhower administration, Alexander urged
greater public investment by the United States and less cordiality toward the region's dictators, noting that the anti-Communist left was the "most significant
obstacle to totalitarianism in the area." In the same issue of this publication,
historian Arthur P. Whitaker expressed the hope that the Eisenhower administration would correct the inconsistency and lack of coordination characteristic
of recent U.S. policy toward Latin America, as evidenced by the "erratic course"
of the State Department in its dealings with Juan Perón. Elsewhere, in October
1953 Whitaker declared that because of the government's "inattention and mis-

takes" and the "indifference" of the public, the United States was headed toward a "first-rate crisis in inter-American relations."[34]

Latin America experienced its first major cold war crisis with the emergence of apparent links between the government of Jacobo Arbenz of Guatemala and that nation's Communist Party (Partido Guatemalteco de Trabajo) and by extension the Soviet Union. Writing in the *Foreign Policy Bulletin* in April 1954, Alexander acknowledged the Communists' penetration of the Guatemalan government but also warned: "Americans must not forget that there is a profound and long-overdue revolution going on in Guatemala, and that only at its own risk can the United States appear to be opposing this revolution." Ronald Schneider, who was given access by the Central Intelligence Agency to more than fifty thousand files from the offices of the Partido Guatemalteco de Trabajo after the overthrow of Arbenz in 1954, unearthed little evidence of Soviet control over Guatemalan Communists, though he asserted their influence in the country's labor movement and agrarian reform apparatus.[35]

At the time of Arbenz's ouster at the hands of the Guatemalan military and the establishment of a new government headed by Carlos Castillo Armas, the full extent of U.S. complicity in these events was not yet known. Latin Americanists, however, tended to criticize overt U.S. actions. Arthur Whitaker, who supervised Schneider's 1958 dissertation titled "Communism in Guatemala," did not condemn the outcome of U.S. actions but was critical of the Eisenhower administration's unilateral approach. Political scientist Philip B. Taylor, Jr., made a similar point in a more extended critique of these events. He concluded that the United States "was intimately involved in a situation of subversion of a constitutional government" and "did not at any time undertake to make the record clear to the people either of the United States or of Latin America."[36]

Early writings for general readers on the Cuban Revolution and related issues by established Latin Americanists were similarly measured. They did not engage in vitriolic denunciations of the Castro government, nor were they among the "political pilgrims," in Paul Hollander's phrase, who trooped to Cuba to admire the achievements of the revolution. As will be seen later, the academics who wrote most positively about the Cuban Revolution in its early phases had not been previously associated with Latin American issues in any significant way.

Latin Americanists certainly deplored the growing ties between Cuba and the Soviet Union and Castro's embrace of Marxism-Leninism. In an article published in March 1961, for example, Russell H. Fitzgibbon concluded that the revolution had "gravitated into a distinctly class movement, and [had] become considerably overlaid with an ugly patina of Communist corrosion." Nevertheless, Fitzgibbon blamed Castro's embrace of the Soviet Union partly on recent

U.S. actions against Cuba: "Whether these were justified or not ... is beside the point at the moment. In terms of consequences, they could not but operate to push Cuban policy closer to the Soviet." The following year Frank Tannenbaum found the Cuban Revolution to have been justified, but he deplored its course: "Castro's political revolution against tyranny, base corruption and governmental indifference to the many needs of the populace was legitimate and inevitable. What was unnecessary and not legitimate was the turning of a political revolution into a totalitarian dictatorship."[37]

Some analysts also expressed the hope that in the future the American government would acknowledge the demand for change sweeping Latin America, even if regional goals did not always coincide with U.S. preferences. In the *New Republic* in June 1961 historian Fredrick B. Pike observed that the region had gained little from its support of the United States since World War II and was in many cases poorer than it had been in 1945. "Latin America's reform advocates," he added, "have, as a consequence, become convinced that formulas of progress for underdeveloped 20th Century countries cannot be borrowed from the United States." In *Current History* (February 1962) Robert Alexander expressed cautious optimism that the Kennedy administration would support the revolution occurring in Latin America that was driven by nationalism and the desire for economic development. Despite "its extremely bad mishandling" of the Cuban problem, he said, the administration was encouraging democracy and turning its back on dictators, such as the late Rafael Trujillo of the Dominican Republic. Moreover, the Alliance for Progress and other initiatives might enable change in Latin America to occur within a democratic framework. Alexander, along with Arthur P. Whitaker, was a member of a task force on Latin America created by the Kennedy administration and chaired by Adolf Berle. Its report, issued in early 1961, warned of the Communist threat to Latin America and emphasized the need for the United States to embrace progressive governments in the region that would undertake social and economic reform.[38]

Established Latin Americanists were not conspicuous among those who emerged as defenders of the Cuban Revolution in the early 1960s. C. Wright Mills, the idiosyncratic Marxist and Columbia University sociologist, had not been noted as a student of Latin America before his two-week visit to Cuba in August 1960. In fact, he admitted in the resulting book, *Listen, Yankee: The Revolution in Cuba* (1960), that he had never been to Cuba before or even thought much about it. *Listen, Yankee* proved to be a best-seller, its effectiveness heightened by Mills's device of addressing the reader in the voice of a Cuban revolutionary. The speaker minimized Communist influence over the government while emphasizing the hope generated by the revolution: "We are building a new society, from top to bottom."[39]

Also influential was *Cuba: Anatomy of a Revolution* (1960) by Leo Huberman and Paul Sweezy, editors of *Monthly Review.* They depicted Cuba as undergoing a genuine socialist revolution though it was led by non-Communists and was occurring in a country that had not experienced a bourgeois national revolution. The diplomatic historian William Appleman Williams of the University of Wisconsin was not a Latin American specialist either but rather was known for his analyses of American imperialism. In 1962 he published *The United States, Cuba, and Castro: An Essay on the Dynamics of Revolution and the Dissolution of Empire.* In that book he contended that prior to 1959 Cuba had been a virtual colony of the United States, which was therefore responsible for the conditions that had brought Castro to power. He also blamed U.S. intransigence for post-1959 problems, including the recent missile crisis.[40]

These writers may not have been dedicated Latin Americanists, but they were sources of inspiration to a younger generation of scholars who were more hostile to capitalism and more suspicious of U.S. intentions in Latin America than their predecessors. Concentrated in political science and the other social sciences, they represented only a minority in the expanding universe of Latin Americanists trained during the 1960s and 1970s, but they made their influence felt through their writings and in professional organizations. Numerous influences—besides the aforementioned writings—contributed to the formation of this younger generation: the contemporary upheavals generated by the civil rights movement and the war in Vietnam as well as continuing controversy produced by U.S. policies toward Latin America, especially the invasion of the Dominican Republic in 1965.

The first direct armed intervention by the United States in a Latin American country in decades, the Dominican affair produced a strong reaction among Latin American specialists. This can be seen in an open letter to President Johnson condemning the invasion because it violated long-standing pledges of nonintervention, was reminiscent of the era of the big stick and gunboat diplomacy, and served to undermine progressive forces in the region. What is notable about the statement is that the 103 signers included not only younger scholars but also established Latin Americanists, among them Robert Alexander, Woodrow Borah, George I. Blanksten, and Robert Burr.[41]

Suspicion of the U.S. government by Americans and of American researchers in Latin America was exacerbated by the controversy surrounding Project Camelot in 1964–65. Originating in the army's Special Operations Research Office, which was housed at American University, the project aimed at employing researchers to study countries in Latin America and elsewhere to determine the conditions conducive to internal revolt and to identify ways of containing or curbing such rebellion. In the end the project was cancelled before it had really begun, after scholars in Chile became aware of its existence and sponsorship. To many Chileans and other Latin Americans, the project smacked of U.S. academic imperialism and interventionism in the internal affairs of their countries. In the words of the magazine *Ercilla*, Chilean social scientists were indignant for two reasons, "one of them patriotic, that of being used as tools in an espionage plan; and another professional, the betrayal to which their own North American colleagues wished to induce them." The fact that the controversy unfolded as the United States was intervening in the Dominican Republic added fuel to the polemics. In the United States debate also revolved around the propriety of army sponsorship of academic research.[42]

One result of the Camelot affair was to encourage efforts by American social scientists to develop collaborative projects with their Latin American counterparts, a goal supported, as noted earlier, by the Ford Foundation and the Joint Committee on Latin American Studies and made possible by the expansion of social science communities within the region. During the 1960s Latin American universities and research institutes grew dramatically in terms of capabilities, sometimes aided by funding from U.S. foundations, and were thus better able to support scholarly projects. Most of the Latin American institutions were represented on the Latin American Council for Social Sciences, which from the mid-1960s was a major promoter and organizer of research within the region.

Despite strains generated by Project Camelot and by the occasionally insensitive or selfish behavior of U.S. scholars, inter-American academic relations remained relatively harmonious, except where members of the Far Left in Latin America were concerned. According to Silvert, they took the position that "any increase in organized social science knowledge is undesirable because Americans know better what to do with such knowledge than Latin Americans do, so that the United States' already great power over its 'colonies' is heightened."[43] When political change hindered academic work, scholars from Latin America often made their way to the United States for periods of varying length. Other opportunities for exchange occurred at LASA meetings and at the many international conferences of the era.

Contact with left-leaning social scientists in Latin America intensified the conviction of some American academics that the interests of the two areas were fundamentally incompatible and led them to embrace dependency theory, which had become a dominant paradigm in social science scholarship by the early 1970s, displacing modernization theory. An amalgam of the ideas of the Argentine economist Raúl Prébisch and his colleagues at the United Nations Economic Commission on Latin America and of neo-Marxists in Latin America, the United States, and Europe, dependency theory explained the underdevelopment and relative poverty of Latin America as a necessary product of the capitalist system as it had evolved in the North Atlantic metropolis since the six-teenth century.

In the *dependistas'* view, the industrialization of the metropolitan center came at the expense of peripheral or satellite areas such as Latin America, from which it extracted agricultural and mineral products. In this system, contrary to classical economic theory, the center expanded, but the periphery remained in an inferior and dependent position. The *dependistas* also repudiated the conten-tion of modernization theorists that changes in traditional values would foster development in Latin America.[44]

An influential popularizer of dependency analysis was André Gunder Frank, a German-born economist trained at the University of Chicago who had worked in Chile and Brazil. In his *Capitalism and Underdevelopment: Historical Stud-ies of Chile and Brazil* (1967), he not only argued the basic tenets of dependency theory but also asserted that the underdeveloped countries would not replicate the experience of the developed nations and that they should instead reject capi-talism. Also influential among *dependistas* was Fernando Henrique Cardoso, so-ciologist and future president of Brazil, who advocated a "historical-structural" approach that analyzed concrete situations and showed how internal political dynamics affected dependent economies.

During the 1960s cohorts of radical young Latin Americanists emerged at several universities. They shared a Marxist or *dependista* orientation and a con-viction that the United States exercised its hegemony in the Western Hemi-sphere solely in the interests of its multinational corporations. They also be-lieved that the content of scholarly production on Latin America in the United States as well as the structure of the field were driven by the very forces of im-perialism that retarded the region's progress. They sought instead to promote scholarship that would not only reflect these convictions but also be relevant to the lives of the exploited masses of Latin America.

In 1966 the North American Congress on Latin America (NACLA) was founded as a direct response to the recent American intervention in the Do-minican Republic. Its founders included individuals associated with Students for a Democratic Society and the University Christian movement as well as many others who shared a "common sense of dismay as we perceive the obstruc-tionist role of the United States in Latin America" and a "common commitment to the necessity of a far-reaching social revolution" in the region.[45]

One of NACLA's primary activities was to investigate and expose the ten-tacles of U.S. imperialism in Latin America. "The projects [NACLA] sponsors will thus attempt to identify in as specific a manner as possible the levers of control which U.S. individuals and institutions exercise over Latin America." Prominent among these institutions, in NACLA's view, were American univer-

sities, which were collaborators in the formulation and execution of American
policy. This was certainly true of Latin American studies, which "from their in-
ception" had "been defined by those possessing power."[46]

A second center for radical Latin Americanists appeared at Stanford University, where they attended lectures by the Marxist economist Paul Baran, recognized as a father of dependency theory. They were associated with the publication of the *Hispanic American Report*, a monthly compilation of news from
Latin America, which was edited by Ronald Hilton, professor of romance languages at Stanford and director of its Institute of Hispanic American and Luso-
Brazilian Studies. The *Report* had gained national notice when its September
1960 issue revealed the existence in Guatemala of a large, well-fortified base
where Cuban exiles were being trained for an invasion of the island. Only the
CIA, Hilton surmised, could provide funds for such an operation.[47]

Among the staff members of the *Report* was Ronald H. Chilcote, who received
a doctorate in political science from Stanford in 1965 and was on the faculty of
the University of California at Riverside. According to Chilcote, the *Report* and
the institute were casualties of Stanford's desire to attract Ford Foundation
funding, which was made contingent on a change in leadership. In reality, Stanford's application and the foundation award included funding for the *Report*,
but it and the institute were slated for reform as part of a large reorganization
and expansion of Latin American studies, especially in the behavioral sciences.
The institute, for example, would no longer be permitted to offer bachelor's or
doctoral degrees. Hilton, called a "rather prickly character" by a foundation official, rendered the issue moot by resigning late in 1964. Hilton himself blamed
the quest for foundation funds for what he called the "debacle":

> It is widely believed that the Ford Foundation, as part of the power elite,
> was interested in suppressing uncensored reporting on international af-
> fairs. While this conclusion was reached gratuitously, it is fair to say that
> when the Ford funds appeared on the horizon, the Stanford crew rushed
> to one side of the ship, causing it to capsize. In general it may be said that
> American universities are in a delicate political balance and that Ford
> Foundation grants have in many cases destroyed that balance in favor of
> those having access to power. Might does not make right, and instead of
> stimulating development Ford grants sometimes have the effect of de-
> stroying creative work which is not supported by a powerful university
> machine such as a major department.[48]

Radicals such as Chilcote were not only dissatisfied with the course of events
at Stanford; they were also unhappy with the direction of LASA and attempted

to air their concerns at the group's meeting in Washington, D.C., in 1970. Students and younger faculty of a radical bent were summoned to the meeting to demand the "total democratization" of what was deemed an elitist organization dominated by "establishment" professionals.[49] These individuals, the radicals asserted, not only worked hand in glove with the U.S. government in co-opting or repressing revolutionary movements in Latin America but also controlled the allocation of research funds from the big foundations and the government.

At the stormy meeting the radicals formed their own organization, the Union of Radical Latin Americanists. In addition, the LASA membership approved several resolutions proposed by the radicals, including a condemnation of the military regime in Brazil. Despite these apparent successes, the radicals remained dissatisfied with their level of representation in the LASA leadership, as a result of which they could exert little influence on the direction of research in the field. "Is it not time for us in LASA to reconsider our research priorities," Chilcote asked, "to reassess the proposition that any research is permissible, . . . except that research which turns the microscope of the social scientists on the forces behind the American empire, . . . which could instruct Latin American governments how to combat the American hegemony?"[50]

Chilcote and other radicals hoped that LASA would fund the establishment of a new alternative journal of opinion and had won support for such a journal from the membership in 1970. Chilcote was invited to draft a proposal, but LASA declined to sponsor the kind of publication he had in mind. In the end the West Coast radicals launched the independent *Latin American Perspectives: A Journal on Capitalism and Socialism* in 1974, with Chilcote as managing editor. Participating editors included several young scholars noted for their socialist and anti-imperialist sympathies, such as political scientists James F. Petras and Susanne Jonas, as well as Latin American scholars such as Fernando Henrique Cardoso and Rodolfo Stavenhagen. "We hope," the editors stated, "to encourage wider and greater theoretical analysis of Latin American reality of the sort which is essential to the formation of viable political strategies. The objective is not merely to draw a clearer picture of the socioeconomic structure, but rather to help find the means by which Latin Americans can transform that structure."[51] The first issue was devoted to a reassessment of dependency theory.

At the same time that radicals were dissatisfied with LASA, others believed that their influence was excessive and deleterious to the interests of the organization. In part the conflict was generational; as one observer put it, the situation was one of "the founding fathers fast fading" versus "the rising radicals raucously ranting." The conflict became glaringly evident at the 1970 business meeting where President John J. Johnson found it impossible to keep order as a "discontented audience kept muttering and speaking out."[52]

A major source of conflict was the wisdom of adopting resolutions relating to political developments in Latin America and to U.S. policy in the region. As noted earlier, the radicals believed that Latin Americanists had an obligation to speak out against unjust and oppressive political and economic systems. At the May 1973 LASA meeting in Madison, Wisconsin, Joel C. Edelstein proposed several resolutions of this type on behalf of the Union of Radical Latin Americanists. Those attending the business meeting adopted modified versions of some of these proposals, notably a resolution condemning repression in Argentina, Bolivia, Colombia, and Uruguay and criticizing U.S. government complicity with these regimes. The resolution also called for the establishment of a Committee on Human Rights and Academic Freedom and of working groups to investigate conditions in the aforementioned countries and to report their findings to the organizations and the mass media. Another resolution condemned U.S. policy toward Cuba and the "invisible blockade" against the Allende government in Chile.[53]

To the radicals' critics, the adoption of resolutions such as these, besides being of doubtful efficacy, were unrelated to the scholarly pursuits that were supposedly LASA's raison d'etre. Critics also pointed out that only a handful of members attended business meetings and voted on resolutions. They asserted, for example, that about sixty-five members, or less than 5 percent of LASA's total membership, were present at the Madison meeting. At the time, LASA bylaws required a mail ballot only if one hundred members requested it. Now the executive council adopted an amendment requiring a mail ballot on all resolutions adopted at future meetings.

Among the critics of LASA was the veteran historian Lewis Hanke, who had been elected to the executive council in 1971. He, with political scientist Federico Gil, organized a drive for a mail ballot on the 1973 resolutions. "We must indeed try to save LASA from becoming a center of political agitation," Hanke wrote. Earlier he had articulated his concerns at greater length in a talk before the Southeastern Council of Latin American Studies, in which he expressed the hope that LASA and other professional groups could avoid "yearly extravaganzas" at their business meetings: "I continue to believe that ... political resolutions are generally counterproductive, that they imply a superior moral position which we have no right to assume, and that they may even be at times a kind of patronizing intervention which a number of our colleagues in Latin America will not welcome. At the very least full discussion and a mail ballot on resolutions should take place."[54]

The most controversial of the 1973 resolutions—those on repressive governments and on U.S. policy toward Cuba and Chile—were approved by narrow majorities of those returning ballots. In subsequent years controversy over

LASA's political posture would continue, and reforms would be undertaken in the 1980s to ensure the kind of extensive debate that Hanke had called for. To its critics, however, LASA remained overly politicized, with members of a radical leftist orientation exercising hegemony over the structure of the organization and its acquiescent or apathetic membership.

A continuing source of annoyance to critics of LASA was the organization's reluctance to condemn violations of human rights or academic freedom in Cuba.[55] The apparent double standard seemed all the more objectionable in the early 1970s as the Cuban regime, which had once seemed a model of an idiosyncratic tropical Socialism, embraced the Soviet political and economic system with its repressiveness and rigidities. European sympathizers such as René Dumont and K. S. Karol publicly expressed doubts about developments in Cuba, only to be roundly condemned by Castro. Maurice Halperin was even more disillusioned by events in Cuba. After fleeing to Mexico in 1953, he had moved to the Soviet Union in 1958 and thence to Cuba in 1962 in the expectation of witnessing a youthful and vibrant revolution that had not yet "gone stale." Over the next six years he was dismayed by the government's economic failures and by the deteriorating cultural climate.[56] After leaving Cuba in 1968, he voiced his criticisms in several books, starting with *The Rise and Decline of Fidel Castro* (1972).

Also sobering was the Cuban experience of Oscar Lewis, who by the early 1960s had attained fame beyond the academy because of his family studies, especially *The Children of Sanchez* (1961), and his controversial concept of the culture of poverty. Always a man of leftist sympathies, Lewis had spent four months in Cuba in 1946 and made brief visits in 1961 and 1968. Late in 1968 he sought funding from the Ford Foundation in order to make a "patient, rigorous field investigation, in a number of spots throughout the island, to determine what the revolution means in terms of the daily lives of the people, particularly the peasants and urban slum dwellers who have been my special interest for many years." In particular, he wished to see whether there had been changes in the "basic traits of the culture of poverty," such as illegitimacy, alcoholism, and fatalism, and to ascertain the degree to which agrarian reform and other revolutionary programs had been successful.[57]

Lewis received a grant of $160,000 from the foundation as well as promises from top Cuban officials, including Castro himself, that he would be able to do his work without government interference and that no Cuban would suffer because of participation in the project. Lewis arrived in Cuba in February 1969 to begin work on the multiyear project, with the help of his wife, Ruth, and several assistants, including ten Cuban students. They conducted research until June 25, 1970, when Cuban officials suddenly terminated the project and confis-

cated thousands of pages of manuscripts and other materials. Despite this set-
back, Lewis hoped to return to Cuba to conclude his fieldwork, but died of a
heart attack in December 1970.[58] In publishing the first of three volumes based
on materials that had not been seized, Ruth Lewis offered several reasons for
the Cuban action, including a contemporaneous crackdown on foreign intellectuals in general and Lewis's decision to interview an individual who was hostile to the government and was subsequently imprisoned. Halperin found Ruth
Lewis's account of the episode "less than satisfactory" and attributed this and
Oscar's confidence that the project could proceed unimpeded to the Lewises' na-
iveté about Socialism and Castro.[59]

The Disciplines: *Plus ça Change . . .*

By the mid-1970s the boom in Latin American studies had clearly ebbed. To the
extent that it was fueled by the fears of U.S. policy makers that Communist expansion in Latin America was a real possibility, the danger now seemed much
less ominous. Fidel Castro's commitment to export the Cuban Revolution had
yielded only failed insurgencies, an outcome dramatized by the capture and execution of Ernesto (Che) Guevara in Bolivia in 1967. In Brazil, Chile, and other
countries, the armed forces had seized power, often with U.S. support, and could
be counted on to keep the Castroite/Communist menace at bay.

Accompanying the diminished salience of Latin America in official circles
was the reduced level of external funding for all area studies programs on the
part of the federal government and the foundations, due in part to financial
constraints and to recurring doubts about the validity of the area studies concept. In 1973, for example, the number of language and area centers that received
support under Title VI was reduced from 107 to 46. By that date, as noted earlier, the Ford Foundation had also ended its support of university area centers.
The diminished level of public interest and funding should not be exaggerated,
however. There was no "bust" in the Latin American field, as had occurred after
World War II, in part because of continued if reduced external funding and in
part because of continued support from the universities.[60]

One can surmise that the staying power of the Latin American field was due
to some extent to occasional bursts of official and public interest generated by
developments in the region, such as events in Chile after 1970. In addition, the
hundreds of specialists created by the boom of the 1960s were now entrenched
in their academic bailiwicks and could not be easily dislodged. The expansion
of the field can be judged by two directories of Latin Americanists compiled by
the Hispanic Foundation and published in 1966 and 1971. Each listed persons
who claimed expertise in the Latin American field and indicated their language

competence. The earlier directory, which included individuals who had received doctoral or equivalent degrees before February 1, 1965, listed 1,884 individuals. The second directory listed 2,695 individuals, an increase of 811 in approximately five to six years.[61] The fact that many of the people listed in the second directory indicated weak language skills suggests that the SSRC and foundation goal of attracting nonspecialists to Latin America had met with some success. Many must have resembled Raymond Vernon, a Harvard economist who took part in a large study of the public and private sectors in developing countries: "Assigned to Mexico, I took off in 1961 with a Spanish grammar under one arm and Prescott's *Conquest of Mexico* under the other."[62]

Data compiled for other surveys around 1970 reveal growth in academic commitment to Latin American studies as well as certain continuities. As of December 31, 1969, 212 colleges and universities in the United States (excluding Puerto Rico) were members of the Consortium of Latin American Studies, which consisted of the institutional members of LASA.[63] Forty-five percent of these institutions offered degrees, minors, or certificates in Latin American studies. Whereas fifty-eight of the schools offered bachelor's degrees in the field and twenty-six offered master's degrees, only nine offered the doctorate, thereby reaffirming the traditional consensus that the doctorate should be earned in a discipline. Also in keeping with tradition, the institutions with the strongest commitment to Latin American studies were located in what was dubbed the "Spanish frontier," made up of Florida and the states bordering Mexico, as well as the remaining western states. The region with the weakest commitment remained the Northeast.

Surveys of course offerings showed a similar pattern of continuity and change. As might be expected, the 212 institutions in the consortium offered more semester hours on the average (89.8) in Spanish language and literature than in any other field. Portuguese language and literature continued to lag far behind, despite the efforts of the 1960s, accounting for an average of only 11.3 semester hours of course work (see table 8.1). Similarly, the 1971 directory of Latin Americanists listed 267 specialists in Spanish American literature but only 56 Brazilianists.[64]

History was the most important discipline after language and literature in the consortium survey, accounting for an average of 14.3 semester hours. A contemporary survey conducted by Richard D. Lambert of a smaller universe of sixty-nine institutions with Latin American interests showed that history represented 18 percent of individual courses devoted to the region, the largest percentage after those related to language and literature (see table 8.2). Historians also made up the largest group represented in the 1971 directory of Latin Americanists, with 552 individuals, or approximately 20 percent of the total.

Table 8.1

Average Number of Semester Hours in Latin American Studies, By Discipline,
Offered in 212 Institutions, circa 1970

Discipline	Semester Hours
Spanish language and literature	89.8
Portuguese language and literature	11.3
History	14.3
Political Science	4.7
Anthropology	4.1
Geography	3.0
Economics	1.7
Sociology	0.9

Source: Martin C. Needler and Thomas W. Walker, "The Current Status of Latin American
Studies Programs," *Latin American Research Review* 6 (Spring 1971): 128.

Table 8.2

Latin American Courses, by Discipline, at Sixty-nine Institutions, circa 1970
(percent of 2,275 courses)

Discipline	Percent
Language related	34.5
History	18.0
Anthropology	11.2
Political Science	9.4
Economics	7.3
Geography	3.2
Sociology	2.9
Other*	13.3

*This category includes courses in the humanities (art, music, philosophy), urban studies,
education, nondisciplinary, and applied and professional courses, among others.
Source: Richard D. Lambert, *Language and Area Studies Review* (Philadelphia: American
Academy of Political and Social Science, 1973), 126–27.

One result of the boom years is that Latin American history appeared to have
shed its image as a marginal field outside the mainstream of historical scholarship. Its new respectability was signaled by the election in 1974 of Lewis Hanke
to be president of the American Historical Association. Hanke was the first Latin
Americanist to be elected to this position since Herbert E. Bolton in 1932. Future

Table 8.3
Fellowships and Postdoctoral Grants, by Discipline (percent)

Discipline	FAFP 1962–70 Fellowships	JCLAS 1959–70 Postdoctoral Grants
History	27.4	26.3
Anthropology	16.2	8.3
Political Science	15.1	13.2
Economics	14.0	15.1
Sociology	10.0	15.6
Geography	3.9	2.9
Language/Literature	1.7	10.7
Other*	6.1	7.8
Number of fellowships	219	205

FAFP, Foreign Area Fellowship Program; *JCLAS*, Joint Committee on Latin American Studies.
*Includes education, psychology, and public administration. The figures in the FAFP table add up to only 94.4 percent.
Source: Michael Potashnik and Bryce Wood, "Government Funding for Research in Latin America, 1970–1971," *Latin American Research Review* 8 (Spring 1973): 137.

historians also fared well, winning 27.4 percent of FAFP dissertation fellowships between 1962 and 1970 and receiving 26.3 percent of postdoctoral grants offered by the Joint Committee on Latin American Studies in the period 1959–70 (see table 8.3). One feature of the historical profession among Latin Americanists had not changed, however. Women remained sorely underrepresented, accounting for only 9 percent of the historians listed in the 1971 directory.

History was less roiled by the controversies of the late 1960s and early 1970s than other disciplines. A few wrote works informed by Marxist or dependency perspectives. Stanley J. Stein and Barbara H. Stein asserted the economic dependence of Latin America in an influential interpretive study (1970) but attributed this condition as much to the Iberian colonial heritage as to the world capitalist system. James D. Cockcroft and Robert P. Millon offered Marxist views of aspects of the Mexican Revolution of 1910, which remained a continuing source of interest to American historians of all political persuasions: for some, a socially and economically significant upheaval that did not result in a Marxist-Leninist regime, but for others, especially after 1968, an incomplete or frustrated popular revolt. John Womack's 1969 study of Zapatismo, called a populist "epic in prose" by one reviewer, spoke to contemporary interest in rural insurgencies in Latin America. Debates related to the U.S. presence in Vietnam were implicit in Neil Macaulay's *Sandino Affair* (1967).[65]

More significant in the long term were several trends that emerged as the 1970s began. These included the adaptation of concepts and methodologies from the social sciences, especially anthropology; an intensified focus on marginal or oppressed groups—African slaves, women, the urban poor—who had been either ignored or slighted in the past; and an effort by colonialists to recount the history of the Indians from their perspective rather than from that of their conquerors. The most important early work in this vein was *The Aztecs under Spanish Rule* (1964) by Charles Gibson, who became president of the American Historical Association in 1977. Historians also used new kinds of sources, such as notarial archives, which were the basis of James Lockhart's *Spanish Peru, 1532–1560* (1968). Lockhart and his students would later be pioneers in the study of the indigenous peoples of colonial Mexico through the use of documents in native languages.

Anthropology in its various subfields also continued to demonstrate strength in the 1960s. Institutions in the consortium survey offered an average of 4.1 semester hours in anthropology related to Latin America, and the Lambert survey showed that anthropology accounted for 11.2 percent of the Latin American content courses offered by the colleges in its sample. The 356 anthropologists listed in the 1971 directory made up the third-largest group of social scientists after historians and economists; 63, or 17.7 percent, were women. Anthropologists won a respectable share of dissertation and postdoctoral fellowships from the FAFP and the Joint Committee in the 1960s, and they benefited from their eligibility for awards made by such federal agencies as the National Science Foundation and the National Institute of Mental Health. Anthropologists associated with Latin America also continued to command respect within the discipline as a whole, as shown by the fact that several were elected to the presidency of the American Anthropological Association: Sol Tax (1959), Gordon R. Willey (1961), John Gillin (1966), George M. Foster (1970), and Charles Wagley (1971).

The 1960s unfolded with anthropology following thematic and conceptual patterns carried over from the previous decade. Ethnographic analysis continued to emphasize peasants and other nontribal groups. Long-term projects continued to be the norm, along with collaboration with Latin American investigators. Just as historians increasingly adopted anthropological principles, so too anthropologists were more likely than before to turn to historical sources, both oral and written, and to examine past societies.[66] As the 1970s began, newer approaches were on the horizon: structuralism, a resurgent Marxism, and a tendency by anthropologists to examine their discipline, the nature of the fieldwork experience, and the ways in which it could be shaped by the researcher's character and values.

Some of these latter tendencies can be linked to the turmoil of the 1960s. Tensions arose within the anthropological community because of opposition to the war in Vietnam and other U.S. foreign policies. Moreover, because anthropologists interested in Latin America or other foreign areas were often dependent on federal funding and might generate findings useful to the government, the Camelot episode had a strong impact. The increase in the number of American anthropologists and their relative affluence exacerbated these problems.

So great was the concern produced by Camelot that the American Anthropological Association appointed a committee headed by Ralph Beals to gather data and prepare a report on research problems and ethics. At a stormy annual meeting in 1966, a Statement on Anthropological Research Problems and Ethics was drafted and submitted in 1967 to the voting members of the association, who overwhelmingly approved it. Among other points, the statement reasserted and strengthened a 1948 resolution regarding the right to conduct research and publish results without censorship; advised anthropologists to provide honest information about the nature and purposes of their research and the sources of their funding and to avoid any involvement in the gathering of intelligence; and warned them of the hazards of doing research for the Department of Defense or other mission-oriented agencies of the U.S. government. The statement did endorse the basic research and training supported by the Smithsonian Institution, the National Science Foundation, and similar agencies.[67]

Archaeology experienced substantial changes in the 1960s and 1970s, among them a new interest in urbanism. In Mesoamerica, a major enterprise was an extensive survey of Teotihuacán by René Millon, William T. Sanders, and others. The Teotihuacán Mapping Project, begun in 1962 under Millon's direction, revealed the site to be a true urban center. In Andean South America the Harvard University Chan Chan–Moche Valley Project, initiated in 1969 and directed by Michael E. Moseley of Harvard's Peabody Museum, mapped and surveyed the capital of the Chimú Empire on Peru's north coast.[68]

Perhaps the most significant development of the 1960s and 1970s was the rise of the so-called New Archaeology. Foreshadowed to some extent by the theories of Walter Taylor in the 1940s and by the work in the Virú Valley and at Tikal, and facilitated by such technical advances as radiocarbon dating and satellite imaging, the New Archaeology was avowedly scientific and aimed at explicating cultural processes with the goal of developing generalizations valid not only for the pre-Columbian past but also for the modern world. The impact of the New Archaeology was felt less strongly in Peru than in Mesoamerica, where it was said to have revolutionized interpretations of Maya civilization, which was now deemed to be more dynamic and complex than was believed in Morley's day. By the 1980s, however, "postprocessualists" were questioning the New Archaeology model and emphasizing the interaction between the contemporary observer and the archaeological record.[69]

The attitudes of governments and institutions in Latin America also affected U.S. archaeologists more strongly than before. The periodic adoption of nationalistic policies in Peru, Mexico, and Colombia hindered or discouraged some Americans from working in these countries. Meanwhile, U.S. archaeologists became more sensitive to illicit trafficking in antiquities and the destruction of archaeological contexts. In 1971, following up on a recent UNESCO convention, the Society of American Antiquities adopted resolutions pledging to support efforts to prevent and penalize illicit trafficking.[70]

The situation of political science within the disciplines remained paradoxical as the 1970s began. In quantitative terms and in influence, it had undeniably made advances over the situation in the early 1960s. Yet criticism of the quality of work on Latin American government and politics persisted, and the prestige of Latin Americanists within the discipline remained low.

At the start of the 1960s, the image of political science related to Latin America remained little changed from that described in chapter 7. In an often-quoted assessment of the field, Merle Kling of Washington University asserted in 1963: "Little capital (funds, talent, or organizational experience) has been invested in political studies of Latin America, and as a result the returns have been relatively meager. Personnel with adequate training and appropriate technical competence have been in scarce supply, research techniques adapted to Latin American studies have been of a relatively primitive nature, and the level of productivity has been low."[71] In addition, the work that had been done on Latin America had not been incorporated into studies of comparative politics, and thus the field and its practitioners remained marginalized within the profession.

By quantitative standards the situation had changed markedly by the end of the 1960s. The 1971 directory listed 251 political scientists (of whom 5 percent were women), an increase of more than 71 percent over the 147 listed only five years earlier. The colleges in the consortium survey offered an average of 4.7 semester hours in political science related to Latin America, and 9.4 percent of the Latin American area courses in the Lambert survey were in political science. Moreover, political scientists won 15.1 percent of the FAFP dissertation fellowships in 1962–70 and 13.2 percent of the Joint Committee postdoctoral grants in 1959–70.

In research and scholarship, too, political science appeared to have made substantial strides. Researchers initially focused on aspects of political development and modernization that would link Latin America more closely with dominant concerns within the field of comparative politics. As a result, there was substantial production of books and articles on political parties and interest groups, such as the armed forces, university students, and the Roman Catholic Church. The use of quantification and statistical techniques also became more widespread.[72]

Despite these advances, the field failed to garner universal respect within the profession. As of the early 1970s no scholar with a strong professional commitment to Latin America had been elected president of the American Political Science Association. In a 1969 essay, Silvert noted that only two of the eleven most prestigious political science departments in the United States had a tenured Latin Americanist on their faculties, though the number was scheduled to double the following year.[73]

After a review of the field in 1971, John D. Martz concluded: "The record would seem to suggest that Latin American political studies have more often than not been unimaginative in concept and pedestrian in approach. A certainly healthy eclecticism has been diluted by a Pavlovian tendency to respond to passing fads within the discipline. Political scientists committed to Latin American studies have in recent years rushed to follow the comparativist pack. They have distinctly been trend-followers rather than trend-setters."[74] Martz failed to mention the newest trend on the horizon—dependency theory, itself in part a product of Latin American dissatisfaction with the modernization approach—or to foresee its impact in the United States. Political scientists were also drawn to the model of the bureaucratic-authoritarian state developed by the Argentine Guillermo O'Donnell in the wake of military coups in Argentina and Brazil. As explained by O'Donnell, this type of regime appeared in relatively modernized states, such as Argentina and Brazil, as a result of crises stemming from the contradictions of import substitution, industrialization, and the expectations of the popular sectors. In short, according to O'Donnell, the result of modernization was not democracy but a new type of authoritarianism. Yet like dependency theory, bureaucratic-authoritarianism, while generating much research, soon found critics.[75]

Given the contemporary interest in problems of Latin American economic and social development, it is not surprising that the region attracted an increasing numbers of economists and sociologists in the 1960s. The 1971 directory of Latin Americanists listed 424 economists, an increase of 39 percent over the 1966 figure; the number of sociologists rose from 82 to 132, or 61 percent, in the same period. As table 8.3 shows, applicants in the two disciplines made a creditable record in winning FAFP and Joint Committee fellowships during the 1960s. The two disciplines lagged behind political science in semester hours and in course offerings both in the consortium and Lambert surveys, but both had made significant gains since the 1940s.

The research interests of economists and sociologists tended to parallel those of political scientists, with much attention devoted to change or the lack thereof.[76] Sociologists evinced continuing interest in rural and agrarian problems and in Latin America's explosive population growth. The former were a focus of the Land Tenure Center established at the University of Wisconsin through a contract with the U.S. Agency for International Development.

During this period U.S. economists and sociologists, as well as those in Latin America, had at their disposal larger amounts of quantitative data that facilitated empirical research. There was also a tendency toward convergence as Latin American economists and sociologists, often trained in the United States, adopted the empirical methods favored there; meanwhile, by the 1970s, many Americans in these disciplines had embraced dependency theory as their conceptual framework and advocated radical solutions for the problems of the region.

The greater availability of statistics encouraged the production of economic history, especially of the national period. In fact, according to Paul Gootenberg, by the 1970s, economic history had become the "queen of Latin American studies," providing a foundation for social history and serving as a link among the various social sciences.[77] The trend was furthered by the compilation of *Latin America: A Guide to Economic History, 1830–1930* (1977), edited by Roberto Cortes Conde and Stanley J. Stein. A major collaborative project sponsored by the Joint Committee and the Latin American Council for Social Sciences, the volume contained annotated entries for the region as a whole and for six nations; each section was preceded by an interpretive essay identifying important works and noting topics yet to be explored.

The relative decline of geography within the universe of Latin American studies, adumbrated in the previous chapter, continued during the 1960s. The 1971 directory listed 174 geographers, an increase of only 28 percent over the 136 included in the 1966 volume; geographers therefore were the smallest group among the social scientists. Geographers also fared poorly among the recipients of awards from the Joint Committee and the FAFP. The field accounted for an average of 3.0 semester hours in the consortium survey and 3.2 percent of the Latin American area courses in the Lambert survey.

By 1969 the community of geographers working on Latin America felt a need to revitalize itself. Their concerns were articulated in plans for a symposium on the future of geographic research on the area:

There appears to be less innovative research in Latin America by North American geographers and less effective adjustments to new political, economic, and social realities in the region. Many researchers have main-

tained a primary concern with native forms of economy and society despite their decreasing importance to Latin American societies. Moreover,
the outstanding developments in spatial analysis of the United States
during the past decade have not been adequately reflected in geographic
analysis of Latin America. The gap between systematic and regional specialization has grown at an alarming rate; there is a danger that both
"sides" will suffer from a lack of communication during the 1970s.[78]

Plans for the symposium grew into a conference at Ball State University in
May 1970 that assessed the state of Latin Americanist geography in the United
States and examined topics that merited further research, such as settlement
geography, frontier zones, and, in general, topics related to development. John
Augelli pointed out that projects related to contemporary problems were most
likely to receive external funding, but he also stressed the need for "research
characterized by sophisticated quantitative techniques and a potential for contributing to theory."[79] One result of the 1970 conference was the formation
of the Conference of Latin American Geographers, which met regularly during the subsequent decades. Like other Latin Americanists, geographers managed to survive and occasionally flourish despite declining support for foreign area studies and continuing differences over the most appropriate research
methods and orientation.

Conclusion

Surveying the state of Latin American studies in the United States in 1966, Lewis Hanke described the current expansion as "staggering": "Never before have so many libraries been able to strengthen their collections on both Brazil and Spanish America. . . . Never before has the academic marketplace been so attractive to graduate students; never before have so many professors and students been able to study and visit Latin America for such prolonged periods; never before have our research facilities and salaries been able to pull to our faculties so many scholars from Latin America as to constitute a kind of 'brain drain' from these countries."[1] Even though the expansionist wave had ebbed by the mid-1970s, its sheer size meant that in subsequent years the academic study of Latin America would exhibit greater vitality than in the post–World War II era of "drought." Even so, throughout its vicissitudes—from its gestation in the nineteenth century through its florescence in the twentieth century—the field of Latin American studies was characterized as much by continuity as by change.

U.S. scholarship on Latin America was always shaped by domestic concerns, as can be seen in early efforts to study the culture of North American Indians by studying those to the south and in the attention given to the "borderlands" by Herbert E. Bolton and others. By the early twentieth century the linkage with state interests became more clearly identifiable as a "boomlet" occurred with the U.S. establishment of protectorates in the Caribbean Basin and efforts to promote trade and investment throughout the region. A second boomlet occurred in the context of the deteriorating international situation of the 1930s and the need to encourage hemispheric solidarity with the United States before and during World War II. The rise of Fidel Castro and the subsequent interjection of the cold war into the region set the stage for the greatest boom of all. Indeed, some have argued that the cold war itself created the area studies concept, regardless of region. In the case of Latin America, earlier chapters have shown that support for area studies existed as far back as the 1930s when the American Council of Learned Societies organized the first Latin American Studies Committee and that the discipline-based study of the region began long before that.

Another example of continuity lies in the dependence of scholars and their institutions on funding from external sources, especially the federal government and the foundations. The Carnegie Corporation and the Rockefeller and Ford foundations, among others, provided funding throughout the period whereas the federal contribution to the study of Latin America peaked during times of perceived emergency, such as World War II and the cold war. Thus the 1940s yielded Nelson Rockefeller's Office of the Coordinator of Inter-American Affairs, and the 1960s brought the Title VI area centers; foundation aid was also high during these periods. When necessary, academics also turned for funding directly to wealthy individuals and corporations, such as Edward Harkness and the United Fruit Company. Only rarely, as in the Camelot episode, did the source of funding arouse ethical concerns.

Dependence on external funding inevitably raises questions about the extent to which sponsors influenced scholars' choices of topics and interpretations. The issue rarely arose during the first half of the twentieth century, but radical scholars of the 1960s, it will be recalled, asserted that the scholarship of their establishment colleagues had traditionally been subservient to the dictates of U.S. policy makers and their corporate backers. For confirmation they merely had to point to the many academics who served in government, if only in an advisory capacity. Gilbert Merkx has asserted, by contrast, that the location of the federally funded Title VI centers in the universities assured their independence: "The relationship of the area studies community to U.S. cold-war policy was therefore not marked by dependence and support but rather by autonomy and even confrontation, as demonstrated by the long history of resolutions denouncing U.S. foreign policy passed by the Latin American Studies Association and other foreign area associations. Foreign area studies served as an independent alternative to information from government agencies, which helped to widen debate over foreign policy alternatives and to fuel opposition to cold war policies."[2] Merkx goes on to state that "the content of area studies came almost entirely from overseas research by U.S. scholars and their foreign colleagues." He is referring to the product of the area centers, and he is undoubtedly correct in arguing that here the direct influence of the government and other sponsors was limited. Nevertheless, scholars who undertook research sponsored by the Agency for International Development and similar federal bodies were constrained by their contracts.

In addition, the nature of the topics selected for investigation, especially by social scientists, was bound to be affected not only by the concerns of these fed-

eral entities but also by the priorities of the learned societies and the foundations that funded them. As early as 1940, Carl Sauer, arguing that researchers
should be free to pursue problems that interested them, declared: "Within [the
field of Latin American studies] the individual student should be allowed to do
things that he wants to do. I am against the breaking down of the field into assignments or projects and I consider that the foundations have done a grave disservice to scholarship insofar as they have lured persons to draw up projects because funds might be offered."[3] Hanke, too, expressed concern in 1966 about the
amount of directed research then under way, citing the case of a university that
offered three-year fellowships but only to those who would write dissertations
relating to social revolution in Latin America.[4]

Evidence of continuity can also be found in the conflicted attitudes of Latin
Americanists toward the region they study. The racialist discourse so common
in the nineteenth and early twentieth centuries had disappeared by the 1960s,
but the tendency to contrast Latin America, either explicitly or implicitly, with
the United States or western Europe remained strong. In a 1964 essay, historian Richard M. Morse described the gulf between the United States and Latin
America as unbridgeable: "Here are two cultures whose historic spiritual trajectories are not merely different . . . but diametrically opposed." The gulf was of
long standing, dating back to colonial times, and had changed little since then:
"Seventeenth-century Ibero America stood for everything that Anglo America
had set itself fiercely against. . . . Our present *doctrinal* diversity and toleration
obscure for us that we are integrally a Protestant nation, insensitive and vaguely
hostile to the *sociological* and *psychological* foundations of a Catholic society."[5]

Not only did scholars continue to emphasize the gulf between the Iberian
heritage of Latin America and that of western Europe, but some saw the former as a major cause of Latin American underdevelopment and an obstacle to
needed change in the region. This was the theme of a 1969 article by historian
Donald E. Worcester, who believed that the Spanish American nations were engaged in a "death-struggle" with their Spanish heritage, which had continued
to shape their political behavior as independent states. In contrast to Spain,
which had introduced medieval cultural values, the colonies founded by the
English and northern Europeans were shaped by the values of the Renaissance
and Reformation: "In the English colonies there was no medieval tradition nor
entrenched nobility or church, and the colonists could reshape their values and
customs in relative freedom from restraint." Worcester concluded that there
was a possibility for change: "When the dam of resistance to change is finally
breached, however, a flood will follow, and the transformation will be revolutionary, uncontrollable, and unpredictable."[6]

In his 1969 economics text William P. Glade also attributed the underdevelopment of Spanish America to the values and institutions introduced during the colonial period:

> By the time independence from the yoke of the Spanish was gained, the Hispanic American institutional structure differed considerably from that of the countries in the North Atlantic cultural continuum. Medieval practices and institutional relics from earlier Mediterranean social organization continued to play a strong role in economic life and were only partly ameliorated by influences emanating from the European commercial revolution and mercantilism. . . . [By the early nineteenth century] the social order which prevailed in Spanish America had become increasingly anachronistic when compared with the culture centers with which the area would primarily interact when the era of republican government replaced the imperial system of Spain.[7]

In their influential 1970 survey Stanley J. Stein and Barbara H. Stein made a similar argument in explaining the economic dependence of Latin America. By 1700 Spain and Portugal, unable or unwilling to modernize their economies and "transform [their] traditional societies of aristocratic values and aspirations," had become dependencies of England and the northern European countries, which had been able to make the required changes.[8] Both traditional values and dependency had been transferred to the New World colonies of Spain and Portugal and bequeathed to the newly independent states of the nineteenth century. Although the Steins' survey ended in 1900, they suggested that the prospects for reform in contemporary Latin America were bleak.

Social scientists who embraced modernization theory agreed that the gulf identified by Morse and his like-minded colleagues existed, but they believed that it could eventually be bridged as traditional societies made their way toward development. To be sure, they, too, frequently asserted that Latin American values and culture, like those of other underdeveloped societies, represented obstacles to change. For the anthropologist John P. Gillin, the middle strata were the groups most in touch with the modern world, yet they lacked the class consciousness and values held by their counterparts in western Europe and the United States. In Latin America the middle groups were characterized by such counterproductive values as a disdain for manual labor, personalism, acceptance of hierarchy, strong family ties, materialism based on tangibles such as real estate, and a sense of fatalism.[9] Latin American scholars and intellectuals made similar points. A volume titled *Obstacles to Change in Latin America* (1965) was made up of essays written entirely by Latin Americans. Of the middle classes, in power for decades, the editor, Chilean Claudio Veliz, wrote: "Far from reforming anything, they have become firm supporters of the Establishment, they have not implemented significant agrarian or fiscal reforms but have displayed remarkable energy trying to become landowners or marry their offspring into the aristocracy."[10]

According to Thomas C. Cochran, various cultural traits, acquired mainly during childhood, differentiated the Latin American entrepreneur from his U.S. counterpart. For example, "the Latin entrepreneur enjoys talk, theory, and speculation, and lacks the compulsion to act. . . . Artistic achievement, professional status, land ownership, and government or military office still outrank anything short of outstanding business success." The sociologist Seymour Martin Lipset discerned a similar set of values among the elites of Latin America (as well as in French Canada and the U.S. South) that were antithetical to entrepreneurship. Lipset, however, believed in the possibility of change: "The value system of much of Latin America, like Quebec, has, in fact, been changing in the direction of a more achievement-oriented, universalistic, and equalitarian value system, and its industrial development both reflects and determines such changes."[11]

Several essays in the Veliz collection adumbrated the advent of dependency theory, in which the Iberian "legacy of doom" became less prominent in explaining Latin American underdevelopment.[12] For *dependistas* and other leftist scholars, Latin America's national bourgeoisies were major culprits, along with the metropole nations, for perpetuating the region's dependence and underdevelopment while the masses remained exploited and oppressed. In this scheme, however, external powers, notably the United States, were assigned the greatest responsibility for Latin America's failings. Criticism of the behavior of the United States toward the region had long been a staple of scholarship, as earlier chapters have shown. These older writings had assumed that certain U.S. policies were merely misguided or misunderstood, a problem that could be corrected by new approaches and greater mutual understanding. To many dependency theorists, this was impossible as the interests of Latin America and the United States were fundamentally opposed.

During the boom years of the 1960s and 1970s there continued to be occasional criticism of the quality of Latin Americanists and the value of their scholarship. In a 1970 essay, for example, Richard Morse complained of the overspecialization and careerism that he thought characterized U.S. historians of Latin America. He also directed some barbs at the superficiality of the work of social scientists, citing as an example the lines by Seymour Martin Lipset quoted above.[13] In 1975 the Brazilian sociologist Gláucio Ary Dillon Soares declared that the "training of Latin Americanists in the United States today is generally poor" and that "much of the research on Latin America carried out in the United States today is second-rate." He considered that Latin Americanists lacked adequate language skills and firsthand experience in the region. More-over, the work of social scientists suffered for several reasons: it was done on an individual basis, it was confined by academic disciplines, and, as a result of the latter, it was ethnocentric in theory and methodology.[14]

By the mid-1970s, such cavils were rare. The ascendancy of dependency theory in the United States answered the last of Dillon Soares's criticisms, be-ing as it was largely of Latin American origin. Indeed, Latin Americanists soon had the novel if short-lived experience of seeing a theoretical approach from their own bailiwick being borrowed and adapted by specialists in other regions of the world. It is not surprising, therefore, that a survey from the mid-1980s that examined production in the social sciences both in the United States and in Latin America over the previous two decades was generally positive, identifying three important advances: "marked increases in analytic power and empirical reach; expansion of interdisciplinary links; and development of inter-American connections." Also notable was a "widespread commitment to focus on what are taken to be hemispheric peoples' most urgent needs."[15]

Another notable change was the increased participation of women in Latin American scholarship and in the institutions associated with it. According to historian Margaret Crahan, she was one of only three women who attended the first LASA conference in 1968. Four years later she was an organizer of the Women's Coalition of Latin Americanists, which secured approval at the 1973 meeting of a resolution endorsing enhanced participation by women in LASA and committing the organization to promoting the study of women in Latin America. The coalition also mounted write-in campaigns to elect women to the presidency and to the executive council. Elected to the council, Crahan en-countered resistance as well as support for her presence. "From the 1980s up to the present, however," she wrote in 2006, "the level of participation in LASA by women, on the program, on committees, on the Executive Council and in the presidency, confirms that there have been major changes."[16] In the case of one discipline, history, a survey of the 2006 directory of the Conference on Latin American History showed that approximately 35 percent of the 802 members were women.

In his 1966 talk Lewis Hanke warned that "Latin Americanists must be prepared for sudden shifts in the winds of circumstance."[17] Indeed, the late twentieth century brought new winds that profoundly affected scholarship and teaching related to Latin America. Trends within individual disciplines, such as the rise of world history and rational-choice theory in the social sciences, had the ef-fect of nudging Latin America once more to a less prominent, if not peripheral, place on the world stage, while the influence of postmodernism, with its emphasis on the fluidity of categories, called the concept of region into question. International developments, such as the collapse of the Soviet Union and the drive toward globalization, had a similar effect. In this context the significance or even the existence of Latin America as a meaningful category of analysis came under scrutiny as never before.[18]

By the mid-1990s the ACLS and the SSRC had concluded that although area studies had made enormous contributions, new frameworks were needed that transcended the traditional regions. In the words of Kenneth Prewitt, president of the SSRC, "Critical problems and critical research issues appear in forms that overwhelm conventional definitions of area and region—from the quality of economic, political, and environmental life around the globe to the conditions for ensuring the security and well-being of all people." Area studies were not to be completely jettisoned, however, but were to be involved in the production of area-based knowledge, "a scholarly enterprise that can interpret and explain the ways in which that which is global and that which is local condition each other."[19] As a result of the new orientation, in 1996 the councils undertook a major reordering of their international programs, which included the decommissioning of the Joint Committee on Latin American Studies and the other area committees. In the new system of committees and networks that was created, regional interests were to be articulated by advisory panels that lacked the authority over research and training once wielded by the joint committees.

At many colleges and universities, such as Florida and Texas, Latin American studies programs and institutes continued despite cuts in federal funding, current academic fashions, and the traditional hostility of departments, what one center director called the "well-guarded disciplinary fiefdoms that comprise the modern university."[20] Offsetting these problems were several trends, both old and new, such as the long-standing commitment to the study of Latin America in history and other disciplines and the burgeoning population in the United States of those of Latin American origin. Accordingly, while the names of programs, centers, or institutes of Latin American studies remained unchanged at many institutions, others responded to the new conditions by adding to the traditional title the words "Caribbean," "Iberian," "Latino," or some combination thereof.[21] Despite the shifting winds, therefore, it seemed likely that teaching and research related to Latin America would continue unabated, building on the strong base laid in the twentieth century.

Notes

Short titles are used within chapter listings after the first citation of a work. Sources frequently cited are identified by the following abbreviations:

AA   *American Anthropologist*
AAAG   *Annals of the American Association of Geographers*
ACLS   American Council of Learned Societies
HAHR   *Hispanic American Historical Review*
JCLAS   Joint Committee on Latin American Studies
LARR   *Latin American Research Review*
SSRC   Social Science Research Council

Preface

1. Unless otherwise noted, the term "American" will be used to refer to a citizen of the United States or as an adjective describing individuals, institutions, and so forth of U.S. origin. The term "North American," long preferred by many writers, is rarely used in ordinary parlance and in any event appears to improperly embrace Canada and perhaps even Mexico since the North American Free Trade Agreement has been in force.

2. For an overview of the development of international studies to 1940, see Robert A. McCaughey, *International Studies and Academic Enterprise: A Chapter in the Enclosure of American Learning* (New York: Columbia University Press, 1984), 3–109. The figures on PhDs appear on page 36. See also Bruce Kuklick, *Puritans in Babylon: The Ancient Near East and American Intellectual Life, 1880–1930* (Princeton, NJ: Princeton University Press, 1996).

3. Martin W. Lewis and Karen W. Wigen, *The Myth of Continents: A Critique of Metageography* (Berkeley and Los Angeles: University of California Press, 1997), 181–82; Aims McGuinness, "Searching for 'Latin America': Race and Sovereignty in the Americas in the 1850s," in *Race and Nation in Modern Latin America*, ed. Nancy P. Appelbaum, Anne S. Macpherson, and Karin Alejandra Rosenblatt (Chapel Hill: University of North Carolina Press, 2003), 87–107.

4. McCaughey, xv. On the growth of academic programs and scholarship about regions other than Latin America, see Thomas Naff, ed., *Paths to the Middle East: Ten Scholars Look Back* (Albany: State University of New York Press, 1993); John King Fairbank, *Chinabound: A Fifty-Year Memoir* (New York: Harper and Row, 1982); C. Martin Wilbur, *China in My Life: A Historian's Own History* (Armonk, NY: M. E. Sharpe, 1996); Jerry Gershenhorn, *Melville J. Herskovits and the Racial Politics of Knowledge* (Lincoln: University of Nebraska Press, 2004).

5. Mark T. Berger, *Under Northern Eyes: Latin American Studies and U.S. Hegemony in the Americas, 1898–1990* (Bloomington: Indiana University Press, 1995); Daniel W. Gade, "North American Reflections on Latin American Geography," in *Latin America*

in the 21st Century: Challenges and Solutions, ed. Gregory Knapp (Austin: Conference of Latin Americanist Geographers and University of Texas Press, 2002), 1–44.

6. Lewis Hanke, "The Early Development of Latin American Studies in the U.S.A.," in *Studying Latin America: Essays in Honor of Preston E. James*, ed. David J. Robinson (Syracuse, NY: Geography Department, Syracuse University, 1980), 103–20; Lewis Hanke, "The Development of Latin American Studies in the United States, 1939–1945," *The Americas* 4 (1947): 32–64; Howard F. Cline, ed., *Latin American History: Essays on Its Study and Teaching, 1898–1965*, 2 vols. (Austin: University of Texas Press, 1967).

7. Lewis Hanke's works include *The Spanish Struggle for Justice in the Conquest of America* (Philadelphia: University of Pennsylvania Press, 1949) and *Bartolomé de Las Casas: Bookman, Scholar, Propagandist* (Philadelphia: University of Pennsylvania Press, 1952). For a complete listing through the mid-1980s, see [Celso Rodríguez, comp.], "The Writings of Lewis Hanke," *Inter-American Review of Bibliography* 36 (1986): 427–51. Howard Cline's published works include "The Aurora Yucateca and the Spirit of Enterprise in Yucatan, 1821–1847," *HAHR* 27 (February 1947): 30–60; "Civil Congregation of the Indians in New Spain, 1598–1606," *HAHR* 29 (August 1949): 349–69; and *The United States and Mexico* (Cambridge, MA: Harvard University Press, 1953). For a complete list of writings published during his lifetime, see John J. Finan, "Howard F. Cline (1915–1971)," *HAHR* 51 (November 1971): 646–53. Cline also edited and was a contributor to the four-volume *Guide to Ethnohistorical Sources* (Austin: University of Texas Press, 1972–75), volumes 12–15 of the *Handbook of Middle American Indians*.

1. Beginnings

1. *Diary of Samuel Sewall* (Boston: Massachusetts Historical Society, 1878–82), 2:52; Stanley Williams, *The Spanish Background of American Literature* (New Haven, CT: Yale University Press, 1955; repr., Hamden, CT: Archon Books, 1968), 1:17–20; Harry Bernstein, *Making an Inter-American Mind* (Gainesville: University of Florida Press, 1961), 6–8, 14.

2. *The Papers of Thomas Jefferson*, ed. Julian P. Boyd (Princeton, NJ: Princeton University Press, 1950), 11:558, 16:208; Bernstein, 14; J. R. Spell, "Spanish Teaching in the United States," *Hispania* 10 (May 1927): 147–48.

3. *Papers of Thomas Jefferson*, 11:668.

4. Harry Bernstein, *Origins of Inter-American Interest, 1700–1812* (Philadelphia: University of Pennsylvania Press, 1945), 53–56.

5. On Robertson, see D. A. Brading, *The First Americans: The Spanish Monarchy, Creole Patriots, and the Liberal State, 1492–1867* (Cambridge: Cambridge University Press, 1991), 432–41, 450–55, and essays by Stewart J. Brown, Bruce P. Lenman, and Nicholas Phillipson in *William Robertson and the Expansion of Empire*, ed. Stewart J. Brown (Cambridge: Cambridge University Press, 1997).

6. Frederick S. Stimson, "William Robertson's Influence on Early American Literature," *The Americas* 14 (July 1957): 37–43.

7. Herbert B. Adams, *The Life and Writings of Jared Sparks* (1893; repr., Freeport, NY: Books for Libraries Press, 1970), 1:297.

8. "Insurrection of Páez in Colombia," *North American Review* 26 (July 1827): 90.

9. *The Writings of Thomas Jefferson* (Washington, DC: Thomas Jefferson Memo-

rial Association, 1904), 21; anonymous review of *Ensayo de la historia civil del Paraguay, Buenos-Ayres, y Tucumán,* by Gregorio Funes, *North American Review* 12 (1821): 433–38.

10. John J. Johnson, *A Hemisphere Apart: The Foundations of U.S. Policy toward Latin America* (Baltimore: Johns Hopkins University Press, 1990), 111, 170.

11. "Traits of Spanish Character," *North American Review* 5 (1817): 30–31; anonymous review of *Journal,* by Charles Stuart Cochrane, *North American Review* 21 (1825): 153–77; anonymous review of *Rough Notes Taken during Some Rapid Journeys across the Pampas and among the Andes,* by F. B. Head, *North American Review* 24 (1827): 295. For a discussion of writing about Spain in the nineteenth century, see Richard L. Kagan, "From Noah to Moses: The Genesis of Historical Scholarship on Spain in the United States," in *Spain in America: The Origins of Hispanism in the United States,* ed. Richard L. Kagan (Urbana: University of Illinois Press, 2002), 21–48.

12. Williams, 1:174–76; Spell, 152; Alfred Coester, "Francis Sales—A Forerunner," *Hispania* 19 (May 1936): 283–302; Robert C. Smith, "A Pioneer Teacher: Father Peter Babad and His Portuguese Grammar," *Hispania* 28 (August 1945): 330–63.

13. David B. Tyack, *George Ticknor and the Boston Brahmins* (Cambridge, MA: Harvard University Press, 1967), 73.

14. George Ticknor, *History of Spanish Literature,* 6th American ed. (1891; repr., New York: Gordian Press, 1965), 3:275. See also Thomas R. Hart, "George Ticknor's *History of Spanish Literature,*" in Kagan, *Spain in America,* 106–21.

15. Washington Irving, *Letters,* ed. Ralph M. Anderson, Herbert L. Kleinfeld, and Jenifer S. Banks (Boston: Twayne Publishers, 1979–82), 2:101, 108.

16. Ibid., 2:236, 3:272.

17. Ibid., 2:171; Washington Irving, *The Life and Voyages of Christopher Columbus,* ed. John Harmon McElroy (Boston: Twayne Publishers, 1981), xxxv–xxxviii.

18. Irving, *Letters,* 2:193.

19. Irving, *Columbus,* lxi–lxx. Irving published several editions of his biography, including a one-volume abridgement in 1829. In 1849 a third revised edition appeared both in New York and in London, the latter under the title of *The Life and Voyages of Christopher Columbus Together with the Voyages of His Companions.* As the title indicates, this edition included Irving's *Voyages and Discoveries of the Companions of Columbus* (1831). See Rolena Adorno, "Washington Irving's Romantic Hispanism and Its Columbian Legacies," in Kagan, *Spain in America,* 96n24.

20. Irving, *Columbus,* lxxviii–lxxxvi.

21. William H. Shurr, "Irving and Whitman: Re-Historicizing the Figure of Columbus in Nineteenth-Century America," *American Transcendental Quarterly* 6 (1992): 237–38; Adorno, 61.

22. Irving, *Columbus,* xci–xcv; Benjamin Keen, *Essays in the Intellectual History of Colonial Latin America* (Boulder, CO: Westview Press, 1998), 186–87.

23. Irving, *Columbus,* 211, 540.

24. Irving, *Letters,* 3:4–5, 708.

25. *The Correspondence of William Hickling Prescott,* ed. Roger Wolcott (Boston: Houghton Mifflin Co., 1925), 32, 127.

26. Ibid., 150, 227–28; *The Literary Memoranda of William Hickling Prescott,* ed. Harvey C. Gardiner (Norman: University of Oklahoma Press, 1961), 2:56–57, 63.

27. *Literary Memoranda*, 2:32. See also Howard F. Cline, C. Harvey Gardiner, and Charles Gibson, eds., *William Hickling Prescott: A Memorial* (Durham, NC: Duke University Press, 1959).

28. *The Complete Works of William Hickling Prescott: History of the Conquest of Peru* (New York: Kelmscott Society, n.d.), 1:118.

29. *Literary Memoranda*, 2:157, 165; *Conquest of Peru*, 1:348, 2:139, 141.

30. Richard L. Kagan, "Prescott's Paradigm: American Historical Scholarship and the Decline of Spain," *American Historical Review* 101 (April 1996): 430, reprinted in Kagan, *Spain in America*, 247–76; *Correspondence of Prescott*, 468.

31. *Correspondence of Prescott*, 533, 571; *The Papers of William Hickling Prescott*, ed. Harvey C. Gardiner (Urbana: University of Illinois Press, 1964), 303, 349; *Literary Memoranda*, 2:199.

32. Irving, *Letters*, 2:234.

33. Robert E. Bieder devotes a chapter (pp. 16–54) to Gallatin in *Science Encounters the Indian, 1820–1880: The Early Years of American Ethnology* (Norman: University of Oklahoma Press, 1986).

34. Ibid., 55–103; Brian W. Dippie, *The Vanishing American: White Attitudes and U.S. Indian Policy* (Middletown, CT: Wesleyan University Press, 1982), 82–83. On Morton and the "American school," see also William Stanton, *The Leopard's Spots: Scientific Attitudes toward Race in America, 1815–1859* (Chicago: University of Chicago Press, 1960).

35. For an account of Stephens's life, see Victor Wolfgang Von Hagen, *Maya Explorer: John Lloyd Stephens and the Lost Cities of Central America and Yucatan* (Norman: University of Oklahoma Press, 1947).

36. John Lloyd Stephens, *Incidents of Travel in Central America, Chiapas, and Yucatan*, ed. Richard L. Predmore (New Brunswick: Rutgers University Press, 1949), 1:334, 2:77.

37. Ibid., 1:81.

38. Ibid., 1:88–99. On "archaeological Monroeism," see Juan Ortega y Medina's essay "Monroismo arqueológico: Un intento de compensación de americanidad insuficiente," in his *Ensayos, tareas, y estudios históricos* (Xalapa: Universidad Veracruzana, 1962), 37–86. R. Tripp Evans makes a similar point in *Romancing the Maya: Mexican Antiquity in the American Imagination, 1820–1915* (Austin: University of Texas Press, 2004), 44–87.

39. E. G. Squier and E. H. Davis, *Ancient Monuments of the Mississippi Valley Comprising the Results of Extensive Original Surveys and Explorations* (1848; repr., New York: AMS Press, 1973), with a new introduction by James G. Griffin, vii–viii, 301. See also Bieder, 104–45, and Terry A. Barnhart, *Ephraim George Squier and the Development of American Anthropology* (Lincoln: University of Nebraska Press, 2005), 30–101.

40. Ephraim George Squier, *Nicaragua* (New York: D. Appleton and Co., 1856), 1:291–95, 368.

41. For a discussion of Squier's activities in Central America, see Barnhart, 150–86, 214–43, and two articles by Charles L. Stansifer: "The Central American Writings of E. George Squier," *Inter-American Review of Bibliography* 16 (1966): 144–60, and "E. George Squier and the Honduras Interoceanic Railroad Project," *HAHR* 46 (1966): 1–27.

42. Quoted in Stansifer, "Central American Writings of Squier," 148.

43. Michael D. Olien, "E. G. Squier and the Miskito: Anthropological Scholarship and Political Propaganda," *Ethnohistory* 32 (1985): 111–33.

44. Stansifer, "Central American Writings of Squier," 151, 153–54.

45. Marian Mould de Pease, "Observaciones a un observador: Hurgando en el tintero de Ephraim George Squier," in *Etnografía e historia del mundo andino: Continuidad y cambio*, ed. Shozo Masuda (Tokyo: Tokyo University, 1986), 35–36. See also Barnhart, 244–80.

46. See the introduction by Gordon R. Willey to the reprint edition (New York: Arno Press, 1973) of Squier's *Peru: Incidents of Travel in the Land of the Incas*, ix.

47. Keith McElroy, "Ephraim George Squier: Photography and the Illustration of Peruvian Antiquities," *History of Photography* 10 (April–June 1986): 99–129.

48. Squier, *Peru*, 433–36.

49. Ibid., 304, 573.

50. Barnhart, 317–32.

51. Adolph Bandelier, "Squier's 'Peru,'" *Nation* 24 (June 21, 1877): 367; Charles H. Lange and Carroll L. Riley, *Bandelier: The Life and Adventures of Adolph Bandelier* (Salt Lake City: University of Utah Press, 1996), 36.

52. See Leslie A. White, *Pioneers in American Anthropology: The Bandelier-Morgan Letters, 1873–1883*, 2 vols. (Albuquerque: University of New Mexico Press, 1940). On Morgan, see also Bieder, 194–246, and Benjamin Keen, *The Aztec Image in Western Thought* (New Brunswick, NJ: Rutgers University Press, 1971), 387–98.

53. Bandelier, "Squier's 'Peru,'" 368; Leslie White and Ignacio Bernal, *Correspondencia de Adolfo F. Bandelier* (Mexico City: INAH, 1960), 124.

54. Madeleine Turrell Rodack, "Adolph Bandelier's *History of the Borderlands*," *Journal of the Southwest* 30 (Spring 1988): 35–46; Russell S. Saxton, "'The Truth about the Pueblo Indians': Bandelier's *Delight Makers*," *New Mexico Historical Review* 56 (July 1981): 261–84.

55. Adolph F. Bandelier, *The Romantic School of American Archaeology* (New York: Trow's Printing and Bookbinding Co., 1885), 10–11; Adolph Bandelier, *The Gilded Man (El Dorado) and Other Pictures of the Spanish Occupancy of America* (New York: D. Appleton and Co., 1893), 262.

56. Adolph Bandelier, "The Truth about Inca Civilization," *Harper's Monthly* 110 (1904–5): 632–40; Adolph Bandelier, *The Islands of Titicaca and Koati* (New York: Hispanic Society of America, 1910), 189, 213, 238.

57. Bandelier, *Islands of Titicaca and Koati*, 19, 219; White and Bernal, 265; Adolph Bandelier, "The Ruins of Casas Grandes," *Nation* 51 (August 28, 1890): 166–68, and *Nation* 51 (September 4, 1890): 185–87.

58. Hubert Howe Bancroft, *Essays and Miscellany*, vol. 38, *Works* (1890, repr., New York: Arno Press and McGraw-Hill Book Co., n.d.), 6–7, 38.

59. See the biography by John Walton Caughey, *Hubert Howe Bancroft: Historian of the West* (Berkeley and Los Angeles: University of California Press, 1946).

60. Howard F. Cline, "Hubert Howe Bancroft, 1832–1918," in *Handbook of Middle American Indians*, ed. Howard F. Cline (Austin: University of Texas Press, 1973), 13: 329–39.

61. Ibid., 341–42.

62. Bancroft, *Literary Industries*, vol. 39, *Works*, 298, 701–2; Bancroft, "Our Treatment of the Native Races," *Essays and Miscellany*, 65–74.

Part I. Laying the Foundations

1. Lars Schoultz, *Beneath the United States: A History of U.S. Policy toward Latin America* (Cambridge, MA: Harvard University Press, 1998), 383.

2. See Mark T. Gilderhus, *The Second Century: U.S.–Latin American Relations since 1889* (Wilmington, DE: Scholarly Resources, 2000), 5–9.

3. James William Park, *Latin American Underdevelopment: A History of Perspectives in the United States, 1870–1965* (Baton Rouge: Louisiana State University Press, 1995), 70.

4. Charles Lyon Chandler, "The Teaching of Hispanic American History from the Practical Standpoint," *HAHR* 2 (August 1919): 398, reprinted in Howard F. Cline, ed., *Latin American History: Essays on Its Study and Teaching, 1889–1965*, 2 vols. (Austin: University of Texas Press, 1967), 1:231–32.

5. Frederick Rudolph, *The American College and University: A History* (New York: Alfred A. Knopf, 1965), 335, 395.

6. Ibid., 406–7.

7. See Donald Fisher, *Fundamental Development of the Social Sciences: Rockefeller Philanthropy and the U.S. Social Science Research Council* (Ann Arbor: University of Michigan Press, 1993).

8. See Nathan Reingold, "National Science Policy in a Private Foundation: The Carnegie Institution of Washington," in *The Organization of Knowledge in Modern America, 1860–1920*, ed. Alexandra Oleson and John Voss (Baltimore: Johns Hopkins University Press, 1979), 313–41.

9. Robert A. McCaughey, *International Studies and Academic Enterprise: A Chapter in the Enclosure of American Learning* (New York: Columbia University Press, 1984), 35–37.

10. J. R. Spell, "Spanish Teaching in the United States," *Hispania* 10 (May 1927): 141–59; Henry Grattan Doyle, "Spanish Studies in the United States," *Bulletin of the Pan American Union* 60 (March 1926): 223–34.

11. For the rise of U.S. interest in Spanish during World War I, see James D. Fernández, " 'Longfellow's Law': The Place of Latin America and Spain in U.S. Hispanism, circa 1915," in *Spain in America: The Origins of Hispanism in the United States*, ed. Richard L. Kagan (Urbana: University of Illinois Press, 2002), 122–41. For a sampling of postwar arguments on both sides of the debate, see the following articles in *School and Society*: J. Warshaw, "Why Spanish?" 9 (April 5, 1919): 409–13; C. E. Seashore, "The Academic Status of Spanish," 20 (October 4, 1924): 442–43; O. K. Boring, "The Academic Status of Spanish," 20 (November 15, 1924): 631–32; Thomas H. Briggs, "Spanish in High Schools," 20 (December 27, 1924): 821–24; Carl E. Seashore, "Elementary Spanish as a Postwar Evil," 33 (May 2, 1931): 590–91.

12. Aurelio M. Espinosa, "Where Is the Best Spanish Spoken?" *Hispania* 6 (October 1923): 244–46; Kenneth McKenzie, "The Question of Spanish Pronunciation," *Modern*

Language Journal 2 (October 1917): 21–27. See also J. Moreno-Lacalle, "The Teaching of Spanish Pronunciation," *Modern Language Journal* 2 (April 1918): 306–7.

13. Alfred L. Coester, *The Literary History of Spanish America* (New York: Macmillan Co., 1916), viii–ix. On Ford, see Henry Grattan Doyle, "Jeremiah Denis Matthias Ford," *Hispania* 19 (May 1936): 153–59, and Urban T. Holmes, Jr., and Alexander J. Denoby, eds., *Medieval Studies in Honor of Jeremiah Denis Matthias Ford* (Cambridge, MA: Harvard University Press, 1948), xv–xxxii. On Coester, see John T. Reid, "Alfred Coester," *Hispania* 25 (1942): 263–71.

14. E. K. Mapes, "The Teaching of Spanish-American Literature in the United States," *Hispania* 14 (November 1931): 393–404.

15. John Casper Branner, "The Importance of the Study of the Portuguese Language," *Hispania* 2 (March 1919): 87–93.

16. Aurelio M. Espinosa, "The Term *Latin America*," *Hispania* 1 (September 1918): 135–43, and "The Term Latin America Is Repudiated by the Second Spanish-American Congress of History and Geography," ibid. 4 (October 1921): 194.

17. Mitchell Codding, "Archer Milton Huntington, Champion of Spain in the United States," in Kagan, *Spain in America*, 142–70; Georgette M. Dorn, "Archer Milton Huntington: Portrait of the Founder," *Archer M. Huntington Newsletter* 1 (Fall 1999): 6–7; Hispanic Society of America, Constitution and By-laws (New York, 1904); Library of Congress, *Hispanic and Portuguese Collections: An Illustrated Guide* (Washington, DC: Library of Congress, 1996).

18. Robert F. Byrnes, *Awakening American Education to the World: The Role of Archibald Cary Coolidge, 1866–1928* (Notre Dame, IN.: University of Notre Dame Press, 1982), 125–26; George P. Hammond and Jerry E. Patterson, "Henry Raup Wagner, 1862–1957," *HAHR* 37 (1957): 486–94.

19. Carlos E. Castañeda and Jack Autrey Dabbs, *Guide to the Latin American Manuscripts in the University of Texas Library* (Cambridge, MA: Harvard University Press, 1939), vii; Felix D. Almaraz, Jr., *Knight without Armor: Carlos Eduardo Castañeda, 1896–1958* (College Station: Texas A&M University Press, 1999), 44, 361–62n4; James A. Robertson, "In Memoriam," *HAHR* 8 (May 1928): 141–42; Manoel Cardoso, "Oliveira Lima and the Catholic University of America," *Journal of Inter-American Studies* 11 (April 1969): 209–22.

20. Byrnes, 104, 113. On Merriman, see Garrett Mattingly, "The Historian of the Spanish Empire," *American Historical Review* 54 (October 1948): 32–48. On Bliss, see Elizabeth Benson, "The Robert Woods Bliss Collection of Pre-Columbian Art: A Memoir," in *Collecting the Pre-Columbian Past*, ed. Elizabeth Hill Boone (Washington, DC: Dumbarton Oaks Library and Collection, 1993), 15–34. See also C. H. Haring to Lewis Hanke, September 6, 1951, Drawer 1, Lewis Hanke Papers, Latin American Library, Tulane University.

2. Early Historians

1. Dexter Perkins and John L. Snell, *The Education of Historians in the United States* (New York: McGraw-Hill Book Co., 1962), 16–17.

2. On Jameson, see Elizabeth Donnen and Leo F. Stock, eds., *An Historian's World: Selections from the Correspondence of John Franklin Jameson* (Philadelphia: American Philosophical Society, 1956), and Morey D. Rothberg, "'To Set a Standard of Workmanship and Compel Men to Conform to It': J. Franklin Jameson as Editor of the *American Historical Review*," *American Historical Review* 89 (1984): 957–75.

3. Lewis Hanke, "The First Lecturer on Hispanic American Diplomatic History in the United States," *HAHR* 16 (1936): 399–402, reprinted in Howard F. Cline, ed., *Latin American History: Essays on Its Study and Teaching, 1889–1965* (Austin: University of Texas Press, 1967), 1:30–32; L. Glen Seretan, *Daniel DeLeon: The Odyssey of an American Marxist* (Cambridge, MA: Harvard University Press, 1979), 12–17.

4. The course was listed in the catalog for 1894–95 and was to be offered in the second term. On Moses, see his "Autobiographical Notes," 78/154c, Bancroft Library, University of California-Berkeley, and James F. Watson, "Bernard Moses' Contribution to Scholarship," *California Historical Society Quarterly* 42 (June 1963): 111–26.

5. His article of that name is reprinted in Cline, *Latin American History*, 1:39–42.

6. Bernard Moses, *The Establishment of Spanish Rule in America* (1898; repr., New York: Cooper Square Publishers, 1965), 302–8.

7. "First Pan-American Scientific Congress," *Bulletin of the Pan American Union* 28 (April 1909): 580–98.

8. On Shepherd, see James Thomson Shotwell, "William R. Shepherd: A Tribute," *Columbia University Quarterly* 26 (December 1934): 339–43, and biographical materials in Box 2, William R. Shepherd Papers, Butler Library, Columbia University.

9. Alfred Hasbrouck to Mrs. Shepherd, August 3, 1934, Box 5, Shepherd Papers.

10. William R. Shepherd, "A Reminiscence of Simancas," *HAHR* 6 (1926): 9–20; William R. Shepherd, "The Teaching of Things Spanish," *School and Society* 21 (June 6, 1925): 663–67; Francisco Casares, "El hispanista Shepherd y su teoría del triángulo de las Españas," *La Epoca* (Madrid), January 10, 1930, clipping in Box 5, Shepherd Papers.

11. *Independent*, May 25, 1914

12. On Bourne, see *American Historical Review* 13 (April 1908): 670, and "Edward Gaylord Bourne," in James Rhodes, *Historical Essays* (New York: Macmillan Co., 1909), 189–200. Bourne's introduction to the Blair and Robertson compilation was published separately as *Discovery, Conquest, and Early History of the Philippine Islands* (Cleveland: Arthur H. Clark Co., 1907).

13. Albert Bushnell Hart to Bourne, February 25, 1902, June 27, 1902, Folder 25, Box 3, Bourne to Hart, June 29, 1902, Folder 55, Box 5, Series 1, Bourne Papers, Sterling Memorial Library, Yale University.

14. Edward Gaylord Bourne, *Spain in America, 1450–1580*, with a new introduction by Benjamin Keen (New York: Barnes and Noble, 1962), 196, 253–54, 280, 311–12. On Bourne's delay in completing the manuscript, see his diary entries for February 4 and April 30, 1904, Folder 74, Box 7, Series 2, Bourne Papers.

15. Shepherd to Bourne, April 4, 1905, Folder 46, Box 4, Series 1, Bourne Papers; *Political Science Quarterly* 20 (1905): 329–30; Keen, introduction to Bourne, *Spain in America*, x.

16. T. N. Carver to Bourne, March 22, 1905, Folder 43, Box 4, Series 1, Bourne diary; June 16, 1905, Folder 75, Box 7, Series 2, Bourne Papers.

17. For details of Bingham's early life, see the biography by his son, Alfred M. Bingham, *Portrait of an Explorer: Hiram Bingham, Discoverer of Machu Picchu* (Ames: Iowa State University Press, 1989).

18. Ibid., 82; Hiram Bingham to Herbert E. Gregory, August 24, 1907, Gregory to Bingham, September 3, 1907, Folder 35-37, Box 35, Series 4, Bingham Family Collection, Sterling Memorial Library, Yale University.

19. Bingham, *Portrait of an Explorer*, 84–92.

20. Ibid., 93–97.

21. See four-page document written by Hardy in 1913 in Folder 35-41, Box 35, Series 4, Bingham Family Collection.

22. P. A. Means to Bingham, March 22, 1914, Bingham to Means, April 1, 1914, Folder 10-141; Means to Bingham, July 31, 1914, Bingham to Means, September 23, 1914, Folder F10-142, Box 10; Means to Bingham, October 26, 1915, Folder 12-175; Bingham to Means, November 1 and 2, 1915, Folder 12-176, Box 12, Yale Peruvian Expedition, Sterling Memorial Library, Yale University.

23. Bingham, *Portrait of an Explorer*, 324–25.

24. Ibid., 312.

25. Lincoln Constance, *Berkeley and the Latin American Connection* (Berkeley, CA: N.p., 1978), 8.

26. Frederick E. Bolton, "The Early Life of Herbert E. Bolton: From Random Memories of an Admiring Brother," *Arizona and the West* 4 (1962): 70. See also John Francis Bannon, *Herbert E. Bolton: The Historian and the Man, 1870–1953* (Tucson: University of Arizona Press, 1978).

27. Russell M. Magnaghi, *Herbert E. Bolton and the Historiography of the Americas* (Westport, CT: Greenwood Press, 1998), 34–35.

28. Herbert E. Bolton to Frederick Jackson Turner, December 27, 1910, Box 134, Part 2, Herbert E. Bolton Papers, Bancroft Library, University of California-Berkeley.

29. Albert L. Hurtado, "Parkmanizing the Spanish Borderlands: Bolton, Turner, and the Historians' World," *Western Historical Quarterly* 26 (Summer 1995): 162; Bolton to Allen Johnson, October 16, 1916, December 5, 1916, Box 136, Part 2, Bolton Papers.

30. Bolton to Johnson, April 28, 1919, March 18, 1920, Box 138, Part 2, Bolton Papers. See also Hurtado, 160–61.

31. Bannon, 141–43; Bolton to Father Peter Guilday, October 15, 1919, Box 138, Part 2, Bolton Papers.

32. Magnaghi, 64–65, 84–87. Bolton's address and related documents can be found in Lewis Hanke, ed., *Do the Americas Have a Common History? A Critique of the Bolton Theory* (New York: Alfred A. Knopf, 1964).

33. Wilbur R. Jacobs, John W. Caughey, and Joe B. Frantz, *Turner, Bolton, and Webb: Three Historians of the American Frontier* (Seattle: University of Washington Press, 1965), 47.

34. Information about Chapman's life comes from "Reminiscences," Folder 1, Box 1, Charles E. Chapman Papers, Bancroft Library, University of California-Berkeley. He dictated these reminiscences after a fire on September 17, 1923, destroyed his home and most of his possessions, diaries, and other records.

35. Ibid.

36. Ibid., Folder 2; J. Fred Rippy, *Bygones I Cannot Help Recalling: The Memoirs of a Mobile Scholar* (Austin, TX: Steck-Vaughn Co., 1965), 100; Osgood Hardy, "Charles E. Chapman," *HAHR* 22 (1942): 2–4.

37. See Chapman diary, entries for June 18–24, 1923, and March 3–9, 1924, Box 2, Chapman Papers.

38. Chapman diary, entries for April 2–8, 9–15, 1923, ibid; statement by Chapman, April 5, 1923, and Bolton to David P. Barrows, April 6, 1923, Part 2, Bolton Papers.

39. "Charles Wilson Hackett: A Biographical Sketch," in *Essays in Mexican History*, ed. Thomas E. Cotner and Carlos E. Castañeda (Austin, TX: Institute of Latin American Studies, 1958), xi–xvi; Bolton tribute, *HAHR* 31 (1951): 547–48.

40. John J. TePaske, "Interview with Irving A. Leonard," *HAHR* 63 (1983): 238.

41. R. A. Humphreys, "William Spence Robertson 1872–1955," *HAHR* 36 (1956): 263–67.

42. Obituary, *American Historical Review* 47 (July 1942): 972–73; Jorge Basadre, introduction to *Latin American Courses in the United States* (Washington, DC: Pan American Union, 1949), reprinted in Cline, *Latin American History*, 2:16–17.

43. Howard F. Cline, "In Memoriam: Clarence Henry Haring, 1885–1960," *The Americas* 17 (1961): 292–97; Haring to Lewis Hanke, September 6, 1951, Drawer 1, Lewis Hanke Papers, Latin American Library, Tulane University.

44. On Castañeda, see Felix D. Almaraz, Jr., *Knight without Armor: Carlos Eduardo Castañeda, 1896–1958* (College Station: Texas A&M University Press, 1999).

45. A. P. Nasatir, introduction to Martin H. Sable, ed., *Guide to the Writings of Pioneer Latinamericanists in the United States* (New York: Haworth Press, 1989), 1–14; Bolton to T. M. Marshall, April 4, 1922, Box 140, Part 2, Bolton Papers; Albert L. Hurtado, "Herbert E. Bolton, Racism, and American History," *Pacific Historical Review* 62 (May 1993): 130–31.

46. A. C. Tilton to Bourne, May 16, 1901, Folder 21, Box 2, Series 1, Bourne Papers; Bolton to Professor McElroy, February 20, 1916, Box 135, Part 2, Bolton Papers.

47. Bannon, 105–6.

48. Ursula Lamb, "Pioneers of Discovery History in the Spanish Archives: Alice Gould and Irene Wright, A Memoir," *Primary Sources and Original Works* 2 (1993): 479–86.

49. Ibid., 486–91.

50. Lillian Estelle Fisher, "Mary Wilhelmine Williams, 1878–1944: In Memoriam," *HAHR* 24 (1944): 365–67; Jacqueline Goggin, "Challenging Sexual Discrimination in the Historical Profession: Women Historians and the American Historical Association, 1890–1940," *American Historical Review* 97 (June 1992): 784.

51. Arthur S. Aiton to Herbert I. Priestley, February 6, 1931, Carton 1; Priestley to Aiton, January 20, 1931, February 13, 1931, Carton 2, Herbert I. Priestley Papers, Bancroft Library, University of California-Berkeley.

52. James A. Robertson, "A Symposium on the Teaching of Hispanic America in Educational Institutions in the United States," *HAHR* 2 (August 1919): 397–418, reprinted in Cline, *Latin American History*, 1:231–44; "Report of a Committee of the Pan American Union on the Teaching of Latin-American History in Colleges, Normal Schools, and Universities of the United States," *HAHR* 7 (1927): 352–61.

53. See Folder 35–34, Box 35, Series 4, Bingham Family Collection.

54. Stetson Conn, "A Topical Analysis of the College Texts on Hispanic American History," *HAHR* 14 (1934): 108–13, reprinted in Cline, *Latin American History*, 1:244–48.

55. Charles E. Chapman, "The Founding of the Review," *HAHR* 1 (February 1918): 8–23.

56. Quoted in Aurelio M. Espinosa, "The Term *Latin America*," *Hispania* 1 (September 1918): 136–39.

57. Bolton to Jameson, September 12, 1921, with Bolton to Edward E. Ayer, September 12, 1921, Box 139, Part 2, Bolton Papers. Bolton hoped that Ayer would aid the struggling journal.

58. These events can be tracked in *HAHR* 3 (1920): 228–29, *HAHR* 8 (1928): 293–98; and *HAHR* 9 (1929): 241–42, the latter two reprinted in Cline, *Latin American History*, 1:265–69.

3. The Rise of Anthropology

1. Alfred L. Kroeber, "Conclusions," in *The Maya and Their Neighbors*, ed. Clarence L. Hay et al. (New York: D. Appleton-Century Co., 1940), 471.

2. Alexander Lesser, "The American Ethnological Society: The Columbia Phase, 1904–1946," in *American Anthropology: The Early Years*, ed. John V. Murra (Minneapolis: West Publishing Co., 1976), 129.

3. See Phoebe Sherman Sheftel, "The Archaeological Institute of America: A Centennial Review," *American Journal of Archaeology* 83 (January 1979): 3–17, and Colin Renfrew, "The Great Tradition Versus the Great Divide: Archaeology as Anthropology?" *American Journal of Archaeology* 84 (July 1980): 287–98.

4. John F. Freeman, "University Anthropology: Early Departments in the United States," *Papers of the Kroeber Anthropological Society* 32 (1965): 78–90; Charles Frantz, "Relevance: American Ethnology and the Wider Society, 1900–1940," in *Social Contexts of American Ethnology, 1840–1984*, ed. June Helm (Washington, DC: American Anthropological Association, 1985), 84–85; Lucy J. Chamberlain and E. Adamson Hoebel, "Anthropology Offerings in American Undergraduate Colleges," *AA* 44 (1942): 527–30.

5. On Boas, see Marshall Hyatt, *Franz Boas, Social Activist: The Dynamics of Ethnicity* (Westport, CT: Greenwood Press, 1990).

6. Donald McVicker, "Prejudice and Context: The Anthropological Archaeologist as Historian," in *Tracing Archaeology's Past: The Historiography of Archaeology*, ed. Andrew L. Christenson (Carbondale: Southern Illinois University Press, 1989), 115–20; R. Berkeley Miller, "Anthropology and Institutionalization: Frederick Starr at the University of Chicago, 1892–1923," *Papers of the Kroeber Anthropological Society* (1978): 49–60; Donald McVicker, "Parallels and Rivalries: Encounters between Boas and Starr," *Curator* 32 (1989): 212–28.

7. On Thompson, see his memoir, *People of the Serpent: Life and Adventures among the Maya* (Boston: Houghton Mifflin, 1932), and the chapter devoted to him in Robert L. Brunhouse, *In Search of the Maya: The First Archaeologists* (Albuquerque: University of New Mexico Press, 1973).

8. McVicker, "Prejudice and Context," 120–23.

9. Ricardo Godoy, "Franz Boas and His Plans for an International School of American Archaeology and Ethnology in Mexico," *Journal of the History of the Behavioral Sciences* 13 (July 1977): 228–42.

10. See Gordon Randolph Willey, *Portraits in American Archaeology: Remembrances of Some Distinguished Americanists* (Albuquerque: University of New Mexico Press, 1988), for sketches of Cummings (3–24) and Vaillant (99–120).

11. Diana Fane, "Reproducing the Pre-Columbian Past: Casts and Models in Exhibitions of Ancient America, 1824–1935," in *Collecting the Pre-Columbian Past*, ed. Elizabeth Hill Boone (Washington, DC: Dumbarton Oaks Research Library and Collection, 1993), 159–63.

12. "Prehistoric Ruins of Copán, Honduras," *Memoirs of the Peabody Museum of American Archaeology and Ethnology* (1896; repr., New York: Kraus, 1970), 5–7; Stephen Louis Black, "Field Methods and Methodologies in Lowland Maya Archaeology" (PhD diss., Harvard University, 1990), 61–67.

13. On Tozzer, see Willey, 267–90.

14. On Morley, see Robert L. Brunhouse, *Sylvanus G. Morley and the World of the Ancient Mayas* (Norman: University of Oklahoma Press, 1971), and *Morleyana: A Collection of Writings in Memoriam, Sylvanus G. Morley, 1883–1948* (Santa Fe: School of American Research and the Museum of New Mexico, 1950). For an overview of CIW archaeological projects in the 1920s and 1930s, see Black, "Field Methods and Methodologies," 75–115.

15. Brunhouse, *Morley*, 74–75, 170–204.

16. Stephen L. Black, "The Carnegie Uaxactun Project and the Development of Maya Archaeology," *Ancient Mesoamerica* 1 (1990): 273.

17. On Kidder, see Willey, 293–315, and Douglas R. Givens, *Alfred Vincent Kidder and the Development of Americanist Archaeology* (Albuquerque: University of New Mexico Press, 1992).

18. Richard E. Greenleaf, "France Vinton Scholes (1897–1979): A Memoir," *HAHR* 60 (1980): 90–94; J. Eric S. Thompson, "Ralph Loveland Roys, 1879–1965," *American Antiquity* 32 (January 1967): 95–99; Pierre Ventur, *Maya Historian: Ralph L. Roys Papers* (Nashville: Vanderbilt University Publications in Anthropology, 1978).

19. Robert L. Brunhouse, *Frans Blom, Maya Explorer* (Albuquerque: University of New Mexico Press, 1976), 40–67; Jacques Soustelle, *The Olmecs: The Oldest Civilization in Mexico*, trans. Helen R. Lane (Garden City, NY: Doubleday and Co., 1984), 9–14. Blom and LaFarge coauthored *Tribes and Temples: A Record of the Expedition to Middle America Conducted by the Tulane University of Louisiana* (New Orleans: Tulane University, 1926).

20. Brunhouse, *Blom*, 75–76, 85.

21. Brunhouse, *Morley*, 245–46; Black, "Field Methods and Methodologies," 103–6; *Piedras Negras Archaeology*, pt. 1, no. 1, introduction by Linton Satterthwaite, Jr. (Philadelphia: University Museum, University of Pennsylvania, 1943), 3–4.

22. Clyde Kluckhohn, "The Conceptual Structure of Middle American Studies," in *Maya and Their Neighbors*, 42.

23. On Uhle, see Gordon R. Willey and Jeremy A. Sabloff, *A History of American Archaeology*, 2nd ed. (San Francisco: W. H. Freeman and Co.), 68–74, and John Howland Rowe, *Max Uhle, 1856–1944: A Memoir of the Father of Peruvian Archaeology*, University

of California Publications in American Archaeology and Ethnology, vol. 46 (Berkeley and Los Angeles: University of California Press, 1963). Dated 1954, the latter work contains a biography of Uhle (1–25), as well as a bibliography, lectures, notes, and photographs.

24. Bingham, Alfred M., *Portrait of an Explorer* (Ames: Iowa St. Univ. Press, 1989), 107–24; Bingham to Minor C. Keith, May 20, 1911, Folder 5-19, Box 5, and Bingham to Edward A. Harkness, March 9, 1914, Folder 10-124, Box 10, Series 2, Yale Peruvian Expedition Papers, Sterling Memorial Library, Yale University (henceforth to be cited as YPE).

25. Bingham, *Portrait of an Explorer*, 186–87, 197–98. See also Richard L. Burger and Lucy C. Salazar, eds., *Machu Picchu: Unveiling the Mystery of the Incas* (New Haven, CT: Yale University Press, 2004).

26. Bingham, *Portrait of an Explorer*, 276–77.

27. "Memorandum of Agreement between the National Geographic Society and Hiram Bingham, on Behalf of Yale University," Folder 2-24, Box 2, Series 1, Bingham to Harkness, April 13, 1912, Folder 6-45, Box 6, Series 2, YPE.

28. "Plan for 1912," Folder 1-2, Box 1, Series 1, YPE.

29. Charles D. Hiller to Huntington Wilson, February 15, 1912, and enclosures, 823.927/1, Reel 30, *Records of the Department of State Relating to Internal Affairs of Peru*, Microcopy 746 (Washington, DC: General Services Administration, 1968) (henceforth to be cited as RDS).

30. H. Clay Howard to President William Howard Taft, April 1, 1912, Folder 6-43, Box 6, Series 1, YPE.

31. Bingham to Wilson, April 11, 1912 (823.927/7) and April 29, 1912 (823.927/12), Reel 30, RDS.

32. Howard to Secretary of State, August 31, 1912, and Wilson to Howard, October 8, 1912 (823.927/20), Reel 30, RDS.

33. *El Comercio*, October 25, 1912, 1; Howard to Secretary of State, November 13, 1912 (823.927/29), and Thomas Barbour and Alfred M. Tozzer to Secretary of State, November 14, 1912 (823.927/23), Reel 30, RDS.

34. *El Comercio*, November 4, 1912, 1; Bingham to Arthur Twining Hadley, October 21, 1912, Folder 7-71, Box 7, Series 2, YPE.

35. "Memorandum of Agreement between the National Geographic Society and Yale University," Folder 2-25, Box 2, Series 1, YPE; Bingham, *Portrait of an Explorer*, 296–97.

36. Bingham, *Portrait of an Explorer*, 304–10. On Valcárcel, see his *Memorias* (Lima: Instituto de Estudios Peruanos, 1981). In an unpublished paper, "Skirmishes Over Cultural Property: Hiram Bingham, Peruvian Indigenistas, and the Enterprise of Knowledge" (2001), Ricardo D. Salvatore attempts to place Bingham's projects and the attacks on them in the context of cultural nationalism and embryonic *indigenismo*.

37. Bingham to Harkness, November 10, 1915, Folder 12-176, Box 12, Series 2, YPE.

38. Dirección General de Instrucción Pública to Ellwood C. Erdis, January 27, 1916, Folder 2-27, Box 2, Series 1; Bingham to W. L. Morkill, February 4, 1916, Folder 12-184, Box 12, Series 2, YPE. On controversy over artifacts from Machu Picchu removed by Bingham, see Arthur Lubow, "The Password," *New York Times Magazine*, June 24, 2007, 42.

39. John Howland Rowe, "Alfred Louis Kroeber," *American Antiquity* 27 (January

1962): 401; Timothy H. H. Thoreson, "Paying the Piper and Calling the Tune: The Beginnings of Academic Anthropology in California," *Journal of the History of the Behavioral Sciences* 11 (July 1975): 257–75. On Kroeber, see also Julian H. Steward, "Alfred Louis Kroeber," *A A* 63 (1961): 1038–87, and Theodora Kroeber, *Alfred Kroeber: A Personal Configuration* (Berkeley and Los Angeles: University of California Press, 1970).

40. Rowe, "Kroeber," 402–5; Patrick H. Carmichael, ed., *The Archaeology and Pottery of Nazca, Peru: Alfred Kroeber's 1926 Expedition* (Walnut Creek, CA: Alta Mesa Press, 1998), 29–33.

41. On Bennett, see Willey, 123–45, and Alfred Kidder II, "Wendell C. Bennett—1905–1953," *A A* 56 (1954): 269–73.

42. Willey, 128.

43. S. K Lothrop, *American Antiquity* 11 (October 1945): 109–12.

44. On Lothrop, see Willey, 195–216. On Bird, see ibid., 147–68, and Junius B. Bird, *Travels and Archaeology in South Chile*, ed. John Hyslop (Iowa City: University of Iowa Press, 1988), xvi–xvii.

45. Brian W. Dippie, *The Vanishing American: White Attitudes and U.S. Indian Policy* (Middletown, CT: Wesleyan University Press, 1982), 231–36.

46. George W. Stocking, Jr., *The Ethnographer's Magic* (Madison: University of Wisconsin Press, 1992), 357.

47. See Clifford Wilcox, *Robert Redfield and the Development of American Anthropology* (Lanham, MD: Lexington Books, 2004), 29–32, 41–49; Robert Redfield, "Among the Middle Americans: A Chicago Family's Adventures as Adopted Citizens of a Mexican Village," *University of Chicago Magazine* 20 (March 1928): 243–47; Ricardo Godoy, "The Background and Context of Redfield's *Tepoztlán*," *Journal of the Steward Anthropological Society* 10 (Fall 1978): 47–77.

48. Stocking, 302–3.

49. Wilcox, 30.

50. Alfred L. Kroeber, review of *Tepoztlán, a Mexican Village: A Study of Folk Life* by Robert Redfield, *A A* 33 (April–June 1931): 236–38; Robert A. Rubinstein, ed., *Fieldwork: The Correspondence of Robert Redfield and Sol Tax* (Boulder, CO: Westview Press, 1991), 67.

51. Robert Redfield, *Tepoztlán, a Mexican Village: A Study of Folk Life* (Chicago: University of Chicago Press, 1930), 83; Robert Redfield, review of *Mexico: A Study of Two Americas*, by Stuart Chase, *International Journal of Ethics* 42 (April 1932): 353–54.

52. On Villa Rojas, see his "Fieldwork in the Mayan Region of Mexico," in *Long-Term Field Research in Social Anthropology*, ed. George Foster et al. (New York: Academic Press, 1979), 45–64. On Hansen, see his "Robert Redfield, The Yucatan Project, and I," in Murra, 167–86. See also Wilcox, 49–58.

53. On Tax, see Rubinstein and Robert Hinshaw, ed., *Currents in Anthropology: Essays in Honor of Sol Tax* (The Hague: Mouton Publishers, 1979).

54. On Parsons, see Louis A. Hieb, "Elsie Clews Parsons in the Southwest," in *Hidden Scholars: Women Anthropologists and the Native American Southwest*, ed. Nancy J. Parezo (Albuquerque: University of New Mexico Press, 1993), 63–75; Peter H. Hare, *A Woman's Quest for Science* (Buffalo, NY: Prometheus Books, 1985); and Desley Deacon, *Elsie Clews Parsons: Inventing Modern Life* (Chicago: University of Chicago Press, 1997).

55. Elsie Clews Parsons, *Mitla: Town of the Souls* (Chicago: University of Chicago Press, 1936), xi–xii.

56. Parezo, 3–37.

57. Kenneth Dauber, "Bureaucratizing the Ethnographer's Magic," *Current Anthropology* 36 (February 1995): 76. On Bunzel, see Deacon, 268–71, and Margaret A. Hardin, "Zuni Potters and *The Pueblo Potter*: The Contributions of Ruth Bunzel," in Parezo, 259–69.

58. Margaret W. Harrison, "Lila Morris O'Neale: 1886–1948," *AA* 50 (1948): 657–65; Margot Blum Schevill, "Lila Morris O'Neale (1886–1948)," in *Women Anthropologists: A Biographical Dictionary*, ed. Ute Gacs et al. (New York: Greenwood Press, 1988), 275–81.

59. Parezo, 3; Hyatt, 49.

60. "The Society for American Archaeology," *American Antiquity* 1 (1935–36): 141–51; Carl E. Guthe, "Reflections on the Founding of the Society for American Archaeology," *American Antiquity* 32 (October 1967): 433–40.

4. Geography and the Other Social Sciences

1. "Report on Instruction in Political Science in Colleges and Universities," *Proceedings of the American Political Science Association* 10 (1913): 249–70.

2. John Kirtland Wright, *Geography in the Making: The American Geographical Society, 1851–1951* (New York: American Geographical Society, 1952), 24, 27–28.

3. Ibid., 270n; Charles Redway Dryer, "A Century of Geographic Education in the United States," *AAAG* 14 (September 1924): 117–49; David Robinson, "On Preston E. James and Latin America: A Biographical Sketch," in *Studying Latin America: Essays in Honor of Preston E. James*, ed. David Robinson (Syracuse, NY: Geography Department, Syracuse University, 1980), 48.

4. See Geoffrey J. Martin, *Mark Jefferson, Geographer* (Ypsilanti: Eastern Michigan University Press, 1968).

5. See Geoffrey J. Martin, *The Life and Thought of Isaiah Bowman* (Hamden, CT: Archon Books, 1980). On Bowman and other early geographers, see also Daniel W. Gade, "North American Reflections on Latin Americanist Geography," in *Latin America in the 21st Century: Challenges and Solutions*, ed. Gregory Knapp (Austin: Conference of Latin American Geographers and University of Texas Press, 2002), 1–44.

6. Wright, 146. See Martin, *Bowman*, 35–53, for the geographical expeditions to South America.

7. Quoted in Martin, *Bowman*, 46.

8. Ibid., 26–27; Homer Aschmann, "George McCutcheon McBride," *AAAG* 62 (1972): 685–88.

9. George M. McBride, *The Land Systems of Mexico* (New York: American Geographic Society, 1923), 173–75.

10. Wright, 185–90.

11. On the expedition, see Martin, *Jefferson*, 145–66.

12. Martin, *Bowman*, 71–72; Raye R. Platt, "The Millionth Map of Hispanic America," *Geographical Review* 17 (April 1927): 301–8.

13. On Sauer's early life, see two pieces by Martin S. Kenzer: "Milieu and the 'Intel-

lectual Landscape': Carl O. Sauer's Undergraduate Heritage," *AAAG* 75 (1985): 258–70, and "Like Father, Like Son: William Albert and Carl Ortwin Sauer," in *Carl O. Sauer: A Tribute*, ed. Martin S. Kenzer (Corvallis: Oregon State University Press, 1987), 40–65.

14. Anne Macpherson, "Preparing for the National Stage: Carl Sauer's First Ten Years at Berkeley," in Kenzer, *Sauer*, 71.

15. Ibid., 75–76; Robert C. West, "A Berkeley Perspective on the Study of Latin American Geography in the United States and Canada," in Robinson, *Studying Latin America*, 146–51. Sauer is quoted in John Leighly, "Carl Ortwin Sauer, 1889–1975," *AAAG* 66 (September 1976): 341.

16. Henry J. Bruman, "Carl Sauer in Midcareer: A Personal View by One of His Students," in Kenzer, *Sauer*, 130.

17. Macpherson, 75–83.

18. Bruman, 126–27; James J. Parsons, "Carl Sauer's Vision of an Institute for Latin American Studies," *Geographical Review* 86 (July 1996): 378; Henry J. Bruman, "Recollections of Carl Sauer and Research in Latin America," ibid., 371.

19. West, 160–63; J. E. Spencer, "A Geographer West of the Sierra Nevada," *AAAG* 69 (1979): 46–49. According to Parsons, Sauer directed thirty-six dissertations, of which only twelve dealt with Latin America (384).

20. David J. Robinson, "On Preston E. James and Latin America: A Biographical Sketch," in Robinson, *Studying Latin America*, 11; Gade, 8–9.

21. Robinson, "On Preston E. James," 12–13.

22. Ibid., 17–19.

23. Ibid., 34.

24. Ibid., 52; Geoffrey J. Martin, "In Memoriam: Preston E. James, 1899–1986," *AAAG* 78 (1988): 171; Kempton E. Webb, "Developments in Brazilian Geography during the Twentieth Century," in Robinson, *Studying Latin America*, 183.

25. On Jones, see John C. Hudson, "In Memoriam: Clarence Fielden Jones, 1893–1991," *AAAG* 83 (1993): 167–72.

26. Clarence F. Jones, *South America* (New York: Henry Holt and Co., 1930), 720–21.

27. On Platt, see Richard Hartshorne, "Robert S. Platt, 1891–1964," *AAAG* 54 (1964): 630–37, and Chauncy D. Harris, "Geography at Chicago in the 1930s and 1940s," *AAAG* 69 (1979): 22, 26–27.

28. "A Memorandum on the Development of Economics in South America," January 7, 1941, Record Group 1: Projects, Series 300: Latin America, Box 8, Rockefeller Foundation Archives, Rockefeller Archive Center, Sleepy Hollow, NY.

29. Charles W. Wagley, ed., *Social Science Research on Latin America* (New York: Columbia University Press, 1964), 15.

30. Paul S. Reinsch, "Parliamentary Government in Chile," *American Political Science Review* 3 (November 1909): 507–38. On Reinsch, see Donald Joseph Murphy, "Professors, Publicists, and Pan Americanism, 1905–1917: A Study in the Use of 'Experts' in Shaping American Foreign Policy" (PhD diss., University of Wisconsin, 1970), passim.

31. On Rowe, see Murphy, 167–215, and David Barton Castle, "The Intellectual Foundations of U.S.-Latin American Policy in the Early Twentieth Century" (PhD diss., University of Oregon, 1991), 21–121.

32. Quoted in Castle, 28.

33. Ibid., 34–36; L. S. Rowe, *The United States and Porto Rico* (New York: Longmans, Green, and Co., 1904), 151–52.

34. L. S. Rowe, "The Renomination of President Díaz," *American Monthly Review of Reviews* 28 (September 1903): 318–20.

35. L. S. Rowe, "The Mexican Revolution: Its Causes and Consequences," *Political Science Quarterly* 27 (June 1912): 281–97.

36. L. S. Rowe, "The Development of Democracy on the American Continent," *American Political Science Review* 16 (February 1922): 1–9.

37. On Munro, see Castle, 122–204.

38. Many years later Munro recalled his experiences in *A Student in Central America, 1914–1916* (New Orleans: Middle American Research Institute, Tulane University, 1983), using letters he wrote at the time to refresh his memory.

39. R. A. Gomez, *The Study of Latin American Politics in University Programs in the United States* (Tucson: University of Arizona Press, 1967), 26–27.

40. On Tannenbaum, see Helen Delpar, "Frank Tannenbaum: The Making of a Mexicanist," *The Americas* 45 (October 1988): 153–71, and Charles A. Hale, "Frank Tannenbaum and the Mexican Revolution," *HAHR* 75 (1995): 215–46.

41. "Sweetened 'Reds' and Rebels of Yesteryear," *Literary Digest* 84 (January 31, 1925): 40.

42. The reviewer was Herbert Heaton in the *Journal of Political Economy* 43 (October 1935): 710–11.

43. James F. King, "Sanford A. Mosk (1904–1960)," *HAHR* 41 (August 1961): 413–18; West, 153–54.

44. T. Lynn Smith, "Sociology," in *Handbook of Latin American Studies: 1951* (Gainesville: University of Florida Press, 1954), 234.

45. Edward A. Ross, *South of Panama* (New York: Century Co., 1915), unpaged preface.

46. Edward A. Ross, *The Social Revolution in Mexico* (New York: Century Co., 1923), 105–6.

47. Smith, 235. Frank W. Fetter was also a member of the commission.

48. *New York Times*, July 2, 1938, 13.

5. Latin Americanists and the World of Policy Making

1. Mark T. Berger, *Under Northern Eyes: Latin American Studies and U.S. Hegemony in the Americas, 1898–1990* (Bloomington: Indiana University Press, 1995), 29.

2. Donald Joseph Murphy uses the term "service intellectual" in his dissertation, especially to refer to a new generation of specialists employed by the government in the 1920s. See "Professors, Publicists, and Pan Americanism, 1905–1917: A Study of the Origin of the Use of 'Experts' in Shaping American Foreign Policy" (PhD diss., University of Wisconsin, 1970), 485–87.

3. John J. TePaske, "An Interview with Irving A. Leonard," *HAHR* 63 (May 1983): 235.

4. Bernard Moses, "Autobiographical Notes," Moses Papers, Bancroft Library, University of California-Berkeley; Glenn Anthony May, *Social Engineering in the Philippines: The Aims, Execution, and Impact of American Colonial Policy, 1900–1913* (Westport, CT:

Greenwood Press, 1980), 10–12, 84, 96; Bernard Moses, "American Control of the Philippines," *Atlantic Monthly* 111 (May 1913): 585–96.

5. TePaske, 237.

6. On Robertson, see Curtis A. Wilgus, "The Life of James Alexander Robertson," in *Hispanic American Essays: A Memorial to James Alexander Robertson*, ed. Curtis A. Wilgus (Chapel Hill: University of North Carolina Press, 1942), 3–14.

7. *Dial* 36 (March 16, 1904): 192–94; J. A. Robertson to Bourne, March 26, 1904, Folder 40; Adolph F. Bandelier to Bourne, March 16, 1905, Folder 42, Box 4, Series 1, Bourne Papers, Yale University Library.

8. E. G. Bourne, *Essays in Historical Criticism* (1901; repr., Freeport, NY: Books for Libraries, 1967), 228. On the Philippine Information Society, see *Letters of Louis D. Brandeis, Volume 1 (1870–1907): Urban Reformer*, ed. Melvin I. Urofsky and David W. Levy (Albany: State University of New York Press, 1971), 148n1, 158n1.

9. David J. Robinson, "On Preston E. James and Latin America: A Biographical Sketch," in *Studying Latin America: Essays in Honor of Preston E. James*, ed. David J. Robinson (Syracuse, NY: Geography Department, Syracuse University, 1980), 5–6, 17; John A. Britton, *Carleton Beals: A Radical Journalist in Latin America* (Albuquerque: University of New Mexico Press, 1987), 14–15.

10. TePaske, 236.

11. For a detailed account, see Charles H. Harris III and Louis R. Sadler, *The Archaeologist Was a Spy: Sylvanus G. Morley and the Office of Naval Intelligence* (Albuquerque: University of New Mexico Press, 2003).

12. Ibid., 269–71, 289–91.

13. Ibid., 60–61, 188–94.

14. Ibid., 109; *New York Times*, May 10, 1915, 7.

15. Harris and Sadler, 52–53. Mason was accompanied by William H. Mechling, who received a doctorate in anthropology from Harvard in 1917.

16. For an account of these events unsympathetic to Boas, see ibid., 284–89. Boas's letter appeared in the *Nation*, December 20, 1919, 797. See also Marshall Hyatt, *Franz Boas, Social Activist: The Dynamics of Ethnicity* (Westport, CT: Greenwood Press, 1990), 131–33.

17. For the resolution, see *AA* 22 (1920): 93–94.

18. See Lawrence E. Gelfand, *The Inquiry: American Preparations for Peace, 1917–1919* (New Haven, CT: Yale University Press, 1963).

19. Ibid., 102.

20. Geoffrey J. Martin, *Mark Jefferson, Geographer* (Ypsilanti: Eastern Michigan University Press, 1968), 148; John T. Reid, "Alfred Coester," *Hispania* 25 (1942): 264.

21. Percy Alvin Martin, *Latin America and the War* (Baltimore: Johns Hopkins Press, 1925), 546–48.

22. Laurence F. Schmeckebier and Gustavus A. Weber, *The Bureau of Foreign and Domestic Commerce: Its History, Activities, and Organization* (Baltimore: Johns Hopkins Press, 1924), 28, 32. The bureau was initially part of the Department of Commerce and Labor, which was divided in 1913.

23. Joseph Brandes, *Herbert Hoover and Economic Diplomacy: Department of Commerce Policy* (Pittsburgh: University of Pittsburgh Press, 1962), 49; Robert Neal Seidel,

"Progressive Pan Americanism: Development and United States Policy toward South America, 1906–1931" (PhD diss., Cornell University, 1973), 2, 4. Seidel provides much information on Klein's early life and on his work at the bureau, especially on pp. 151–87.

24. Robinson, "Preston E. James," 54–59.

25. Murphy, 444–46. On the Pan-American Conference and the International High Commission, see Seidel, 72–103.

26. Percy A. Martin, "The Second Pan American Financial Conference," *HAHR* 3 (May 1920): 202–13.

27. For a review of Munro's State Department career, see David Barton Castle, "The Intellectual Foundations of U.S.-Latin American Policy in the Early Twentieth Century" (PhD diss., University of Oregon, 1991), 158–91. See also Andrew J. Bachevich, Jr., "The American Electoral Mission in Nicaragua, 1927–28," *Diplomatic History* 4 (1980): 241–61.

28. See Leo S. Rowe to Mr. Davis, July 28, 1920, 817.51/1223, in *Records of the Department of State, Internal Affairs of Nicaragua, 1910–1929*, Reel 81 (Washington, DC: General Services Administration, 1966).

29. W. W. Cumberland to Secretary of State, March 10, 1928, 817.51/1921, Reel 89, ibid. See also Walter C. Thurston to Secretary of State, September 17, 1924, 817.51/1517, Reel 85, ibid.

30. Seidel emphasizes this distinction in his dissertation; see especially pp. 30–37.

31. Chester Lloyd Jones, *Caribbean Interests of the United States* (New York: D. Appleton and Co., 1916), 3; Charles W. Hackett, "Relations between the United States and Latin America since 1898," *Current History* 26 (September 1927): 833–47.

32. Hiram Bingham, *The Monroe Doctrine: An Obsolete Shibboleth* (New Haven, CT: Yale University Press, 1913), 55. See also Thomas L. Karnes, "Hiram Bingham and his Obsolete Shibboleth," *Diplomatic History* 3 (1979): 39–57.

33. Clarence H. Haring, *South America Looks at the United States* (Cambridge, MA: Harvard University Press, 1928), 102.

34. Bingham, 109–11; C. E. Chapman, "A Monroe Doctrine Divided: Suggestion for a Presidential Message," *Political Science Quarterly* 37 (March 1922): 75–82.

35. Jones, 3–4.

36. Dana G. Munro, "The Basis of American Intervention in the Caribbean," *Current History* 26 (September 1927): 857–61; Herbert J. Spinden, "Shall the United States Intervene in Cuba?" *World's Work* 41 (March 1921): 465–83.

37. Charles W. Hackett, *The Mexican Revolution and the United States, 1910–1926*, World Peace Foundation Pamphlets, vol. 9, no. 5 (Boston: World Peace Foundation, 1926), 341; Isaac J. Cox, "The Mexican Problem: Self-Help or Intervention," *Political Science Quarterly* 36 (June 1921): 226–44; Moisés Sáenz and Herbert I. Priestley, *Some Mexican Problems* (Chicago: University of Chicago Press, 1926); J. Fred Rippy, *The United States and Mexico* (New York: Alfred K. Knopf, 1926), 360–61.

38. Rippy, 363–64; foreword to Samuel Guy Inman, *Intervention in Mexico* (New York: George H. Doran Co., 1919), x–xi; Hackett, *Mexican Revolution*, 401–2.

39. Abstract of address, February 1919, William R. Shepherd Papers, Columbia University; Sáenz and Priestley, 163–64.

40. Rippy, 351–58; Sáenz and Priestley, 144.

41. Rippy, 363–64; Sáenz and Priestley, 151–54.

42. Jones, 351; J. Fred Rippy, "Literary Yankeephobia in Hispanic America," *Journal of International Relations* 12 (April 1922): 538.

43. William R. Shepherd, "New Light on the Monroe Doctrine," *Political Science Quarterly* 31 (1916): 583; William R. Shepherd, "Uncle Sam, Imperialist: A Survey of Our Encroachments in the Caribbean, 1898–1927," *New Republic* 49 (January 26, 1927): 269. See also Shepherd, "America Again Rouses Her Latin Neighbors," *New York Times*, January 23, 1927, xx5.

44. Leo S. Rowe, "Some Fundamental Misconceptions Concerning South America," *Proceedings of the American Political Science Association* 4 (1907): 28–33.

45. Karnes, 41–42, 54–57.

46. Haring, 75, 122–23.

47. Barnes wrote a similar introduction to each volume in the series. In addition to the three mentioned here, two others relating to Latin America appeared in the series, both published by the Vanguard Press of New York in 1928: Melvin M. Knight, *The Americans in Santo Domingo*, and Margaret Alexander Marsh, *The Bankers in Bolivia*. Chapman's review of Jenks's book is in *HAHR* 9 (May 1929): 224–28, and is followed by his equally acerbic review of Knight's volume (228–30). For a rebuttal by Jenks, see *HAHR* 10 (February 1930): 58–60.

48. The events surrounding the writing and publication of the book are described in Chapman's diaries for 1924–27 and in his travel diary of his visits to Cuba, Box 2, Chapman Papers, Bancroft Library, University of California-Berkeley. See also Louis A. Perez, Jr., "Scholarship and the State: Notes on a History of the Cuban Republic," *HAHR* 54 (November 1974): 682–90.

49. Charles E. Chapman, *A History of the Cuban Republic: A Study in Hispanic-American Politics* (New York: Macmillan, 1927), vii.

50. Guerra's review appeared in Havana's *Diario de la Marina* on April 10, 1927. The clipping as well as other newspaper articles and letters related to the book can be found in a scrapbook (volume 7) in the Chapman Papers.

51. Ortiz to Chapman, March 22, 1927, Box 1, José Estrada Palma y Guardiola, February 2, 1928, scrapbook, Chapman Papers.

52. Williams to Chapman, October 5, 1927, and Pierson to Chapman, July 16, 1927, scrapbook, ibid. Williams reviewed the book favorably in *HAHR* 8 (May 1928): 224–26.

53. *New York Evening Post Literary Review*, April 23, 1927, clipping in Box 5, Shepherd Papers.

6. A Decade of Expansion, 1935–1945

1. Cf. James William Park, *Latin American Underdevelopment: A History of Perspectives in the United States, 1870–1965* (Baton Rouge: Louisiana State University Press, 1995), 145–47, and Claude Curtis Erb, "Nelson Rockefeller and United States-Latin American Relations, 1940–1945" (PhD diss., Clark University, 1982), 284.

2. J. Manuel Espinosa, *Inter-American Beginnings of United States Cultural Diplomacy, 1936–1948* (Washington, DC: U.S. Department of State, 1976), 78–87, 111–13, 124–25; Frank A. Ninkovich, *The Diplomacy of Ideas: U.S. Foreign Policy and Cultural Relations, 1938–1950* (Cambridge: Cambridge University Press, 1981), 24–34.

3. Donald Fisher, *Fundamental Development of the Social Sciences: Rockefeller Philanthropy and the United States Social Science Research Council* (Ann Arbor: University of Michigan Press, 1993), 45–47.

4. Raymond B. Fosdick, *The Story of the Rockefeller Foundation* (New York: Harper and Brothers, 1952), 239–42.

5. "Latin America in the Humanities Program," March 1, 1938, Record Group 1.2, Series 300R, Folder 116, Rockefeller Foundation Archives, Rockefeller Archive Center (henceforth to be cited as RF).

6. "Survey of Cultural Activities, South America (West Coast), May–September 1937," Record Group 1.1, Series 300R, Box 8, Folder 53, RF.

7. JCLAS, Proceedings, September 8–9, 1944, 81–83, Folder 16-9, Container 811, Central Files, Library of Congress, Manuscript Division, Library of Congress (henceforth to be cited as CFLC). See also Lewis Hanke, "The Early Development of Latin American Studies in the U.S.A.," in *Studying Latin America: Essays in Honor of Preston E. James,* ed. David J. Robinson (Syracuse, NY: Geography Department, Syracuse University, 1980), 109–10.

8. ACLS, *Proceedings Number,* October 1934, Bulletin No. 22 (Washington, 1934), 78–81.

9. Hanke, 110–12; C. H. Haring, preface to *Handbook of Latin American Studies, 1935* (1936; repr., Gainesville: University Press of Florida, 1963), xi–xii.

10. Lewis Hanke, introduction to *Handbook,* 1935, xiii.

11. See No. 38048, Record Group 1.1 Projects, Series 200, U.S., Box 195, Folder 2338, RF.

12. ACLS, Committee on Latin-American Studies, Minutes, Box 126, Howard F. Cline Papers, Manuscript Division, Library of Congress. See also ACLS, *Proceedings Number,* Bulletin No. 31 (Washington, 1940), 260–64.

13. No. 40339, Record Group 1.1 Projects, Series 200, U.S., Box 195, Folder 2340, RF; Humanities Grants for Latin America, Record Group 1.2, Series 300R, Box 15, Folder 116, RF; Rockefeller Foundation, *Annual Reports, 1940,* 308–9; Arthur S. Aiton, "Institute of Latin-American Studies," *HAHR* 19 (1939): 561–63; Charles W. Hackett, "The Special Institute of Latin-American Studies at the University of Texas in the Summer of 1940," *HAHR* 20 (1940): 650–54.

14. "Hispanic Foundation of the Library of Congress," *Hispania* 23 (October 1940): 256–62; Mario Pedrosa, "Portinari: From Brodowski to the Library of Congress," *Bulletin of the Pan American Union* 76 (May 1942): 258–66; Library of Congress, *Hispanic and Portuguese Collections: An Illustrated Guide* (Washington, DC: Library of Congress 1996), 17–18.

15. Helen Delpar, "Lewis Hanke and Latin American History: The Legacy of an 'Old Christian,'" *SECOLAS Annals* 34 (2002): 141–55.

16. Rockefeller Foundation, *Annual Report, 1939,* 331; idem, *Annual Report, 1941,* 282–83; idem, *Annual Report, 1943,* 206–7; Folder 11-1, Container 804, CFLC.

17. JCLAS, Minutes, March 29, 1942, Box 253, Folder 2984, SSRC Archives, Rockefeller Archive Center.

18. Rockefeller Foundation, *Annual Report, 1941,* 249–50; idem, *Annual Report, 1944,* 225–26; David H. Stevens to Waldo G. Leland, October 15, 1943, and Leland to Ross G. Harrison and Robert T. Crane, October 16, 1943, Box 253, Folder 2985, SSRC Archives;

David J. Robinson, "On Preston E. James and Latin America: A Biographical Sketch," in Robinson, *Studying Latin America*, 67–68.

19. Carl O. Sauer, *Andean Reflections: Letters from Carl O. Sauer while on a South American Trip under a Grant from the Rockefeller Foundation, 1942*, ed. Robert C. West (Boulder, CO: Westview Press, 1982), 87, 121.

20. Rockefeller Foundation, *Annual Report, 1942*, 209–10; idem, *Annual Report, 1943*, 204–5; idem, *Annual Report, 1944*, 235–36; Leland to Charles A. Thomson (mimeograph), Folder 17-4, Container 813, and Hamilton report, Folder 3-2, 1942, Container 793, CFLC.

21. On the CIAA, see Erb, 74–75, and *History of the Coordinator of Inter-American Affairs* (Washington, DC: Government Printing Office, 1947).

22. Espinosa, 274; *Notes on Latin American Studies*, No. 1 (April 1943): 56–57; JCLAS, report of meeting, May 9, 1943, Folder 3, 1943, Container 791, CFLC.

23. Robinson, "Preston E. James," 75–76; Earl Parker Hanson, ed., *New World Guides to the American Republics*, 3 vols. (New York: Duell, Sloan and Pearce, 1943); idem, *Index to the Millionth Map of Hispanic America* (Washington, DC: Government Printing Office, 1943); "Strategic Index of Latin America," Folder 3, 1942, Box 791, CFLC. For an overview of scholarly projects undertaken during the war, see Lewis Hanke, "The Development of Latin-American Studies in the United States, 1939–1945," *The Americas* 4 (1947): 32–64.

24. Erb, 278; Espinosa, 308; Park F. Wollam, "Summary of the Report on the Activities of the Institute of Latin-American Studies at the University of Texas, 1940–41," *HAHR* 22 (1942): 229–35.

25. Erb, 76; *Notes on Latin American Studies*, No. 1 (April 1943): 47; William Duncan Strong, *Cross Sections of New World Prehistory: A Brief Report on the Work of the Institute of Andean Research, 1941–1942*, Smithsonian Miscellaneous Publications, vol. 104 (Washington, DC: Smithsonian Institution, 1943); Gordon Randolph Willey, *Portraits in American Archaeology: Remembrances of Some Distinguished Americanists* (Albuquerque: University of New Mexico Press, 1988), 86–90, 147, 156–57.

26. Sauer, 81.

27. Willey, 181–84; Theodora Kroeber, *Alfred Kroeber: A Personal Configuration* (Berkeley and Los Angeles: University of California Press, 1970), 151–54; A. L. Kroeber, *Peruvian Archaeology in 1942* (New York: Viking Fund, 1944), 5.

28. On Steward, see Willey, 219–41, and Virginia Kerns, *Scenes from the High Desert: Julian Steward's Life and Theory* (Urbana: University of Illinois Press, 2003), 218–32. See also Steward's introduction to the first volume of the *Handbook of South American Indians* (Washington, DC: Government Printing Office, 1946). On Métraux, see Charles Wagley, "Alfred Métraux, 1902–1963," *AA* 66 (June 1964): 603–13.

29. George M. Foster, "The Institute of Social Anthropology," in *The Uses of Anthropology*, ed. Walter Goldschmidt (Washington, DC: American Anthropological Association, 1979), 205–15; Julian H. Steward, *Area Research: Theory and Practice* (New York: Social Science Research Council, 1950), 33–37.

30. Quoted in Foster, 211.

31. Ibid.

32. Hanke to Luther Evans, May 11, 1943, Folder 4-11, 1940–54, and "American Library Association: Its Participation and Contribution to the U.S. Program of Rehabilitation of the National Library of Peru," November 22, 1948, Folder 4-11-1, Container 795, CFLC.

For Basadre's account of the fire and its aftermath, see his *La vida y la historia: Ensayos sobre personas, lugares y problemas* (Lima: Fondo del Libro del Banco Industrial del Perú, 1975), 355–425.

33. Espinosa, 170, 303–4; William S. Stokes to Charles A. Thomson, February 3, 1942, Folder 17-4, Container 813, CFLC.

34. Espinosa, 167, 176, 284–85; Hanke, "Latin-American Studies, 1939–45," 37.

35. Hanke, "Latin-American Studies, 1939–1945," 39–42; C. Harvey Gardiner, *Samuel Putnam: Latin Americanist: A Bibliography* (Carbondale: The Library, Southern Illinois University, 1970). See also J. H. D. Allen, Jr., "Portuguese Studies in the United States," *Hispania* 25 (February 1942): 94–100.

36. Robinson, "Preston E. James," 71. Robinson discusses James's work for the OSS on pp. 61–73.

37. Don S. Kirschner, *Cold War Exile: The Unclosed Case of Maurice Halperin* (Columbia: University of Missouri Press, 1995), 67–71; Robin W. Winks, *Town and Gown: Scholars in the Secret War, 1939–1961*, 2nd ed. (New Haven, CT: Yale University Press, 1996), 89.

38. Maurice Halperin, "Mexico the Incredible," *Current History* 45 (November 1936): 50.

39. Kirschner, 86–94; John Earl Haynes and Harvey Klehr, *Venona: Decoding Soviet Espionage in America* (New Haven, CT: Yale University Press, 1999), 101–2.

40. Edwin M. Shook, *Incidents in the Life of a Maya Archaeologist* (Guatemala City: Southwestern Academy Press, 1998), 79–92; Ruben E. Reina, "John Phillip Gillin, 1907–1973," *AA* 78 (March 1976): 82.

41. Wendell Clark Bennett, *The Ethnogeographic Board*, Smithsonian Miscellaneous Collections, vol. 107 (Washington, DC: Smithsonian Institution, 1947).

42. Ernesto Yepes, ed., *Mito y realidad de una frontera: Perú-Ecuador 1942–1949. El Informe McBride: Un testimonio inédito del Departamento de Estado* (Lima: Ediciones Análises, 1996), 7–8, 10–12. This book contains a Spanish translation of McBride's report.

43. Espinosa, 334–38.

44. Susan M. Rigdon, *The Culture Façade: Art, Science, and Politics in the Work of Oscar Lewis* (Urbana: University of Illinois Press, 1988), 18–20.

45. Carl C. Taylor, "Early Rural Sociological Research in Latin America," *Rural Sociology* 25 (1960): 1–8; Lowry Nelson, "Rural Sociology: Some Inter-American Aspects," *Journal of Inter-American Studies* 9 (July 1967): 326–30; Lowry Nelson, *In the Direction of His Dreams: Memoirs* (New York: Philosophical Library, 1985), 228–31, 306–11. Whetten spent three years in Mexico.

46. Hanke, "Latin-American Studies, 1939–1945," 35.

47. Lewis Hanke, "Plain Speaking about Latin America," *Harper's Magazine*, November 1940, reprinted in *Selected Writings of Lewis Hanke on the History of Latin America* (Tempe: Center for Latin American Studies, Arizona State University, 1979), 417–18. According to Samuel Putnam, Hanke's article constituted "one of the first forthright criticisms" of the newly established Rockefeller program. Putnam, a Marxist of the Far Left, publicly attacked the program and Rockefeller, whom he called the embodiment of Yankee imperialism in the eyes of Latin Americans. See two articles on the subject by

Putnam in *New Masses*: "Whose Culture for Latin America?" 38 (January 28, 1941): 13–15, and "Oil and Culture Don't Mix," 38 (February 4, 1941): 3–5. Putnam offered to quit the *Handbook of Latin American Studies* because of these articles and one attacking the Vargas government in Brazil ("Brazil's Master Demagogue: Dr. Vargas," *New Masses* 37 [December 17, 1940]: 12–13) but did stay on. See Putnam to Hanke, December 11, 1940, and Haring to Lewis [Hanke], January 13, 1941, Box 126, Cline Papers.

48. Dana G. Munro, "Postwar Problems in Our Latin-American Relations," *American Political Science Review* 38 (June 1944): 521–30; Arthur P. Whitaker, "Latin America and Postwar Organization," *Annals of the American Academy* 240 (July 1945):109–15; Frank Tannenbaum, "An American Commonwealth of Nations," *Foreign Affairs* 22 (July 1944): 576–88.

7. Marking Time, 1945–1958

1. Lewis Hanke, "Studying Latin America: The Views of an 'Old Christian,'" in *Selected Writings of Lewis Hanke on the History of Latin America* (Tempe: Center for Latin American Studies, Arizona State University, 1979), 237; Howard F. Cline, "The Latin American Studies Association: A Summary Survey with Appendix," *LARR* 2 (Autumn 1966): 60. Hanke's essay first appeared in the *Journal of Inter-American Studies* 9 (January 1967): 43–64.

2. Leonard's report, which first appeared in *Notes on Latin American Studies*, No. 1 (April 1943): 7–46, is reprinted in Howard F. Cline, ed., *Latin American History: Essays on Its Study and Teaching in the United States, 1889–1965*, 2 vols. (Austin: University of Texas Press, 1967), 1:289–316.

3. Cline, *Latin American History*, 1:291–300.

4. Ibid., 315–16.

5. *Courses on Latin America in Institutions of Higher Learning in the United States, 1948–1949*, comp. Estellita Hart (Washington, DC: Department of Cultural Affairs, Division of Education, Pan American Union, 1949), v–vi. Jorge Basadre's long introduction to this survey (ix–lxxiii) is reprinted in Cline, *Latin American History*, 2: 413–60.

6. *Courses on Latin America*, xxxi.

7. Ibid., 1.

8. Ibid.

9. Cline, *Latin American History*, 1:310–11.

10. Cline to Charles C. Griffin, December 8, 1948, Folder Correspondence C-M, Box 127, Howard F. Cline Papers, Manuscript Division, Library of Congress.

11. James F. King and Samuel Everett, "Latin American History Textbooks," in *American Council on Education, Latin America in School and College Teaching Materials* (Washington, DC: 1944), reprinted in Cline, *Latin American History*, 1: 336–49.

12. For a review of the literature on the Black Legend, as well as a debate on its accuracy, see Benjamin Keen, "The Black Legend Revisited: Assumptions and Realities," *HAHR* 49 (1969): 703–19, and Lewis Hanke, "A Modest Proposal for a Moratorium on Grand Generalizations: More Thoughts on the Black Legend," *HAHR* 51 (1971): 112–27.

13. "The Academy of American Franciscan History," *HAHR* 24 (1944): 541–43.

14. Lewis Hanke, "Experiencias con Silvio Zavala, 1933–1949: Algunos Recuerdos al

Azar," *Historia Mexicana* 38 (1989): 603–5; Ruth Lapham Butler, "Notes on the First Congress of Historians of Mexico and the United States," *HAHR* 29 (1949): 634–39.

15. Cline, *Latin American History*, 1:269–73.

16. Ibid., 309; *Courses on Latin America*, lxvi.

17. Kirchhoff's article, "Mesoamerica," was first published in *Acta Americana* 1 (1943). An English translation appears in *Heritage of Conquest: The Ethnology of Middle America*, ed. Sol Tax (Glencoe, IL: Free Press, 1952), 17–30. Kirchhoff was a German-born scholar resident in Mexico.

18. Walter W. Taylor, *A Study of Archaeology, Memoir No. 69* ([Menasha, WI:] American Anthropological Association, 1948), 59–60; Black, "Field Methods and Methodologies," 115–17.

19. Black, "Field Methods and Methodologies," 117–26. On Pollock, see Gordon Randolph Willey, *Portraits in American Archaeology: Remembrances of Some Distinguished Americanists* (Albuquerque: University of New Mexico Press, 1988), 341–62.

20. Char Solomon, *Tatiana Proskouriakoff: Interpreting the Ancient Maya* (Norman: University of Oklahoma Press, 2002), 137–38.

21. Black, "Field Methods and Methodologies," 138–45, 155–63.

22. Ibid., 127–29, 145–54. See also Edwin M. Shook et al., *Tikal Reports, Numbers 1–4* (Philadelphia: University Museum, University of Pennsylvania, 1958). For Shook's candid account of his work at Tikal, see his *Incidents in the Life of a Maya Archaeologist* (Guatemala City: Southwestern Academy Press, 1998), 119–54.

23. See Joyce Marcus and Ronald Spores, "The *Handbook of Middle Americans*: A Retrospective Look," *AA* 80 (1978): 85–100.

24. Willey, 132–42, 236–37; Gordon R. Willey and Jeremy A. Sabloff, *A History of American Archaeology*, 2nd ed. (San Francisco: W. H. Freeman and Co., 1980), 146–48; Richard P. Schaedel and Izumi Shimada, "Peruvian Archaeology, 1946–80: An Analytic Overview," *World Archaeology* 13 (February 1982): 359–60.

25. Ruth Benedict, "The Viking Fund," *AA* 49 (1947): 527–30; Emil W. Haury, "Axel L. Wenner-Gren, 1881–1961," *American Antiquity* 29 (July 1963): 90–91; John W. Dodds, "Eulogy for Paul Fejos," *Current Anthropology* 4 (October 1963): 405–6. The U.S. government blacklisted Wenner-Gren in January 1942 for doing business with the Axis (*New York Times*, January 15, 1942, 1, and November 25, 1961, 1).

26. Richard N. Adams, "Ricocheting through Half a Century of Revolution," *LASA Forum* 29 (Fall 1998): 14–15.

27. In 1949 the Committee on Latin American Anthropology of the National Research Council recommended the study of what it considered a cultural type peculiar to modern Latin America, namely, *criollo* culture. This culture type was not to be found among those whose mode of life was predominantly Indian or among "high society" sophisticates. See "Research Needs in the Field of Modern Latin American Culture," *AA* 51 (1949): 149–54. See also Ronald R. McIrvin, "Latin American Culture: Reality or Anthropological Myth?" *SECOLAS Annals* 16 (1985): 21–35.

28. Julian H. Steward, *Area Research: Theory and Practice* (New York: Social Science Research Council, 1950), 57–66. See also Daniel Rubín de la Borbolla and Ralph Beals, "The Tarasca Project: A Cooperative Enterprise of the National Polytechnic Institute, Mexican Bureau, Indian Affairs and the University of California," *AA* 42 (1940): 708–

12, and George M. Foster, "Fieldwork in Tzintzuntzan: The First Thirty Years," in *Long-Term Field Research in Social Anthropology*, ed. George M. Foster et al. (New York: Academic Press, 1979), 165–84.

29. Susan M. Rigdon, *The Culture Façade: Art, Science, and Politics in the Work of Oscar Lewis* (Urbana: University of Illinois Press, 1988), 20, 200–201; Clifford Wilcox, *Robert Redfield and the Development of American Anthropology* (Lanham, MD: Lexington Books, 2004), 65–66; Oscar Lewis, *Life in a Mexican Village: Tepoztlán Restudied* (Urbana: University of Illinois Press, 1951), 435.

30. Steward, *Area Research*, 126–49; Julian Steward et al., *The People of Puerto Rico* (Urbana: University of Illinois Press, 1956).

31. Willey, 238; Virginia Kerns, *Scenes from the High Desert: Julian Steward's Life and Theory* (Urbana: University of Illinois Press, 2003), 251–52.

32. There is an extensive literature on the Vicos project. See Henry L. Dobyns, Paul L. Doughty, and Harold D. Laswell, eds., *Peasants, Power, and Applied Social Change: Vicos as a Model* (Beverly Hills, CA: Sage Publications, 1971), and William Mangin, "Thoughts on Twenty-Four Years of Work in Peru: The Vicos Project and Me," in Foster et al., 65–83. The quoted lines appear in Allan R. Holmberg, "Changing Community Attitudes and Values in Peru: A Case Study in Guided Change," in *Social Change in Latin America Today: Its Implications for U.S. Policy*, ed. Richard N. Adams et al. (New York: Vintage Books, 1960), 97.

33. *Courses on Latin America*, li; Neil Smith, "'Academic War over the Field of Geography': The Elimination of Geography at Harvard, 1947–1951," *AAAG* 77 (1987): 155–72; Susan Schulten, *The Geographical Imagination in America, 1880–1950* (Chicago: University of Chicago Press, 2001), 134–35.

34. James J. Parsons, "The Later Sauer Years," *AAAG* 69 (1979): 9.

35. Robert C. West, "A Berkeley Perspective on the Study of Geography in the United States and Canada," in *Studying Latin America: Essays in Honor of Preston E. James*, ed. David J. Robinson (Syracuse, NY: Geography Department, Syracuse University, 1980), 145–46, 154–58.

36. David J. Robinson, "On Preston E. James and Latin America: A Biographical Sketch," 76–91, and Harold A. Wood, "Preston E. James and the Pan American Institute of Geography and History," 121–34, in Robinson, *Studying Latin America*.

37. John C. Hudson, "Clarence Fielden Jones, 1893–1991," *AAAG* 83 (1993): 169–70.

38. Allen D. Bushong, "Raymond E. Crist: A Biographical Essay," *Journal of Cultural Geography* 9 (1989): 121–32.

39. David W. Dent, ed., *Handbook of Political Science Research on Latin America: Trends from the 1960s to the 1990s* (Westport, CT: Greenwood Press, 1990), 2.

40. *American Political Science Review* 36 (1942): 342; Committee on Latin American Affairs, Minutes, February 2, 1945, Folder 3, 1945, Container 791, CFLC. The Committee on Latin American Affairs, as the group was renamed, became a committee of the American Political Science Association but apparently did not survive a reorganization of the association in 1953.

41. John Lloyd Mecham to Russell H. Fitzgibbon, March 7, 1946, and JCLAS, Minutes, May 2 and 3, 1946, both in Folder 3, 1946, Container 792, CFLC. See also JCLAS, Proceedings, September 8–9, 1944, pp. 137–54, Folder 16-9, 1942–53, Container 811, CFLC.

42. Miron Burgin, "Research in Latin American Economics and Economic History," *Inter-American Economic Affairs* 1 (December 1947): 5.

43. JCLAS, Minutes, May 1946.

44. John D. French, "The Robert J. Alexander Interview Collection," *HAHR* 84 (May 2004): 315–26.

45. Sanford A. Mosk, "Latin American Economics: The Field and Its Problems," *Inter-American Economic Affairs* 3 (Autumn 1949): 62–63.

46. Cline, *Latin American History*, 1: 311; *Courses on Latin America*, lvii.

47. William Nelson Fenton, *Area Studies in American Universities* (Washington, DC: American Council on Education, 1947), v–vii; Jerome S. Rauch, "Area Institute Programs and African Studies," *Journal of Negro Education* 24 (Autumn 1955): 410–11. For a discussion of the definition of an area, see Steward, *Area Research*, 6–8.

48. Charles Wagley, *Area Research and Training: A Conference Report on the Study of World Areas* (New York: Social Science Research Council, 1948), 8.

49. Ibid., 11–13, 50–51.

50. Ibid., 39.

51. Wendell C. Bennett, *Area Studies in American Universities* (New York: Social Science Research Council, 1951), 7–9, 75–80. Criteria for an integrated area program included intensive language instruction, opportunities to interact with natives of the target area, joint seminars, group research projects, combination of the humanities and social sciences, and the acquisition of books, newspapers, films, and other material pertinent to the target area.

52. Carnegie Corporation of New York, *Annual Report*, 1947, 29.

53. Preston E. James, quoted in Cline, "Latin American Studies Association," 72n13.

54. Fenton, 27–28.

55. Bennett, 10–11, 13–15.

56. Hanke to Haring, December 16, 1943, Folder Haring, C. H. (1943–44), Box 126, Cline Papers. See also Haring to Hanke, December 11, 1943, ibid.

57. "Report of the Exploratory Committee on Latin American Studies to the Conference Board of the Associated Research Councils," April 10, 1948, Folder 534, Box 101, Subseries XIV, Latin America, Series 1: Committee Projects, Accession 1, SSRC Archives.

58. Cline, "Latin American Studies Association," 61.

59. "Conference on Latin American Affairs," Folder ALAS, Sagamore Conference, Box 4, Cline Papers.

60. The Doherty Fellowships: Report for the Years, 1947–1957, Box 32, Frank Tannenbaum Papers, Columbia University. Tannenbaum was a member of the selection committee for twenty years.

61. Cline to Haring, November 11, 1948, December 15, 1949, Folder Haring, C. H. (1950–51), Box 126, and Cline to Gray C. Boyce, November 20, 1952, Folder Correspondence A-B, Box 127, Cline Papers.

62. Cline, "Latin American Studies Association," 61; J. F. Wellemeyer to Cline, March 14, 1958, Box 129, and "Latin American Studies in the United States," Folder ACLS, Box 1, Cline Papers.

63. *Latin American Studies in the United States: Proceedings of a Meeting Held in Chicago, November 6–8, 1958*. Hispanic Foundation Survey Reports of Teaching and Re-

search Resources and Activities in the United States on Latin America, No. 8 (Washington, DC: Library of Congress, 1959), 3–4.

64. Ibid., 55, 57–58.

65. Ibid., 38–39.

8. The Boom Years, 1958–1975

1. *ACLS Newsletter* 10 (January 1959): 6.

2. See George Sullivan, *The Story of the Peace Corps* (New York: Fleet Publishing Corp., 1964) and Morris I. Stein, *Volunteers for Peace: The First Group of Peace Corps Volunteers in a Rural Community Development Program in Colombia, South America* (New York: John Wiley and Sons, 1966). See also Brian E. Schwimmer and D. Michael Warren, eds., *Anthropology and the Peace Corps: Case Studies in Career Perspectives* (Ames: Iowa State University Press, 1993), which includes accounts by several anthropologists who were volunteers in Latin America.

3. Donald N. Bigelow and Lyman H. Legters, *NDEA Language and Area Centers: A Report on the First 5 Years* (Washington, DC: Government Printing Office, 1964), 5. The term "Third World" initially identified the Asian and African nations that organized the neutralist, nonaligned movement of the 1950s. Latin America was added later, and the movement's agenda was broadened to include economic issues. See Philip W. Porter and Eric S. Sheppard, *A World of Difference: Society, Nature, Development* (New York: Guilford Press, 1998), 3–4.

4. *ACLS Newsletter*, 7.

5. Howard F. Cline, ed., *Latin American History: Essays on Its Study and Teaching, 1898–1965*, 2 vols. (Austin: University of Texas Press, 1967), 2:806. For a discussion of modernization theory, see Michael E. Latham, *Modernization as Ideology: American Social Science and "Nation-Building" in the Kennedy Era* (Chapel Hill: University of North Carolina Press, 2003), 1–68; James William Park, *Latin American Underdevelopment: A History of Perspectives in the United States, 1870–1965* (Baton Rouge: Louisiana State University Press, 1995), 197–201; and Peter F. Klaren and Thomas J. Bossert, eds., *Promise of Development: Theories of Change in Latin America* (Boulder, CO: Westview Press, 1986), 9–14.

6. In discussing the beginnings of the *LARR*, anthropologist Richard N. Adams recalled "that halcyon period when funding such things seemed almost effortless." See Adams, "Some Personal Trivia about the Early Days," *LASA Forum* 37 (Spring 2006): 14–15.

7. Barbara Barksdale Clowse, *Brainpower for the Cold War: The Sputnik Case and the National Defense Education Act of 1958* (Westport, CT: Greenwood Press, 1981); Charles Everett Wilson, "A Study of the Background and Passage of the National Defense Education Act of 1958" (PhD diss., University of Alabama, 1960); James Vachel Dougherty, "A History of Federal Policy Concerning College or University-Based Foreign Language and Area Studies Centers, 1941–1980" (PhD diss., University of Maryland, 1993).

8. Bigelow and Legters, 27, 77, 119.

9. *Hispania* 44 (1961): 687–88. Program A was targeted toward Asian, African, and European languages.

10. For a discussion of government-sponsored programs, see Michael Potashnik and Bryce Wood, "Government Funding for Research in Latin America, 1970–1971," *LARR* 8 (Spring 1973): 135–46. See also *Subliminal Warfare: The Role of Latin American Studies* (New York: North American Congress on Latin America, 1970), 25–31.

11. William W. Marvel to Howard F. Cline, May 25, 1954, Folder: Travel. Carnegie Corporation of New York, Box 128, Howard F. Cline Papers, Manuscript Division, Library of Congress.

12. Frederick Burkhardt and Pendleton Herring to William W. Marvel, April 29, 1959, Folder 3105, Box 264, Subseries 64, Committee on Latin America, Series 1: Committee Projects, Accession 2, SSRC Archives, Rockefeller Archives Center. See also Florence Anderson to Herring, May 22, 1959, and June 13, 1962, Folder 3105, ibid.

13. Burkhardt and Herring to Marvel.

14. JCLAS, "Program of Grants to Individuals for Research on Latin America, 1959–60 through 1962–63," Folder 543, Box 101, Subseries 14. Latin America, Series 1: Committee Projects, Accession 2, SSRC Archives.

15. JCLAS, "Conference on Research and Training in Sociology," Folder 2987, Box 254, Subseries 14, Latin America, Series 1: Committee Projects, SSRC Archives. CHEAR, an affiliate of the Institute of International Education, received funding from the Carnegie Corporation, the Ford Foundation, and other sources. See *Subliminal Warfare*, 59.

16. John J. Johnson, ed., *Continuity and Change in Latin America* (Stanford, CA: Stanford University Press, 1964), 3, 232.

17. See Charles Wagley, ed., *Social Science Research on Latin America* (New York: Columbia University Press, 1964). Geography was omitted from the seminar topics, but James J. Parsons was invited to submit a chapter on U.S. contributions to the field for the printed volume.

18. Ibid., 290.

19. Ford Foundation, *Annual Report, October 1, 1958–September 30, 1959* (New York: Ford Foundation, 1960), 66. For an overview of the activities of the various foundations in promoting area studies, see George M. Beckmann, "The Role of the Foundations," *Annals of the American Academy of Political and Social Science* 356 (November 1964): 12–22.

20. International Training and Research, "Latin American Studies," No. 06490153, Reel 0674, Ford Foundation Archives, New York (henceforth to be cited as FFA). For the evolution of the Ford Foundation's university-based foreign area programs, see Robert A. McCaughey, *International Studies and Academic Enterprise: A Chapter in the Enclosure of American Learning* (New York: Columbia University Press, 1984), 141–95.

21. See Spaeth's reports: Reports 000083 (1963) and Reports 000327 (1964), FFA.

22. The Ford Foundation's programs to advance Latin American studies in the United States can best be traced in its annual reports. The discussion of foundation activities in this chapter does not include the many programs it sponsored in Latin America itself or its training programs for Latin Americans at U.S. universities. For a partial listing, see *Subliminal Warfare*, 7–9.

23. Anita Isaacs, "The Ford Foundation, the Social Science Research Council and Its Joint Committee for Latin American Studies: A Historical Overview," 5–6, Reports 013947, FFA.

24. Ibid.; 3 On the Ford Foundation grants to the SSRC for support of the committee, see memos from Bryce Wood to the JCLAS, January 3, 1963, Folder 543, and December 30, 1965, Folder 545, Box 101, Subseries 14. Latin America, Series 1: Committee Projects, Accession 2, SSRC Archives.

25. Manuel Diégues Júnior and Bryce Wood, eds., *Social Science in Latin America* (New York: Columbia University Press, 1967), 7–8. See also Bryce Wood, "Transnational Collaborative Research," *ACLS Newsletter* 23 (Winter 1972): 26–30.

26. Kalman H. Silvert to William D. Carmichael, February 24, 1975, File 0690062, Reel 1270, FFA. See also Isaacs, 14–15.

27. Bryce Wood, "Transnational Collaborative Research"; John M. Thompson, "Foreign Area Fellowship Program to Merge with Other Area Programs of the ACLS and SSRC," *Items* 26 (December 1972): 41–44.

28. Howard F. Cline, "The Latin American Studies Association: A Summary Survey with Appendix," *LARR* 2 (Autumn 1966): 66–68.

29. Documents related to the Sagamore conference and ALAS can be found in Box 4, Cline papers.

30. Cline, "Latin American Studies Association," 63.

31. Ibid., 66–69.

32. For the LASA constitution, see ibid., 75–79. On the organization of LASA, see also JCLAS, Minutes, February 9, 1965, and November 12, 1965, Folder 544, Box 101, Subseries 14, Latin America, Series 1: Committee Projects, Accession 2, SSRC Archives, and Paul Doughty, "Words from the Eighth President of LASA," *LASA Forum* 37 (Spring 2006): 16–18. On the Ford Foundation grant, see *LARR* 3 (Spring 1968): 189–90.

33. Don S. Kirschner, *Cold War Exile: The Unclosed Case of Maurice Halperin* (Columbia: University of Missouri Press, 1995), 118–40; "An Interview with John V. Murra," *HAHR* 64 (November 1984): 639; Keith Haynes, "Benjamin Keen (1913–2002)," *HAHR* 83 (May 2003): 357–59. See also David H. Price, *Threatening Anthropology: McCarthyism and the FBI's Surveillance of Activist Anthropologists* (Durham, NC: Duke University Press, 2004), 372n4.

34. "Foreign Policy Forum: What Should the New Administration Do about Latin America?" *Foreign Policy Bulletin* 32 (April 15, 1953): 4, 5; Arthur P. Whitaker, "Latin America: Disillusioned Neighbors," *Current History* 25 (October 1953): 232.

35. Robert J. Alexander, "The Guatemalan Revolution and Communism," *Foreign Policy Bulletin* 33 (April 1, 1954): 7; Stephen Schlesinger and Stephen Kinzer, *Bitter Fruit: The Untold Story of the American Coup in Guatemala* (Garden City, NY: Doubleday, 1982), 220; Nick Cullaher, *Secret History: The CIA's Classified Account of Its Operations in Guatemala, 1952–1954* (Stanford, CA: Stanford University Press, 1999), 106–7. See also Ronald M. Schneider, *Communism in Guatemala* (New York: Praeger, 1958).

36. Arthur P. Whitaker, "Foreign Policy Forum: Guatemala, OAS and US," *Foreign Policy Bulletin* 33 (September 1, 1954): 4–7; Philip B. Taylor, Jr., "The Guatemalan Affair: A Critique," *American Political Science Review* 50 (1956): 787–806.

37. Russell H. Fitzgibbon, "The Revolution Next Door: Cuba," *Annals of the American Academy of Political and Social Science* 334 (March 1961): 113–22; Frank Tannenbaum, "Castro and Social Change," *Political Science Quarterly* 77 (June 1962): 178–204.

38. Fredrick B. Pike, "That Nebulous Monroe Doctrine," *New Republic* 144 (June 26,

1961): 10; Robert J. Alexander, "New Directions: The United States and Latin America," *Current History* 42 (February 1962): 65–70; Arthur M. Schlesinger, Jr., *The Thousand Days: John F. Kennedy in the White House* (New York: Fawcett Crest, 1967), 184–85.

39. C. Wright Mills, *Listen, Yankee: The Revolution in Cuba* (New York: McGraw-Hill, 1960), 116.

40. Van Gosse, *Where the Boys Are: Cuba, Cold War America and the Making of the New Left* (London: Verso, 1993), discusses the work of Mills, Williams, Huberman, and Sweezy in the context of the debate over Cuba in 1959–61. His focus is on the Fair Play for Cuba Committee, which he argues was "truly germinal" in the formation of the New Left (176).

41. *New York Times*, May 23, 1965, E6; Ronald H. Chilcote, "The Legacy of the Sixties and Its Impact on Academics," *LASA Forum* 37 (Spring 2006): 22–24.

42. The *Ercilla* quotation appears in Kalman H. Silvert, "American Academic Ethics and Social Research Abroad: The Lesson of Project Camelot," *Background* 9 (November 1965): 220. Silvert's article is reprinted in Irving Louis Horowitz, ed., *The Rise and Fall of Project Camelot: Studies in the Relationship between Social Science and Practical Politics* (Cambridge, MA: MIT Press, 1967), 80–106. Some controversy arose in 1966 about a U.S.-sponsored program in Colombia, Operation Simpático, which was intended to study the effects of military and civilian civic action programs. See articles in the *New York Times*: January 28, 1966, 11; February 4, 1966, 12; February 11, 1966, 14; February 13, 1966, 2.

43. Kalman H. Silvert, "Politics and Studying Societies: The United States and Latin America," *Essays in Understanding Latin America* (Philadelphia: Institute for the Study of Human Issues, 1977), 134.

44. The literature on dependency theory is vast. See, for example, C. Richard Bath and Dilmus D. James, "Dependency Analysis of Latin America," *LARR* 11 (1976): 3–54; Fernando Henrique Cardoso, "The Consumption of Dependency Theory in the United States," *LARR* 12 (1977): 7–24; Tulio Halperin-Donghi, "'Dependency Theory' and Latin American Historiography," *LARR* 17 (1982): 115–30; and Klaren and Bossert, 14–26. Robert A. Packenham offers a critical appraisal of the impact of dependency theory in the United States in *The Dependency Movement: Scholarship and Politics in Development Studies* (Cambridge, MA: Harvard University Press, 1992). For a rejection of the view that a "harmony of interests" exists between the United States and Latin America, see James Petras, "U.S.-Latin American Studies: A Critical Assessment," *Science and Society* 32 (Spring 1968): 148–68.

45. Brady Tyson, "NACLA as Coalition," *NACLA Newsletter* 1 (March 1967): 4–5; Pierre LaRamée, preface to *North American Congress on Latin America (NACLA) Archive of Latin America: Guide to the Scholarly Resources Microfilm Edition*, ed. Peter T. Johnson (Wilmington, DE: Scholarly Resources, 1999).

46. *NACLA Newsletter* 1 (April 1967): 8; *Subliminal Warfare*, 1.

47. Marjorie Woodford Bray, "Latin American Studies," in *Encyclopedia of the American Left*, ed. Mari Jo Buhle, Paul Buhle, and Dan Georgakas, 2nd ed. (New York: Oxford University Press, 1998), 431–32; Ronald H. Chilcote, "U.S. Hegemony and Academics in the Americas," *Latin American Perspectives* 24 (January 1997): 75; *Hispanic American Report* 13 (September 1960): 583, and 14 (March 1961): 213–16; Ronald Hilton, "The Cuba Trap," *Nation* 192 (April 29, 1961): 364–66.

48. Chilcote 76: Ronald Hilton, "The 'Hispanic American Report' (1948–1964)," *Hispania* 48 (March 1965): 89–97. The characterization of Hilton appears in a memo from John B. Howard to Henry T. Heald, December 7, 1964, and Hilton's statement in a confidential assessment of proposals to revive the *Hispanic American Report* and the Institute of Hispanic-American Studies (May 5, 1965). These and other relevant documents can be found in No. 06500031, Reel 1770, FFA.

49. See the announcement in *NACLA Newsletter* 3 (February 1970): 15.

50. Ronald H. Chilcote, "The Latin American Challenge to U.S. Scholarship in Latin America," *LASA Newsletter* 4 (June 1973): 31.

51. "Our Views," *Latin American Perspectives* 1 (1974): 3–4; Ronald H. Chilcote, "LAP at 25: Retrospective and New Challenges," *Latin American Perspectives* 25 (November 1998): 5–6.

52. Packenham, 270–71; Henry A. Landsberger, "When a LASA President Was Only 66 Percent 'PC,'" *LASA Forum* 26 (Winter 1996): 7; Peter H. Smith, "Memoirs from LASA's 14th President," *LASA Forum* 37 (Spring 2006): 21; Alfred G. Cuzan, *Dictatorships and Double Standards: The Latin American Studies Association on Cuba*, Paper No. 13 (Miami, FL: Endowment for Cuban American Studies, 1995), 23n4.

53. "Fourth National Meeting Resolutions," *LASA Newsletter* 5 (March 1974): 9–12; Joseph C. Edelstein to Felicity Trueblood, April 18, 1973, Box 20, Lewis Hanke Papers, Latin American Library, Tulane University.

54. Lewis Hanke to Arturo Morales Carrión, September 20, 1973, Box 20, Hanke Papers; Lewis Hanke, "Four Genuine Generalizations on Academic Pollution Created by U.S. Latin Americanists," *SECOLAS Annals* 5 (March 1974): 5–15, reprinted in Lewis Hanke, *Selected Writings on the History of Latin America* (Tempe: Center for Latin American Studies, Arizona State University, 1979), 467–76.

55. Cuzan, 9–14; Packenham, 281.

56. Kirschner, 177–249.

57. Oscar Lewis to Harry E. Wilhelm, November 1, 1968, No. 06900121, Reel 4204, FFA. This letter is reprinted in Susan Rigdon, *The Culture Façade: Art, Science, and Politics in the Work of Oscar Lewis* (Urbana: University of Illinois Press, 1988), 275–78. See also Rigdon, 99–106, for an account of Lewis's experiences in Cuba.

58. Oscar Lewis to Joseph B. Casagrande, December 12, 1970, No. 06900121, Reel 4204, FFA.

59. Oscar Lewis, Ruth M. Lewis, and Susan Rigdon, *Four Men: Living the Revolution: An Oral History of Contemporary Cuba*, 3 vols. (Urbana: University of Illinois Press, 1977), 1:xvii–xxii; Maurice Halperin, *The Taming of Fidel Castro* (Berkeley and Los Angeles: University of California Press, 1981), 141–46. See also *New York Times*, October 26, 1981, 19. For a subsequent assessment by a Ford Foundation staff member, see a memo from Barry R. Schuman to William D. Carmichael, March 5, 1984, No. 06900121, Reel 4204, FFA.

60. Richard D. Lambert, *Language and Area Studies Review*, Monograph No. 17 (Philadelphia: American Academy of Political and Social Science, 1973), 2–3; idem, *Beyond Growth: The Next Stage in Language and Area Studies* (Washington, DC: Association of American Universities, 1984), 10–13.

61. Hispanic Foundation, comp., *National Directory of Latin Americanists* (Wash-

ington, DC: Library of Congress, 1966), and idem, *National Directory of Latin Americanists* (Washington, DC: Library of Congress, 1971). Work on the 1971 edition began on April 10, 1967, and continued through most of 1970. Eighteen new subject specialties were added for the 1971 directory, including accounting, banking, folklore, religion, and theater (6–7).

62. Raymond Vernon, "The Foundations Came Last," in *Journeys through World Politics: Autobiographical Reflections of Thirty-Four Academic Travellers*, ed. Joseph Kruzel and James N. Rosenau (Lexington, MA: Lexington Books, 1988), 441. Vernon also wrote *The Dilemma of Mexico's Development* (Cambridge, MA: Harvard University Press, 1963).

63. Martin C. Needler and Thomas W. Walker, "The Current Status of Latin American Studies Programs," *LARR* 6 (Spring 1971): 119–39.

64. The directories included lists of Latin Americanists by field of specialization; some individuals were listed in more than one field. The total for each discipline given here and in the following pages is based on the number of individuals listed under it in the directory indexes.

65. The review quoted, by Mark Mancall, appears in the *Journal of Interdisciplinary History* 1 (Winter 1971): 341. For overviews of historiographical currents in the United States and Latin America in the 1960s and 1970s, see Charles W. Bergquist, "Recent United States Studies in Latin American History: Trends since 1965," *LARR* 9 (Spring 1974): 3–35; Tulio Halperin Donghi, "The State of Latin American History," in *Changing Perspectives in Latin American Studies: Insights from Six Disciplines*, ed. Christopher Mitchell (Stanford, CA: Stanford University Press, 1988), 13–62; Marshall C. Eakin, "Latin American History in the United States: From Gentlemen Scholars to Academic Specialists," *History Teacher* 31 (August 1998): 547–50. Thomas E. Skidmore reviews work by those he calls radicals in "Studying the History of Latin America: A Case of Hemispheric Convergence," *LARR* 33 (1998): 111–15.

66. See, for example, Richard S. MacNeish, "Mesoamerican Archaeology," *Biennial Review of Anthropology* 5 (1967): 306–31; John V. Murra, "Current Research and Prospects in Andean Ethnohistory," *LARR* 5 (Spring 1970): 3–36; and Robert M. Carmack, "Ethnohistory: A Review of Its Development, Definitions, Methods, and Aims," *Annual Review of Anthropology* 1 (1972): 227–46.

67. Ralph L. Beals, "International Research Problems in Anthropology: A Report from the U.S.A.," *Current Anthropology* 8 (December 1967): 470–75. See also *New York Times*, November 18, 1966, 1, November 21, 1966, 11, and Thomas C. Patterson, *A Social History of Anthropology in the United States* (Oxford: Berg, 2001), 124–33.

68. See René Millon, R. B. Drewitt, and G. L. Cowgill, *Urbanization at Teotihuacán, Mexico* (Austin: University of Texas Press, 1973), and Michael E. Moseley and Kent C. Day, eds., *Chan Chan, Andean Desert City* (Albuquerque: University of New Mexico Press, 1981).

69. Charles L. Redman, "The Development of Archaeological Theory: Explaining the Past," in *Companion Encyclopedia of Archaeology*, ed. Graeme Barker, 2 vols. (London: Routledge, 1999), 1:60–69; Richard L. Burger, "An Overview of Peruvian Archaeology (1976–1986)," *Annual Review of Anthropology* 18 (1989): 37; Jeremy A. Sabloff, *The New Archaeology and the Ancient Maya* (New York: Scientific American Library, 1990); David

Freidel, "A Conversation with Gordon Willey," *Current Anthropology* 35 (February 1994): 63–68.

70. Burger, 42–43; Jaime Litvak King, "Mesoamerica: Events and Processes, The Last Fifty Years," *American Antiquity* 50 (April 1985): 378–79; "Society Action against Illicit Antiquities Traffic," *American Antiquity* 36 (July 1971): 253–54.

71. Merle Kling, "The State of Research on Latin America: Political Science," in Wagley, 168.

72. See Arturo Valenzuela, "Political Science and the Study of Latin America," in Mitchell, 63–86, and David W. Dent, ed., *Handbook of Political Science Research on Latin America: Trends from the 1960s to the 1990s* (Westport, CT: Greenwood Press, 1990), 2–5.

73. Silvert, "Politics and Studying Societies," 137.

74. John D. Martz, "Political Science and Latin American Studies: A Discipline in Search of a Region," *LARR* 6 (Spring 1971): 94.

75. See Guillermo A. O'Donnell, *Modernization and Bureaucratic-Authoritarianism: Studies in South American Politics* (Berkeley: Institute of International Studies, University of California, 1973), and "Reflections on the Patterns of Change in the Bureaucratic-Authoritarian State," *LARR* 13 (1978): 3–38. For a critique, see Karen L. Remmer and Gilbert W. Merkx, "Bureaucratic-Authoritarianism Revisited," *LARR* 17 (1982): 3–40; O'Donnell's reply is in the same issue (pp. 41–50).

76. See Albert Fishlow, "The State of Latin American Economics" (87–119) and Alejandro Portes, "Latin American Sociology in the Mid-1980s: Learning from Experience" (121–42) in Mitchell.

77. Paul Gootenberg, "Between a Rock and a Softer Place: Reflections on Some Recent Economic History of Latin America," *LARR* 39 (2004): 239–40. See also William Paul McGreevy, "Recent Research in the Economic History of Latin America," *LARR* 3 (1968): 89–117.

78. "Symposium on the Future of Geographic Research in Latin America," Folder 2982, Box 253, Subseries 64: Committee on Latin America, Series 1: Committee Projects, Accession 2, SSRC Archives, Rockefeller Archive Center.

79. John P. Augelli, "Future Research in Latin America: Changing Professional Viewpoints and Issues," in *Geographic Research in Latin America: Benchmark 1970*, ed. Barry Lentnek, Robert L. Carmin, and Tom L. Martinson (Muncie, IN: Ball State University, 1971), 432. See also James J. Parsons, "Latin America," in *Geographers Abroad: Essays on the Prospects and Problems of Research in Foreign Areas*, ed. Marvin W. Mikesell (Chicago: Geography Department, University of Chicago, 1973), 16–46.

Conclusion

1. Lewis Hanke, "Studying Latin America: The Views of an 'Old Christian,'" *Journal of Inter-American Studies* 4 (January 1967): 44.

2. Gilbert W. Merkx, "Foreign Area Studies: Back to the Future?" *LASA Forum* 26 (Summer 1995): 6

3. James J. Parsons, "Carl Sauer's Vision of an Institute for Latin American Studies," *Geographical Review* 86 (July 1996): 380.

4. Hanke, 52.

5. Richard M. Morse, "The Strange Career of Latin American Studies," in *New World Soundings: Culture and Ideology in the Americas* (Baltimore: Johns Hopkins University Press, 1989), 170, 175 (Morse's italics).

6. Donald E. Worcester, "The Spanish American Past—Enemy of Change," *Journal of Inter-American Studies* 11 (January 1969): 71, 75.

7. William P. Glade, *The Latin American Economies: A Study of Their Institutional Evolution* (New York: American Book Co., 1969), 148.

8. Stanley J. Stein and Barbara H. Stein, *The Colonial Heritage of Latin America: Essays on Economic Dependence in Perspective* (New York: Oxford University Press, 1970), 19.

9. John P. Gillin, "Some Signposts for Policy," in *Social Change in Latin America Today: Its Implications for U.S. Policy*, ed. Richard N. Adams et al. (New York: Vintage Books, 1960), 28–47.

10. Claudio Veliz, ed., *Obstacles to Change in Latin America* (London: Oxford University Press, 1965), 2. The essays in the volume were prepared for a conference in London in 1965.

11. Thomas C. Cochran, "Cultural Factors in Economic Growth," *Journal of Economic History* 20 (December 1960): 518; Seymour Martin Lipset, "Values, Education and Entrepreneurship," in *Elites in Latin America*, ed. Seymour Martin Lipset and Aldo Solari (New York: Oxford University Press, 1967), 32.

12. Tulio Halperin Donghi uses this expression in "Dependency Theory and Latin American Historiography," *LARR* 17 (1982): 120.

13. Richard M. Morse, "Stop the Computers, I Want to Get Off," in *New World Soundings*, 177–86.

14. Gláucio Ary Dillon Soares, "Latin American Studies in the United States: A Critique and a Proposal," *LARR* 11 (1976): 51–69.

15. Christopher Mitchell, ed., *Changing Perspectives in Latin American Studies: Insights from Six Disciplines* (Stanford, CA: Stanford University Press, 1988), 3, 8.

16. Margaret E. Crahan, "Lest We Forget: Women's Contribution to Making LASA an Organization for All Its Members by One of the First Women to Serve on the LASA Executive Council (1973–1975)," *LASA Forum* 37 (Spring 2006): 19–20.

17. Hanke, 43.

18. See also Arturo Escobar, "Revisioning Latin America and Caribbean Studies: A Geopolitics of Knowledge Approach," *LASA Forum* 37 (Spring 2006): 11–14.

19. Kenneth Prewitt, "Presidential Items," *Items* 50 (June–September 1996), 31–32. See also Bruce Cummings, "Boundary Displacement: The State, the Foundations, and Area Studies after the Cold War," in *Learning Places: The Afterlives of Area Studies*, ed. Masao Miyoshi and H. D. Harootunian (Durham, NC: Duke University Press, 2002), 261–302.

20. See "Center Directors Discuss the Future of Latin American Studies," *LASA Forum* 32 (Summer 2001): 10–16.

21. For examples, see the Web page of the Consortium of Latin American Studies Programs, which itself now includes the Caribbean within its purview: www.claspprograms.org/members.htm.

Select Bibliography

Unpublished Manuscripts

The Bancroft Library, University of California, Berkeley

Herbert Eugene Bolton Papers (MSS C-B 840, Pt. 2)
Charles Edward Chapman Papers (MSS C-B 883)
Bernard Moses Papers (MSS 78/154)
Herbert Ingram Priestley Papers (MSS C-B 1053)

Rare Book and Manuscript Library, Butler Library, Columbia University

William R. Shepherd Papers
Frank Tannenbaum Papers

Research Center, Ford Foundation

Ford Foundation Archives

Manuscript Division, Library of Congress

Central Files, Library of Congress
Howard F. Cline Papers

Rockefeller Archive Center

Rockefeller Foundation Archives
Social Science Research Council Archives

Latin American Library, Tulane University

Lewis Hanke Papers

Manuscripts and Archives, Yale University Library

Bingham Family Papers
E. G. Bourne Papers
Yale Peruvian Expedition Papers

General Works

Beckmann, George M. "The Role of the Foundations." *Annals of the American Academy of Political and Social Science* 356 (November 1964): 12–22.

Byrnes, Robert F. *Awakening American Education to the World: The Role of Archibald Cary Coolidge, 1866–1928.* Notre Dame, IN: University of Notre Dame Press, 1982.

Fairbank, John King. *Chinabound: A Fifty-Year Memoir.* New York: Harper and Row, 1982.

Fenton, William Nelson. *Area Studies in American Universities.* Washington, DC: American Council on Education, 1947.

Fisher, Donald. *Fundamental Development of the Social Sciences: Rockefeller Philanthropy and the United States Social Science Research Council.* Ann Arbor: University of Michigan Press, 1983.

Freeman, John F. "University Anthropology: Early Departments in the United States." *Papers of the Kroeber Anthropological Society* 32 (1965): 78–90.

Gelfand, Lawrence E. *The Inquiry: American Preparations for Peace, 1917–1919.* New Haven, CT: Yale University Press, 1963.

Gershenhorn, Jerry. *Melville J. Herskovits and the Racial Politics of Knowledge.* Lincoln: University of Nebraska Press, 2004.

Kagan, Richard L., ed. *Spain in America: The Origins of Hispanism in the United States.* Urbana: University of Illinois Press, 2002.

Kuklick, Bruce. *Puritans in Babylon: The Ancient Near East and American Intellectual Life, 1880–1930.* Princeton, NJ: Princeton University Press, 1996.

Lambert, Richard D. *Beyond Growth: The Next Stage in Language and Area Studies.* Washington, DC: Association of American Universities, 1984.

———. *Language and Area Studies Review.* Monograph No. 17. Philadelphia: American Academy of Political and Social Science, 1973.

Lewis, Martin W., and Karen W. Wigen. *The Myth of Continents: A Critique of Metageography.* Berkeley and Los Angeles: University of California Press, 1997.

McCaughey, Robert A. *International Studies and Academic Enterprise: A Chapter in the Enclosure of American Learning.* New York: Columbia University Press, 1984.

Miller, R. Berkeley. "Anthropology and Institutionalization: Frederick Starr at the University of Chicago, 1892–1924." *Kroeber Anthropological Society Papers* (1978): 49–60.

Miyoshi, Masao, and H. D. Harootunian, eds. *Learning Places: The Afterlives of Area Studies.* Durham, NC: Duke University Press, 2002.

Murphy, Donald Joseph. "Professors, Publicists, and Pan Americanism, 1905–1917: A Study in the Use of 'Experts' in Shaping American Foreign Policy." PhD diss., University of Wisconsin, 1970.

Murra, John V., ed. *American Anthropology: The Early Years.* Minneapolis: West Publishing Co., 1976.

Naff, Thomas, ed. *Paths to the Middle East: Ten Scholars Look Back.* Albany: State University of New York Press, 1993.

Patterson, Thomas C. *A Social History of Anthropology in the United States.* Oxford: Berg, 2001.

Rauch, Jerome S. "Area Institute Programs and African Studies." *Journal of Negro Education* 24 (Autumn 1955): 409–25.

Reingold, Nathan. "National Science Policy in a Private Foundation: The Carnegie Institution of Washington." In *The Organization of Knowledge in Modern America, 1860–1920,* edited by Alexandra Oleson and John Voss, 319–41. Baltimore: Johns Hopkins University Press, 1979.

Steward, Julian H. *Area Research: Theory and Practice.* New York: Social Science Research Council, 1950.

Stocking, George W., Jr. *The Ethnographer's Magic*. Madison: University of Wisconsin Press, 1992.

Thoreson, Timothy H. H. "Paying the Piper and Calling the Tune: The Beginnings of Academic Anthropology in California." *Journal of the History of the Behavioral Sciences* 11 (July 1975): 257–75.

Wagley, Charles. *Area Research and Training: A Conference Report on the Study of World Areas*. New York: Social Science Research Council, 1948.

Wilbur, C. Martin. *China in My Life: A Historian's Own History*. Armonk, NY: M. E. Sharpe, 1996.

Williams, Stanley T. *The Spanish Background of American Literature*. 2 vols. New Haven, CT: Yale University Press, 1955; reprint, Hamden, CT: Archon Books, 1968.

Wright, John Kirtland. *Geography in the Making: The American Geographical Society, 1851–1951*. New York: American Geographical Society, 1952.

Latin America and Latin American Studies

Bath, C. Richard, and Dilmus D. James. "Dependency Analysis of Latin America: Some Criticisms, Some Suggestions." *Latin American Research Review* 11 (1976): 3–54.

Berger, Mark T. *Under Northern Eyes: Latin American Studies and U.S. Hegemony in the Americas, 1898–1990*. Bloomington: Indiana University Press, 1995.

Bernstein, Harry. *Making an Inter-American Mind*. Gainesville: University of Florida Press, 1961.

———. *Origins of Inter-American Interest, 1700–1812*. Philadelphia: University of Pennsylvania Press, 1945.

Black, Stephen Louis. "Field Methods and Methodologies in Lowland Maya Archaeology." PhD diss., Harvard University, 1990.

Burgin, Miron. "Research in Latin American Economics and Economic History." *Inter-American Economic Affairs* 1 (December 1947): 3–22.

Castle, David Barton. "The Intellectual Foundations of U.S.-Latin American Policy in the Early Twentieth Century." PhD diss., University of Oregon, 1991.

Chilcote, Ronald H. "LAP at 25: Retrospective and New Challenges." *Latin American Perspectives* 25 (November 1998): 5–27.

———. "U.S. Hegemony and Academics in the Americas." *Latin American Perspectives* 24 (January 1997): 73–77.

Cline, Howard F. "The Latin American Studies Association: A Summary Survey with Appendix." *Latin American Research Review* 2 (Autumn 1966): 57–79.

———, ed. *Latin American History: Essays on Its Study and Teaching in the United States, 1889–1965*. 2 vols. Austin: University of Texas Press, 1967.

Constance, Lincoln. *Berkeley and the Latin American Connection*. Berkeley, CA: N.p., 1978.

Dent, David W., ed. *Handbook of Political Science Research on Latin America: Trends from the 1960s to the 1990s*. Westport, CT: Greenwood Press, 1990.

Diégues Júnior, Manuel, and Bryce Wood, eds. *Social Science in Latin America*. New York: Columbia University Press, 1967.

Dobyns, Henry L., Paul L. Doughty, and Harold D. Lasswell, eds. *Peasants, Power, and Applied Social Change: Vicos as a Model.* Beverly Hills, CA: Sage Publications, 1971.

Eakin, Marshall C. "Latin American History in the United States: From Gentleman Scholars to Academic Specialists." *History Teacher* 31 (August 1998): 539–61.

Erb, Claude Curtis. "Nelson Rockefeller and United States-Latin American Relations, 1940–1945." PhD diss., Clark University, 1982.

Espinosa, J. Manuel. *Inter-American Beginnings of United States Cultural Diplomacy, 1936–1948.* Washington, DC: U.S. Department of State, 1976.

Foster, George M. "The Institute of Social Anthropology." In *The Uses of Anthropology,* edited by Walter Goldschmidt, 205–15. Washington, DC: American Anthropological Association, 1979.

Gomez, R. A. *The Study of Latin American Politics in University Programs in the United States.* Tucson: University of Arizona Press, 1967.

Hanke, Lewis. "The Development of Latin American Studies in the United States, 1939–1945." *The Americas* 4 (1947): 32–64.

———. "Four Genuine Generalizations on Academic Pollution Created by U.S. Latin Americanists." *SECOLAS Annals* 5 (1974): 5–15.

———. *Selected Writings of Lewis Hanke on the History of Latin America.* Tempe: Center for Latin American Studies, Arizona State University, 1979.

———. "Studying Latin America: The Views of an 'Old Christian.'" *Journal of Inter-American Studies* 7 (January 1967): 43–64.

Hart, Estellita, comp. *Courses on Latin America in Institutions of Higher Learning in the United States, 1948–1949.* Washington, DC: Department of Cultural Affairs, Division of Education, Pan American Union, 1949.

Horowitz, Irving Louis, ed. *The Rise and Fall of Project Camelot: Studies in the Relationship between Social Science and Practical Politics.* Cambridge, MA: MIT Press, 1967.

Johnson, John J., ed. *Continuity and Change in Latin America.* Stanford, CA: Stanford University Press, 1964.

Knapp, Gregory, ed. *Latin America in the 21st Century: Challenges and Solutions.* Austin: Conference of Latin Americanist Geographers and University of Texas Press, 2002.

Latin American Studies in the United States: Proceedings of a Meeting Held in Chicago, November 6–8, 1958. Hispanic Foundation Survey Reports of Teaching and Research Resources and Activities in the United States on Latin America. Washington, DC: Library of Congress, 1959.

Lentnek, Barry, Robert L. Carmin, and Tom L. Martinson, eds. *Geographic Research in Latin America: Benchmark 1970.* Muncie, IN: Ball State University, 1971.

Martz, John D. "Political Science and Latin American Studies: A Discipline in Search of a Region." *Latin American Research Review* 6 (Spring 1971): 73–99.

McGreevey, William Paul. "Recent Research in the Economic History of Latin America." *Latin American Research Review* 3 (1968): 89–117.

Mitchell, Christopher, ed. *Changing Perspectives in Latin American Studies: Insights from Six Disciplines.* Stanford, CA: Stanford University Press, 1988.

Morse, Richard M. *New World Soundings: Culture and Ideology in the Americas.* Baltimore: Johns Hopkins University Press, 1989.

Mosk, Sanford A. "Latin American Economics: The Field and Its Problems." *Inter-American Economic Affairs* 3 (Autumn 1949): 55–64.

Needler, Martin C., and Thomas W. Walker. "The Current State of Latin American Studies Programs." *Latin American Research Review* 6 (Spring 1971): 119–39.

Packenham, Robert A. *The Dependency Movement: Scholarship and Politics in Development Studies.* Cambridge, MA: Harvard University Press, 1992.

Park, James William. *Latin American Underdevelopment: A History of Perspectives in the United States, 1870–1965.* Baton Rouge: Louisiana State University Press, 1995.

Petras, James. "U.S.-Latin American Studies: A Critical Assessment." *Science and Society* 32 (Spring 1968): 148–68.

Potashnik, Michael, and Bryce Wood. "Government Funding for Research in Latin America, 1970–1971." *Latin American Research Review* 8 (Spring 1973): 135–46.

Robinson, David J., ed. *Studying Latin America: Essays in Honor of Preston E. James.* Syracuse: Geography Department, Syracuse University, 1980.

Sable, Martin, ed. *Guide to the Writings of Pioneer Latinamericanists in the United States.* New York: Haworth Press, 1989.

Seidel, Robert Neal. "Progressive Pan Americanism: Development and United States Policy toward South America, 1906–1931." PhD diss., Cornell University, 1973.

Silvert, Kalman H. *Essays in Understanding Latin America.* Philadelphia: Institute for the Study of Human Issues, 1977.

Soares, Gláucio Ary Dillon. "Latin American Studies in the United States: A Critique and a Proposal." *Latin American Research Review* 11 (1976): 51–69.

Subliminal Warfare: The Role of Latin American Studies. New York: North American Congress on Latin America, 1970.

Taylor, Carl C. "Early Rural Sociological Research in Latin America." *Rural Sociology* 25 (1960): 1–8.

Wagley, Charles W., ed. *Social Science Research on Latin America.* New York: Columbia University Press, 1964.

Studies of Individual Latin Americanist Scholars

Almaraz, Felix D., Jr. *Knight without Armor: Carlos Eduardo Castañeda, 1896–1958.* College Station: Texas A&M University Press, 1999.

Bannon, John Francis. *Herbert E. Bolton: The Historian and the Man, 1870–1953.* Tucson: University of Arizona Press, 1978.

Barnhart, Terry A. *Ephraim George Squier and the Development of American Anthropology.* Lincoln: University of Nebraska Press, 2005.

Bingham, Alfred M. *Portrait of an Explorer: Hiram Bingham, Discoverer of Machu Picchu.* Ames: Iowa State University Press, 1989.

Brunhouse, Robert L. *Sylvanus G. Morley and the World of the Ancient Mayas.* Norman: University of Oklahoma Press, 1971.

Bushong, Allen D. "Raymond E. Crist: A Biographical Essay." *Journal of Cultural Geography* 9 (1989): 121–32.

Caughey, John Walton. *Hubert Howe Bancroft: Historian of the West.* Berkeley and Los Angeles: University of California Press, 1946.

"Charles Wilson Hackett: A Biographical Sketch." In *Essays in Mexican History*, edited by Thomas E. Cotner and Carlos E. Castañeda, xl–xvi. Austin, TX: Institute of Latin American Studies, 1958.

Cline, Howard F. "In Memoriam: Clarence Henry Haring, 1885–1900." *The Americas* 17 (1961): 292–97.

Cline, Howard F., C. Harvey Gardiner, and Charles Gibson. *William Hickling Prescott: A Memorial.* Durham, NC: Duke University Press, 1959.

Deacon, Desley. *Elsie Clews Parsons: Inventing Modern Life.* Chicago: University of Chicago Press, 1997.

Delpar, Helen. "Lewis Hanke and Latin American History: The Legacy of an 'Old Christian.'" *SECOLAS Annals* 34 (2002): 141–55.

———. "Frank Tannenbaum: The Making of a Mexicanist. *The Americas* 45 (Oct. 1988): 153–71.

Finan, John J. "Howard F. Cline (1915–1971)." *Hispanic American Historical Review* 51 (1971): 646–53.

Foster, George M., Thayer Scudder, Elizabeth Colson, and Robert W. Kemper. *Long-Term Field Research in Social Anthropology.* New York: Academic Press, 1979.

Harris, Charles H., III, and Louis R. Sadler. *The Archaeologist Was a Spy: Sylvanus G. Morley and the Office of Naval Intelligence.* Albuquerque: University of New Mexico Press, 2003.

Harrison, Margaret W. "Lila Morris O'Neale: 1886–1948." *American Anthropologist* 50 (1948): 657–65.

Hudson, John J. "In Memoriam: Clarence Fielden Jones, 1893–1991." *Annals of the American Association of Geographers* 83 (1993): 167–72.

Kenzer, Martin S., ed. *Carl O. Sauer: A Tribute.* Corvallis: Oregon State University Press, 1987.

Kerns, Virginia. *Scenes from the High Desert: Julian Steward's Life and Theory.* Urbana: University of Illinois Press, 2003.

Kirschner, Don S. *Cold War Exile: The Unclosed Case of Maurice Halperin.* Columbia: University of Missouri Press, 1995.

Kroeber, Theodora. *Alfred Kroeber: A Personal Configuration.* Berkeley and Los Angeles: University of California Press, 1970.

Lamb, Ursula. "Pioneers of Discovery History in the Spanish Archives: Alice Gould and Irene Wright, A Memoir." *Primary Sources and Original Works* 2 (1993): 479–91.

Lange, Charles H., and Carroll L. Riley. *Bandelier: The Life and Adventures of Adolph Bandelier.* Salt Lake City: University of Utah Press, 1996.

Magnaghi, Russell M. *Herbert E. Bolton and the Historiography of the Americas.* Westport, CT: Greenwood Press, 1998.

Martin, Geoffrey J. *The Life and Thought of Isaiah Bowman.* Hamden, CT: Archon Books, 1980.

———. *Mark Jefferson, Geographer.* Ypsilanti: Eastern Michigan University Press, 1968.

McFarland, Philip. *Sojourners.* New York: Atheneum, 1978.

Munro, Dana G. *A Student in Central America, 1914–1916.* New Orleans: Middle American Research Institute, Tulane University, 1983.

Nelson, Lowry. *In the Direction of His Dreams: Memoirs.* New York: Philosophical Library, 1985.

Parsons, James J. "The Later Sauer Years." *Annals of the American Association of Geographers* 69 (1979): 9–15.

Rigdon, Susan M. *The Culture Façade: Art, Science, and Politics in the Work of Oscar Lewis.* Urbana: University of Illinois Press, 1988.

Rippy, J. Fred. *Bygones I Cannot Help Recalling: The Memoirs of a Mobile Scholar.* Austin, TX: Steck-Vaughn Co., 1965.

Robinson, David J. "On Preston E. James and Latin America: A Biographical Sketch." In *Studying Latin America: Essays in Honor of Preston E. James,* edited by David J. Robinson, 76–91. Syracuse, NY: Geography Department, Syracuse University, 1980.

Sauer, Carl O. *Andean Reflections: Letters from Carl O. Sauer while on a South American Trip under a Grant from the Rockefeller Foundation,* edited by Robert C. West. Boulder, CO: Westview Press, 1982.

Shook, Edwin M. *Incidents in the Life of a Maya Archaeologist.* Guatemala City: Southwestern Academy Press, 1998.

Solomon, Char. *Tatiana Proskouriakoff: Interpreting the Ancient Maya.* Norman: University of Oklahoma Press, 2002.

Steward, Julian H. "Alfred Louis Kroeber." *American Anthropologist* 63 (1961): 1038–87.

TePaske, John J. "Interview with Irving A. Leonard." *Hispanic American Historical Review* 63 (1983): 233–53.

Von Hagen, Victor Wolfgang. *Maya Explorer: John Lloyd Stephens and the Lost Cities of Central America and Yucatan.* Norman: University of Oklahoma Press, 1947.

West, Robert C. *Carl Sauer's Fieldwork in Latin America.* Ann Arbor, MI: University Microfilms International, 1979.

Wilcox, Clifford. *Robert Redfield and the Development of American Archaeology.* Lanham, MD: Lexington Books, 2004.

Wilgus, Curtis A. "The Life of James Alexander Robertson." In *Hispanic American Essays: A Memorial to James Alexander Robertson,* edited by Curtis A. Wilgus, 3–14. Chapel Hill: University of North Carolina Press, 1942.

Willey, Gordon Randolph. *Portraits in American Archaeology: Remembrances of Some Distinguished Americanists.* Albuquerque: University of New Mexico Press, 1988.

Index

Looking South